317

AS IS

THE BASIC BAKUNIN

WRITINGS 1869–1871

Frontispiece. Photograph of Mikhail Alexandrovich Bakunin by Valerian Mroczowski. "To the venerable brother, Patriarch Meuron of Le Locle. His brother and friend, M. Bakounine. February 1869." Photograph courtesy of International Institute for Social History.

THE BASIC BAKUNIN

WRITINGS 1869–1871

Translated and Edited by
Robert M. Cutler

GREAT BOOKS IN PHILOSOPHY

PROMETHEUS BOOKS
Buffalo, New York

To the memory of P. E. C.
and
for all those whose freedom does not depend
on others' lack thereof.

Published 1992 by Prometheus Books

Editorial offices located at 700 East Amherst Street, Buffalo, New York 14215,
and distribution facilities at 59 John Glenn Drive, Amherst, New York 14228.

Library of Congress Cataloging-in-Publication Data

Bakunin, Mikhail Aleksandrovich, 1814–1876.
[Selections. English. 1992]
The basic Bakunin : writings, 1869–1871 / translated and edited by Robert M. Cutler.
p. cm. — (Great books in philosophy)
Originally published: From out of the dustbin. Ann Arbor, Mich. : Ardis, © 1985.
ISBN 0–87975–745–0
1. Anarchism. I. Series.
HX914.7.B34A25 1992
335′.83—dc20 92–5386
CIP

Printed on acid-free paper in the United States of America

Additional Titles on Social and Political Philosophy in Prometheus's Great Books in Philosophy Series

Aristotle
The Politics

Edmund Burke
Reflections on the Revolution in France

John Dewey
Freedom and Culture

G. W. F. Hegel
The Philosophy of History

Thomas Hobbes
The Leviathan

Sidney Hook
Paradoxes of Freedom

Sidney Hook
Reason, Social Myths, and Democracy

John Locke
Second Treatise on Civil Government

Niccolo Machiavelli
The Prince

Karl Marx and Frederick Engels
The Economic and Philosophic Manuscripts of 1844 and *The Communist Manifesto*

John Stuart Mill
Considerations on Representative Government

John Stuart Mill
On Liberty

John Stuart Mill
On Socialism

John Stuart Mill
The Subjection of Women

Thomas Paine
Rights of Man

Plato
The Republic

Plato on Homosexuality: Lysis, Phaedrus, and *Symposium*

Jean-Jacques Rousseau
The Social Contract

Mary Wollstonecraft
A Vindication of the Rights of Women

For a complete list of titles in Prometheus's Great Books in Philosophy and Great Minds Series, see the order form at the back of this volume.

Every revolt is a cry of innocence
and an appeal to the essence of being.

—Albert Camus, *The Rebel*

Contents

Acknowledgments

A decade ago William Watson introduced me to Bakunin, and he and Suzanne Berger supervised my Bachelor's thesis at the Massachusetts Institute of Technology, where I developed the interpretations presented in the Introduction here. A Youthgrant from the National Endowment for the Humanities sustained me during the summer of 1975, when the major work of the initial translations was completed. This was done at the Pennsylvania State University, in space provided by the Slavic and Soviet Language and Area Center. I am indebted to the Center's Director, Vernon Aspaturian, for his hospitality and support. Other colleagues at the Slavic Center, who never permitted me to forget my interest in Bakunin, deserve more than I can give them.

A graduate seminar in methods of working with historical sources, taught by S. V. Utechin, is at the origin of the Comment on Texts and Translation. His generous counsel and enduring interest in this project provided a continuity through all its phases. The image of judicious scholarship to which I have tried to be faithful in this volume is no less sharp for his example.

During 1979-80, in connection with other work, I was Albert Gallatin Fellow at the Graduate Institute for International Studies in Geneva, Switzerland. The Institute, located only a few hours' train ride from where Bakunin wrote most of these texts, provided, through its expertise in the First International and its hospitality, the ideal environment for completing this project. Urs Luterbacher and his associates contributed signficantly to making that year especially productive.

I wish to thank the staffs of the libraries whose services assisted my research: the Internationaal Instituut voor Sociale Gescheidnis, Amsterdam; the Graduate Library of the University of Michigan, Ann Arbor, particularly the Joseph A. Labadie Collection and the Inter-Library Loan Office; the Bibliothèque publique et universitaire, Geneva; the British Library, London; and the Bibliothèque nationale, Paris.

Marion Blakely, of the National Endowment for the Humanities, and Carl Proffer, of Ardis Publishers, generously refrained from insisting that different stages of the project be completed before the time was right. Jackie Allen, Monarch Cutler, Marianne Enckell, Claudine Fuhrimann, Raymond Grew, Monica Irwin, Jaap Kloosterman, and Miklós Molnár provided various kinds of encouragement and support. I thank also other persons too numerous to count, let alone mention, who have expressed interest in this project. However, no one but myself can be responsible for how I have used the advice and resources available to me.

Milestones in Bakunin's Life

1814 May 18	Born at Priamukhino, in Tver province, Russia.
1828-1833	Studies at St. Petersburg Artillery School.
1833-1835	Serves in Minsk and Grodno as lieutenant in an artillery brigade.
1835 March	Meets Stankevich during a visit to Moscow.
October	Begins participating in Stankevich's study circle.
December	Resigns military commission.
1836-1840	Settles in Moscow, making frequent visits to Priamukhino. From 1837 on, plunges into philosophical studies, especially Hegel. Knows Belinsky, Botkin, Granovsky, Katkov, and others in the Stankevich circle.
1839/40 Winter	Becomes friends with Herzen and Ogaryov.
1840 June 29	Leaves Russia to study philosophy in Berlin.
1840-1842	Attends lectures by Schelling, Werder, and Ranke in Berlin.
1842 October	"Reaction in Germany" is published under the pseudonym Jules Elysard.
1843	Moves to Zürich and Berne. Associates with Weitling and Fröbel.
1844 February	Summoned by Tsar to return to Russia. Leaves instead for Paris, stopping in Brussels en route.
1844 December	Stripped of noble title by Russian Senate.
1844-1847	Remains in Paris, in contact with representatives of French, Polish, and European democracy.
1847 November 18	Speaks at a banquet commemorating the Polish insurrection of 1830.
December	Expelled by French government. Leaves for Brussels. His expulsion is contested in the French Parliament.
1848 February	Louis-Philippe overthrown; France proclaimed a Republic. Bakunin returns to Paris, publishes several letters in the press.
March	Leaves Paris. Travels to Frankfurt, Mainz, Mannheim, Heidelberg. Tries unsuccessfully to reach Poland. Goes to Berlin, Leipzig, Breslau.

June	Attends Slav Congress in Prague, where he speaks and presents papers. Participates in the Whitsuntide insurrection there.
June-December	Travels to Breslau, Berlin, Breslau again, and Dresden. Finally finds freedom from political harassment in Köthen.
December	*Appeal to the Slavs* appears.
1849 April	Brochure on "Russian Conditions" appears; articles in *Dresdner Zeitung.*
May	Participates in the revolt in Dresden. Arrested and incarcerated.
July	Transferred to Königstein fortress.
1850 January 14	Condemned to death by Saxon tribunal.
June	Sentence commuted to life imprisonment. Extradited and delivered to Austria. Imprisoned in Prague.
1851 March 14	Transferred to Olmütz fortress.
May	Tried in Prague and condemned to death. Sentence commuted to life imprisonment. Extradited and delivered to Russian authorities. Thrown into the Alexis ravelin of the Peter-and-Paul fortress in St. Petersburg.
1854 March	Transferred to Schlüsselberg.
1857 February	Imprisonment commuted to Siberian exile.
1858 October 5	Marries Antonia Ksaverievna Kwiatkowska.
1859 Spring	Leaves for Irkutsk.
1861 June	Escapes from Siberia. Regains Europe via the Amur River, Yokohama, San Francisco, the Panama Canal, and New York.
December	Arrives in England. Goes to London to the house of Herzen.
1862 Summer	Writes brochures *The People's Cause* and *To Russian, Polish, and All Slav Friends.*
1863 March	Participates in expedition to Poland in support of insurrection there. The revolt is crushed and the party docks instead in Sweden.
April-October	Sojourn in Sweden.
1863/64 Winter	Passes to Italy via London, Paris, Brussels, Geneva, Berne.
1864-1865	In Florence. Founds the Brotherhood.
1864 Sept.-October	Trip to Stockholm. Meets Marx in London on return trip.
1865-1867	Sojourn in Naples. Founds the International Brotherhood.

1867 September	Attends, in Geneva, First Congress of League of Peace and Freedom; enters its Central Committee.
1867/68 Winter-Spring	In Vevey, Switzerland. Meets Utin, Zhukovsky. Writes *Federalism, Socialism, and Anti-Theologism.*
1868 July	Joins the Geneva section of the International Working-Men's Association.
Autumn	Attends, in Berne, Second Congress of the League of Peace and Freedom. Withdraws from the League with associates and founds the International Association of Socialist Democracy. Moves to Geneva.
1869 March-Sept.	Collaboration with Nechaev and Ogaryov on Russian propaganda. Writes articles for *L'Égalité* and *Le Progrès.* These activities are kept separate from one another.
September	Basle Congress of the International. Bakunin delivers speeches there, succeeds in defeating recommendation of the General Council on the right of inheritance.
October	Moves to Lugano.
1870 June	Breaks with Nechaev.
September	Participates in Lyons insurrection. Seeks to establish a free federation of communes in France, on the ruins of the Second Empire, which fell in the Franco-Prussian War.
Sept.-October	Travels to Marseilles, Locarno.
1871 Spring	Travels in French Switzerland.
May	Gives "Three Lectures to Swiss Members of the International."
September	London Conference of the International.
November	Publishes "The Organization of the International."
1872 September	Expelled from the International by its Hague Congress.
1873 August	Settles in the villa Baronata, near Locarno, Switzerland.
1874 August	Participates in attempted insurrection in Bologna.
1876 June	Goes to Berne.
July 1	Dies in Berne hospital.
July 3	Buried in Bremgarten cemetery, Berne, Switzerland.

"The Social Question. The equalization of individuals is not possible!!! (demonstated by M. B[akunin] in his speech)." A caricature of the falsification of Bakunin's position by the leadership of the League of Peace and Freedom. After Bakunin withdrew from the League in 1868, the League's journal editorialized: " . . . collectivism, which was so very carefully distinguished from communism, cannot lead to the *equalization of classes and individuals* any more than can individualism itself, for the more collectivism is differentiated from communism, the more it tends to establish inequality among groups, that is, among individuals belonging to different groups." (*Les Etats-Unis d'Europe* [Geneva], no. 39 [30 September 1868]: 155, emphasis in the original.) In the drawing Goegg, a leading member of the League, and Bakunin are shown trying to fit into each other's clothes. Source: Pittorino [pseud.], *Congrès de la Paix à Berne: Album* (Geneva: Braun et Cie. for Ch. T. Montaniar, [1868]).

Introduction

Mikhail Alexandrovich Bakunin, the anarchist, was a political thinker; his reputation, based partly on his appetite for action and partly on unsympathetic historiography, obscures this. Bakunin's social milieu influenced the manner in which he expressed his ideas, because he tried always to tailor them to those to whom he spoke, promoting so far as possible the revolutionary consciousness and socialist instincts of his audience. That is still another reason, without even mentioning Bakunin's unyielding antidoctrinairism, why it has been hard to delineate a Bakuninist "doctrine."

The works included in this volume nevertheless have a certain unity, because they all were intended for the same audience. The texts presented here date from the period of Bakunin's propaganda on behalf of the International Working-Men's Association. They thus belong to a phase of his activity which is central to his anarchism, which is generally agreed to be one of his most significant projects, and which marks the height of his influence during his life.[1] Most of the items first appeared in the Swiss newspapers *L'Égalité* and *Le Progrès* in 1869.[2] Isaiah Berlin, no great partisan of Bakunin's, has called him a "gifted journalist," and Amédée Dunois considers these articles the best of Bakunin's written works.[3] Only one of them, however, has ever before appeared unabridged in English.

A reasoned examination of Bakunin's ideas is complicated, too, by the fact that he did not leave an organized body of written work: "My life itself is a fragment," he once replied when the disarray of his manuscripts was mentioned to him.[4] By making available in English an important and coherent set of Bakunin's writings, it is hoped to contribute to a more careful reevaluation of his thought.

There are any number of ways to approach an interpretation of Bakunin's ideas. One of the most fruitful, but least frequently adopted, is to attempt to understand their evolution from his pre-anarchist through his anarchist period. A dichotomy between a pre-anarchist "early Bakunin" and an anarchist "late Bakunin," each distinct from and related only superficially to the other, is as helpful as one between a humanistic "early Marx" and a deterministic "late Marx"—but also, in the end, as unenlightening. Both suppositions belong in the dustbin of hypotheses.

For historical reasons, and also because contrast is a convenient method of clarification, it is nevertheless useful to compare some of Bakunin's ideas with those of Karl Marx. This Introduction attempts to suggest the fruitfulness both of the evolutionary perspective and of the Bakunin-Marx comparison. One hopes it will be clear, moreover, that the two approaches are mutually complementary and can, together, yield useful insights.

I

Bakunin first encountered philosophy through the romantic poems and letters of Venevitinov, whose passion had been Schelling.[5] At the suggestion of Nicholas Stankevich, "the bold pioneer who opened to Russian thought the vast and fertile continent of German metaphysics,"[6] whom he met in 1835, Bakunin read Kant's *Critique of Pure Reason*; soon, however, he turned to Fichte. He published a translation of the *Lectures on the Vocation of the Scholar* (the first of the philosopher's works to appear in Russian), and *The Way to a Blessed Life* became his favorite book. Fichte's ideas gave Bakunin the inspiration for his religious but extra-ecclesiastical immanentism, and Bakunin's Russian Orthodox upbringing provided the originally Christian terminology in which this was expressed. An August 1836 letter to his sisters strikingly illustrates this development; in it, Bakunin exhorts them to

> . . . [l]et religion become the basis and reality of your life and your actions, but let it be the pure and single-minded religion of divine reason and divine love, and not . . . that religion which strove to disassociate itself from everything that makes up the substance and life of truly moral existence. . . . Look at Christ, my dear friend; . . . His life was divine through and through, full of self-denial, and He did everything for mankind, finding His satisfaction and His delight in the dissolution of His material being. . . .Because we have been baptized in this world and are in communion with this heavenly love, we feel that we are divine creatures, that we are free, and that we have been ordained for the emancipation of humanity, which has remained a victim of the instinctive laws of unconscious existence . . . . Absolute freedom and absolute love—that is our aim; the freeing of humanity and the whole world—that is our purpose.[7]

That there are "instinctive laws of unconscious existence" is a postulate of the series of articles on "Physiological or Natural Patriotism" that Bakunin wrote as an anarchist, and which are translated here. This series also shows the long-lasting influence on Bakunin of Feuerbach, in the assumption that man progresses through history from animality to humanity.

Less than a year after Bakunin wrote this letter to his sisters, Hegelian terminology began to predominate in his style, though sometimes only cloaking Fichtean ideas.

> Finite man is separated from God. . . . Such a man fears and even hates reality. But that means he hates God and does not know Him. For reality is the will of God.[8]

Nevertheless, from such a point it was a short step to acquiesce in Hegel's *dictum* that "the real is rational and the rational is real." The consistent unity of Hegel's system urged this acceptance, aided by the philosopher's profound sense of concrete existence and abetted by his idealistic interpretation of that existence. Having read Fichte, Bakunin was already prepared to see, in concrete existence, the immanence of the Absolute.

By the time Bakunin left Moscow in 1840, for the fount of idealist philosophy in Berlin, he had translated into Russian the first of Hegel's works to appear in that language (a series of lectures), and published an article expressing the orthodox Hegelianism that he and Belinsky had propagated after Stankevich's death. The sequel to that article, which remained unpublished until nearly a century later, suggested a new direction by portraying man as the realization of the universal and transforming him into an instrument of Spirit, such that Spirit is in fact animated by the activity of the individual human being in concrete reality.[9]

Following the direction indicated by this way of thinking, Bakunin found its limit by 1842, the year in which, under the pseudonym Jules Elysard, his sensational article, "The Reaction in Germany," was published. It marked the full transformation of the philosophical orthodoxy of his Moscow days into the most radical Left Hegelianism. The conception of the dialectic that Bakunin presents in this article animated his revolutionary activities for the rest of his life. Neither his resolutely uncompromising attitude, nor his idea of social revolution as the total destruction and entire razing of the existing order, nor perhaps even his *self*-conception, can be fully fathomed without an understanding of these roots in German philosophy.

For Hegel, the dialectic began with the thesis (the Positive), which was negated, creating the antithesis, which was then in its turn negated, yielding the third element of the dialectical triad: the synthesis. As a negation of a negation, Hegel's synthesis represented the superposition of the Positive; Marx's dialectic shares this basic feature. Bakunin, in his 1842 article, establishes the *Negative,* rather than the Positive, as the motive force of the dialectic. This aspect of Bakunin's thought is important enough to deserve elaboration.

The contradiction between Positive and Negative was, to Bakunin,

> ... not an equilibrium but a preponderance of the Negative, which is its encroaching dialectical phase. The Negative, as determining the life of the Positive itself, alone includes within itself the totality of the contradiction, and so it alone has absolute justification.[10]

At first the Positive appears restful, immobile. The Positive, in its inertia, not only contains nothing negative; it must also, furthermore, resist the Negative and exclude the Negative from itself in order to maintain its own positive nature. But, Bakunin asserts, this exclusion of the Negative is motion, and in ending its immobility the Positive becomes negative. If it subsequently denies the Negative, then it only denies itself. The "significance and irrepressible power" of the Negative, on the other hand,

> ... is in the annihilation of the Positive; but along with the Positive it leads itself to destruction as this evil, particular existence which is inadequate to its essence. ... The Negative ... exists only in contradiction to the Positive. Its whole being, its content and its vitality are simply the destruction of the Positive.[11]

For Bakunin, the resolution of the dialectical contradiction signifies the victory of the Negative. In this victory, *both* parties are vanquished; *neither* is superposed on the other in the outcome. The Negative and the Positive disappear, together and totally, in the final conflagration to which their struggle leads.

In Marx's dialectic, as in Hegel's, the resolution of the dialectical contradiction comprehends not only the destruction and transcendence of thesis and antithesis but also their preservation: for Marx, one thing in particular which should survive the destruction of the existing social order is the communitarian essence which, according to him, the State, despite its alienating aspect, expresses. In Bakunin's vision of the contradiction, however, the Positive and the Negative mutually destroy one another, leading to the transcendence of both but preserving nothing of either. Thus Bakunin, in his revolutionary exhortations, foresees no aspect of existing society, based on the institution of the State, to survive the universal insurrection.

Bakunin's dialectic acquires substantive meaning in his 1842 article, when he sociomorphizes the Positive into social reactionaries and the Negative into social revolutionaries; and here his anarchist rejection of compromise with bourgeois opponents has its origin. The reactionaries, Bakunin explains, are composed of two trends: the consistent ones and the compromising ones. The consistent reactionaries flee from the present conflict by taking refuge in the past, although it is mistaken to believe that the historical totality of the past, which existed before the emergence of the revolutionary movement, can be recreated. The compromising reactionaries, on the other hand, do not unconditionally reject the revolutionary movement: "... they maintain that two opposing trends are as such one-sided and therefore untrue; but, they argue, if the two members of the contradiction are untrue when taken abstractly in themselves, then the truth must lie in their middle, and so one must intercorrelate them to arrive at the truth."[12] Thus the compromisers wish to prohibit to the Positive the act of excluding the Negative, thus they desire to rob the contradiction of its vitality. The articles "The Hypnotizers" and "*La Montagne* and Mr. Coullery," among others, find Bakunin inveighing against the bourgeois socialists—compromising Positives—who wish to prohibit to the workers the act of excluding the bourgeois world. The uncompromising revolutionaries, however, of whom Bakunin undoubtedly was one, are animated by "the energy of [the contradiction's] all-embracing vitality," itself the source of the "pure fire" of the Negative, which, "through this storm of destruction, powerfully urges sinful, compromising souls to repentance."[13]

Bakunin's anarchist attitude toward political participation, one of the most salient questions of revolutionary tactics, reflects his refusal to compromise. He viewed acceptance of universal suffrage as participation in the bourgeois world and hence compromise with it.[14] In contrast to Bakunin, Marx and Engels encouraged proletarian participation in bourgeois politics. Believing the proletariat to be the class that would inevitably comprise the vast majority of humanity, they had no complaint about majoritarian balloting. Engels called the democratic republic "the highest form of the State," because it "officially knows nothing any more of property distinctions." It was, he wrote, the only form of the State in which "the last decisive struggle between proletariat and bourgeoisie can be fought out."[15] Said Engels *contra* Bakunin in 1871:

> Complete abstention from political action is impossible. . . . Living experience, the political oppression of the existing government compels the workers to occupy themselves with politics whether they like it or not, be it for political or for social goals. . . .
>
> We want the abolition of classes. What is the means of achieving it? The only means is the political domination of the proletariat.[16]

Bakunin believed, on the contrary, that the workers should strive to create their future world in the very heart of the existing bourgeois world, alongside but altogether separate from it. As he explains below in his article "On Cooperation," it was up to the workers themselves to create cooperative organizations, which would replace the erstwhile political distribution of goods and services with a more just social distribution of them.

Establishing cooperatives was thus one tactic the workers could use in their struggle to resist the deleterious influences of the bourgeois world. Another was the strike, which Bakunin discusses in "Geneva's Double Strike." In a pamphlet he wrote in 1870, Bakunin argues that strikes facilitate the work of socialist-revolutionary propagandists.

> Strikes are necessary . . . to such an extent that without them it would be impossible to rouse the masses to the social struggle, nor would it be possible to organize them.
>
> Strikes awaken, in the masses of the people, all the socialist-revolutionary instincts that reside deep in the heart of every worker . . . [and] when those instincts, stirred by the economic struggle, are awakened in the masses of the workers, who are arising from their own slumber, then the propagation of the socialist-revolutionary idea becomes quite easy. For that idea is simply the pure and faithful expression of the instincts of the people. If it does not correspond fully to their instincts, then it is false; . . . if that idea represents the *genuine thought of the people,* then it will quickly and unquestionably take hold among the popular masses in revolt; and once it so infuses the people, it will not hesitate to triumph in reality.[17]

This "theoretical propaganda of socialist ideas [is spread] among the masses" by "the International[, which] prepares the elements of the revolutionary organization but does not fulfill [that role]."[18] Thus whereas Marx's activities as well as his writings suggest that *he* conceived the International to be a sort of federation, the general line of which would unite different national parliamentary workers' parties in their electoral struggles with their respective national bourgeoisies, Bakunin saw the International as the midwife of an uncompromisingly revolutionary movement in the form of an alternative society of the world of the workers, unpolluted by bourgeois intrusions and institutions.

II

Bakunin's interpretation of history suggests two principal elements of his anarchist political philosophy: (1) that the essence of the State is first and foremost coercive; and (2) that the modern State, being the contemporary form assumed by coercion, is a child of the Reformation—or, as he wrote elsewhere, "The State is the younger brother of the Church."[19] These two tenets conflict fundamentally with two of Marx's most basic ideas about the State: (1) that the essence of the State is not coercion but alienation; and (2) that the modern State, being the contemporary form assumed by alienation, is a child not of the Reformation but of the French Revolution.

Bakunin explicitly disconnects the creation of the modern State from the ascendance of the bourgeoisie in his "Three Lectures to Swiss Members of the International." These lectures are the most concise and careful survey of the history of Western Europe, from the Reformation through the Paris Commune, to be found in his writings. Bakunin believed that the most significant characteristic of the era prior to the French Revolution was the usurpation, by the State, of the power of the Church and feudal lords: the raging battle between the Pope and the crowned sovereigns having been decided in favor of the latter, they claimed their titles directly by divine right, without the intercession of religious authorities.

According to Marx, however, the "so-called Christian State" of the Middle Ages was only the "constable of the Catholic Church." In such a State, Marx continues, "what counts is . . . alienation";[20] this tendency is developed further, he concludes, when the French Revolution alienates private property from the community in the creation of the modern State. Marx interpreted the Constitution of the French bourgeoisie as the "independent form of the State, divorced from the real interests of the individual and community." The State became "a separate entity beside and outside civil society" by virtue of "the emancipation of private property from the community."[21] Because he felt that inheritance would disappear naturally in the future with the establishment of communism, which he had defined in 1844 as the "positive overcoming of private property,"[22] Marx opposed the abolition of the right of inheritance, in the 1860s, as unnecessary.

With that position Bakunin disagreed. His interpretation of history led him to regard the right of inheritance as one of the foundations of social inequality: thanks to it, human beings are unequal at birth. The minoritarian founders of even the most primitive State bequeath to their offspring superior social status and all its concomitant advantages, including the "right" to exploit. The "Report of the Committee on the Question of Inheritance" and the "Speeches to the Basle Congress" in this volume illustrate this perspective, according to which the bourgeoisie, in seizing State power by toppling the monarch, did not change the coercive nature of the State but rather became its new usufructuaries.

These differences between Bakunin and Marx, over the basic notion of the State, are rooted in their divergent understandings of Hegel. Both men believed that Democracy was the motive force of history, the real form of Hegel's world-historical Spirit; but that is as far as their agreement went on the issue. According to Hegel, Monarchy was the generic form of the State. Bakunin agreed, and in his analysis Monarchy and Democracy opposed each other, with the result that the State had to be *destroyed* in a general conflagration. For Marx, however, the essence of the State was Democracy itself; he conceived Democracy to be embodied in a constitution hierarchically superior to other political forms, and therefore concluded that the State had to be *realized* to its highest degree.[23]

Bakunin the Left Hegelian had written in 1842, "Democracy not only stands in opposition to the government and is not only a particular constitutional or politico-economic change, but a total transformation of the world condition and a herald of an original, new life which has not yet existed in history."[24] In his eyes, social emancipation did not exist in degrees; either it existed or it did not. For Bakunin the anarchist, therefore, all forms of government were merely various forms of Monarchy, that is, different forms of the despotism of some small number exercised against the vast majority. Political constitutions could not be differentiated as more or less democratic.

If for Marx the carrier of Democracy was the German proletariat, for Bakunin this was the Russian peasantry. Bakunin always had faith in the instincts and the inclinations of the Russian people, believing that they merely needed appropriate inspiration to break into revolt. "The Russian people," he wrote in 1845, "are altogether democratic in their instincts and habits [and] . . . they still have a great mission to perform in the world."[25] He was aware, however, that the Russian people would not rise spontaneously against the Tsar, whose "unlimited will" is the "[only] law in Russia" and whom we may consider to be, according to Bakunin's reading of Hegel, the perfect monarch, "uniting all political powers in his own person, free from any control."[26]

In a speech in Paris in November 1847, Bakunin declared that Russia "is everywhere a synonym for brutal oppression and slavery,"[27] and reasoned that Polish and Russian peasants have a common interest to free themselves from the Tsar's oppression. (This idea reappears in the article here on "Panslavism.") Uniting the themes of Polish nationalism and Russian democracy, Bakunin conjures for his audience a situation in Russia where the army, the peasants, "a very numerous intermediate class composed of quite diverse elements," and the enlightened aristocratic youth are all on the verge of open rebellion. (See "On Russia" and "A Few Words to My Young Brothers in Russia.") What is needed for them to break into revolt, he concludes, is a Russo-Polish revolutionary alliance, which would foretoken the deliverance of all Slavs from the Tsar's domination, and announce the arrival of democracy for all the peasants of Eastern Europe and Russia.

> The reconciliation of Russia and Poland is a great cause and worthy of our wholehearted devotion. It means the liberation of sixty million people, the liberation of all the Slav peoples who groan under a foreign yoke. It means, in a word, the fall, the irretrievable fall, of despotism in Europe.[28]

At the Slav Congress (1848) in Prague, Bakunin tried unsuccessfully to form an international revolutionary committee to foment an insurrection in Bohemia, where he hoped to strike the spark that would inflame the Slavs in a wave rolling eastward to Russia. Whenever Bakunin called for an uprising of the Poles or other Slavs in the 1840s, or for one of the Spanish or the Italians in the 1860s, this was in the hope that such an insurrection would spread, and in the belief that if it spread far enough, it could catalyze the revolutionary sentiments of the Russian peasants. In 1851, Bakunin recalled his attitudes at the Congress three years earlier:

> It is true that without Russia Slav unity is not complete and there is no Slav strength; but it would be senseless to expect salvation and assistance for the Slavs from present-day Russia. What is left for you? First, unite outside of Russia, not excluding her but waiting, hoping for her liberation near at hand; and she will be carried away by your example and you will be the liberators of the Russian people, who in turn will then be your strength and your shield.[29]

It is useful to interpose here Engels's critique of Bakunin's *Appeal to the Slavs,* for it also contains his criticism of democratic Panslavism more generally. Writing in 1849, Engels argues that the Slavs cannot be revolutionary.

> [Panslavism] . . . has in reality no other aim than to give the Austrian Slavs . . . a basis of support . . .
>
> . . . [T]he Southern Slavs [are] necessarily counterrevolutionary owing to the whole of their historical position . . .
>
> Peoples which have never had a history of their own . . . are not viable and will never be able to achieve any kind of independence.
>
> And that has been the fate of the Austrian Slavs. . . .
>
> The same thing holds for the Southern Slavs proper.[30]

This criticism is based not only on the premise that bourgeois capitalist development is a prerequisite to the formation of a nation-state, but also on a not always latent German nationalist undercurrent.

> [If the Panslavist program were realized,] the eastern part of Germany would be torn to pieces like a loaf of bread that has been gnawed by rats! And all that by way of thanks for the Germans having given themselves the trouble of civilizing the stubborn Czechs and Slovenes . . .[31]

Bakunin's mature anarchism was built on a foundation of international, not just Slav, revolution; his advocacy of Panslavism in Prague in 1848 is perhaps best understood as an aspect of this developing cosmopolitanism, a stage evolving from his strictly Polish sympathies of the mid-1840s. Nevertheless, there are continuities with his later period. Bakunin's *Appeal to the Slavs* of 1848, as well as the three papers he submitted to the Prague Congress, on which the *Appeal* is based, express his belief (1) that although the future hopes of revolution lay with the working class, both peasantry and proletariat, still the peasantry, especially the Russian peasantry, would prove the decisive force in bringing about the final and successful revolution; and (2) that the Austrian Empire had to be broken up and a federation of free Slav republics established in Central and Eastern Europe, based on common ownership of the land. These arguments undergird his discussion of events in his 1869 article, "The Agitation of the Socialist-Democratic Party in Austria."

It is easy to misinterpret the contrasts between this practical revolutionary program, proposed by Bakunin, and that of Marx's, because the social classes each man conceives have, as a set, contrasting and different relationships to the concept of social revolution that he holds. By the time of the revolution, according to Marx, society will have been dichotomized into "two great hostile camps": the bourgeoisie, who are the "owners of the means of production and employers of wage-labor"; and the proletariat, who are reduced by the former "to selling their labor-power in order to live."[32] As for the peasants, "their natural ally [is] the proletariat, whose task is the overthrow" of the bourgeois order.[33] Despite Marx's admission late in life that even in Germany "the majority of the 'toiling people' . . . consists of peasants, and not of proletarians," the world-historical role of the proletariat remained for him an article of faith; and he believed that, since the peasantry would cease to exist because of the inevitable universalization of the condition of the proletariat, the peasants' only hope was to forsake their own interests and to identify with those of the proletariat.[34] Bakunin objected to this very idea, foreseeing "nothing more nor less than a new aristocracy, that of the workers in the factories and towns, to the exclusion of the millions who constitute the proletariat of the countryside and who . . . will become the subjects in this great so-called People's State" proclaimed in the name of the urban proletariat.[35] Bakunin considered the proletariat to comprise the urban-industrial workers and the rural-agricultural workers *together*; their union he often simply referred to as "the people." Moreover, the workers and the peasants—to call them that—had, in Bakunin's eyes, not only common but also *interdependent* interests. Bakunin agreed with Marx that the workers had a more highly developed revolutionary consciousness than did the peasants, and he affirmed that the peasants needed the workers' guidance. But he stressed that no revolution could succeeed without an uprising by the people, of whom the peasants were the vast majority. "There is more thought, more revolutionary consciousness in the proletariat of the cities, but there is more natural force in the countryside."[36] These are the main themes of his article on "The Policy of the International."

In "All-Round Education" Bakunin discusses what he calls the "equalization of classes" with respect to knowledge. It is because Bakunin did not believe that the proletariat would become a universal class, and so put an end to history, that he used that phrase in preference to Marx's "abolition of classes." By the equalization of classes, Bakunin meant equalizing not so much the classes themselves as the individuals who compose them; Marx, however, appeared to interpret the phrase in the former, more abstract sense. "The equalization of classes," Marx wrote,

> ... results in the harmony of capital and labor, so obtrusively preached by the bourgeois specialists. The great goal of the International is not the equalization of classes, a logical contradiction, but on the contrary the abolition of classes, the real secret of the proletarian movement.[37]

But "the proletariat ... presented as *class*, and not as *mass*" seemed to Bakunin not only to exclude the peasantry but also to fail to recognize as individuals the individuals who compose it.[38] The issue for Bakunin was the death of the bourgeoisie as a separate class, as a political body economically separated from the working class—not the death of an aggregation of individuals who, as individuals, could join the proletariat by following the program set out in "The Policy of the International." His analysis of this situation may be found in "The International Working-Men's Movement."

Because Bakunin and Marx disagreed over the nature of the principal ill of the existing social order, they meant different things when they wrote of "classes." In brief: (1) Marx defined classes by their relation to the means of production, and (2) he characterized political power as "merely the organized power of one class for oppressing another,"[39] from which (3) he concluded that the proletariat's economic appropriation of the means of production would constitute the foundation of a new political order. By contrast, (1) Bakunin saw the bourgeoisie's political power as having resulted from their denial of political liberty to the people, whose poverty made freedom a fiction for them and licensed to the bourgeoisie alone that liberty,[40] which (2) he believed they obtained through their *own* revolt against the monarchy, in which they seized State power in the *name* of the people, whence (3) he concluded that economic relations between politically defined classes did not change when merely the form of government was altered.

III

The programs of revolution espoused by Bakunin and by Marx are superficially similar; each man believed that the productive forces of society, reappropriated by revolution, would sustain social life thereafter. Each man also believed that transformation of the productive forces of society into collective property to be a *conditio sine qua non* of the revolution. The difference between them lies in the fact that, whereas that transformation did not serve Bakunin as a characteristic definition of social revolution, it did so serve for Marx.

Bakunin would have been a partisan of any spirit or any power that could have realized a genuine and wholehearted revamping of social conditions. The violence or peacefulness of the transformation was less important than its immanence and thoroughgoingness. This he asserted as early as his 1845 letter to *La Réforme* in Paris, and it accounts for his willingness (which disappeared after 1863) to allow the Tsar a role in accomplishing the social transformation. Following his imprisonment in the 1850s and subsequent escape from exile, Bakunin, in 1862, wrote and published a pamphlet in which he examined three possible forms that he then conceived a revolution in Russia could take: a bloodless revolution sponspored by the Tsar, a peasant uprising such as Pugachev's, and an insurrection modelled on the Decembrist movement.[41] Discounting a revolt of the intelligentsia as incapable of bringing about a true revolution, Bakunin confronted the same tactical choice as a decade and a half earlier.

In *To Russian, Polish, and All Slav Friends,*[42] another pamphlet he wrote in 1862, Bakunin renovated, from the perspective of his experiences in 1848-49, his belief that a peasant revolution in Russia could be catalyzed by the right combination of national insurrections in Europe. Acting on this belief the following year, he left London for Poland, where a widespread rebellion was being heralded, joining an eclectic legion of sympathizers who sailed to reinforce the insurgents. The insurrection, however, was suppressed before the brigade reached Poland, and the ship docked instead in Sweden. From there Bakunin moved to Italy, where he spent the middle years of the decade of the 1860s: first in Florence, where he formed a circle called the Brotherhood (really a discussion group in which he propagandized future Italian socialists), and later in Naples, where he created a new society which he called the International Brotherhood. The program that Bakunin wrote for the latter, the "Revolutionary Catechism," was the first document in which he outlined the program of his mature anarchism.[43]

Leaving Italy in 1867, Bakunin attended, in September of that year, the First Congress of the League of Peace and Freedom (LPF), in Geneva. He spoke to the assembled delegates and joined the organization's Central Committee, which accepted the program he outlined in the brochure *Federalism, Socialism, and Anti-Theologism.*[44] At the League's Berne Congress the following year, however, Bakunin found himself accused of communism by the rank-and-file bourgeois delegates when he introduced a resolution concerning "the economic and social equalization of classes and individuals." He defended himself as a collectivist and not a communist:

> I am not a communist, because communism concentrates and swallows up in itself for the benefit of the State all the forces of society, because it inevitably leads to the concentration of property in the hands of the State, whereas I want the abolition of the State[.] . . . I want to see society and collective or social property organized from below upwards, by way of free association, not from above downwards, by means of any kind of authority whatever. . . . That is the sense, gentlemen, in which I am a collectivist, but not a communist.[45]

Bakunin's motion was nevertheless defeated, and after the Congress finished its business he withdrew from the League with his associates. With them he then founded the International Alliance of Socialist Democracy, which considered itself a branch of the International Working-Men's Association (IWMA) and, applying to the latter's General Council for corporate admission, accepted its statutes. The Council refused this application, contending that an international body within the IWMA would create confusion, and citing its refusal of a similar application which Bakunin had convinced the LPF Central Committee to make. The General Council of the IWMA declared null and void those articles of the Alliance pertaining to their mutual relations, but allowed the individual sections of the Alliance to become sections of the International after the Alliance had altered its statute on the "equalization of classes" to read "abolition of classes," and had dissolved itself as a corporate organization.

From the fact that Bakunin tried to merge, with the IWMA, first the League of Peace and Freedom and then the International Alliance of Socialist Democracy, it can be claimed (as many have done) that he was seeking to take control of Marx's organization. This interpretation is one-sided, betraying an insufficient degree of comprehension of Bakunin's tactical program. The purpose that Bakunin gave the Alliance was to provide the International with a real revolutionary organization. In order to understand fully the logic of this tactic, it is necessary to recall Bakunin's philosophical orientation, particularly the conception of dialectical contradiction as he discussed it in his 1842 article.

Briefly put, Bakunin respected Marx's scholarship but believed the man to be, in the language of "Reaction in Germany," a compromising

Negative. Marx's advocacy of participation in bourgeois politics, including parliamentary suffrage, would have been proof of this. It would have been Bakunin's duty, following the script defined by his dialectic, to bring the IWMA to a recognition of its true role. His desire to merge first the League and then the Alliance with the International derived from a conviction that the revolutionaries in the International should never cease to be penetrated to every extremity by the spirit of Revolution. Just as, in Bakunin's dialectic, the consistent Negatives needed the compromisers in order to vanquish them and thereby realize the Negative's true essence, so Bakunin, in the 1860s, needed the International in order to transform its activity into uncompromising Revolution.

Why did the revolutionary organization itself, within the International, have to remain secret? Bakunin argues that it would otherwise divorce itself from the life of the people and become a new State by imposing on them (like a "vanguard" party) its thenceforth authoritarian will. A secret organization was essential to the revolution, but wide participation by the masses was necessary to its success. Still, even the most widespread insurgency would accomplish nothing unless it were skillfully organized and prepared; therefore the secret revolutionary organization draws its strength from the life of the people. Its members "go to the people."[46] The "powerful but always invisible revolutionary collectivity" leaves the "full development [of the revolution] to the revolutionary movement of the masses and the most absolute liberty to their social organization, . . . but always seeing to it that this movement and this organization should never be able to reconstitute any authorities, governments, or States and always combatting all ambitions, collective (such as Marx's) as well as individual, by the natural, *never official,* influence of every member of our Alliance."[47] Animated by the secret revolutionary organization, the International would provide a base of operations for stirring popular sentiment, taking on the crucial role of disseminating propaganda. Bakunin's conception of the revolutionary role of the International, and of its tactics, is elaborated below in the very important text, "The Organization of the International."

Both Bakunin's Panslavism and his anarchism were *democratic*. It is worthwhile to recall, in this connection, how he first conceived Democracy, under the influence of German philosophy, in his 1842 article: "Democracy is a religion[; its partisans should be] religious, that is, *permeated* by its true principle not only in thought and reasoning, but true to it also in real life down to life's smallest manifestations . . ."[48] When Bakunin concluded that "we must not only act politically, but in our politics act religiously,"[49] he meant that action must be permeated, penetrated through and through, by the principle of Democracy. In the same way, the members of the secret revolutionary organization were to be penetrated by the spirit of Revolution, which would transmit itself, through them, among the people.

Many observers find it difficult to reconcile the democratic current in Bakunin's thought with the seemingly authoritarian streak inferred from passages such as the following, which dates from 1851:

> I thought that in Russia, more than anywhere else, there would be necessary a strong dictatorial power [*vlast*], exclusively concerned with the elevation and public education of the masses; a power with a free spirit, free to follow any path, but without parliamentary forms; with the printing of books free in content, but without the freedom of printing; surrounded by like-minded persons and enlightened by their advice, strengthened by their free assistance but not limited by anyone or anything. I told myself that the whole difference between such a dictatorship and monarchical power was that the former, through the spirit that sets it in place, strives to render its own existence unnecessary as soon as possible, having in view only the freedom, independence, and progressive maturation of the people; monarchical power, on the contrary, must endeavor to prevent its [own] existence from ever becoming unnecessary, and therefore must maintain its subjects in unalterable childhood.[50]

Such a notion is fundamentally different from Marx's "dictatorship of the proletariat." In the midst of a popular upheaval, Bakunin explained in the early 1870s, the members of the secret revolutionary organization, "firmly united and inspired with a single idea, a single aim, applicable everywhere in different ways according to the circumstances," would disperse themselves "in small groups throughout the empire." The "dictatorial power" of the secret revolutionary organization, democratic in this immanent sense, would have for its chief aim and purpose to "help the people towards self-determination, without the least interference from any sort of domination, *even if it be temporary or transitional.*"[51] In this respect, the contrast with Marx's vision of the dictatorship of the proletariat could not be more clearly drawn. Bakunin seemed instinctively to recognize that pre-revolutionary organizational tactics are imprinted on post-revolutionary social relations.

If we now understand, first, that the revolution, according to Bakunin, will be animated by a secret revolutionary organization immanent in the people, one that "goes to the people" and draws its strength from their life, acting as lightning rods to electrify them with the current of Revolution; and, second, that the members of the secret revolutionary organization, animated by the same revolutionary spirit and working with similar purpose, organize the people of every region around the *local* issues closest to them, assuring nonetheless that each local uprising take on the character of the true popular revolution into which, erupting universally, they will all merge: then *the ideational nexus of (1) the secret revolutionary organization with (2) its own anti-Statist "dictatorship," which is in fact (3) immanent in the people,* ceases to resemble the incoherent ravings of a "demon of pan-destruction"[52] and *takes on the appearance of the nucleus of a structured system of thought* which the vagaries of the history of Bakunin's time aided in obscuring, and which the vagaries of historiography since then have not much helped to clarify.

It is incorrect to believe that, because Bakunin was an anarchist, he was opposed to all laws. He detested man-made law, but natural law was something else again. "All things are governed by laws that are inherent to them[, that]... are the natural and real processes... through which everything exists."[53] Human society being a thing of nature, it follows immanent natural laws. "In obeying the laws of nature, man... only obeys laws which are inherent in his own nature."[54] Animated by the spirit of Revolution, the members of the secret revolutionary organization catalyze the appearance of the real laws which are inherent in the life of the people but which are obscured by artificial laws. Where human beings oppose *man-made law* that has been forced on them by others, and attempt instead to follow their own inherent human nature, there Revolution is itself nothing less than *natural law*.

Comment on Texts and Translation

Many of the items in this collection either have not appeared in English before or have appeared only in disconnected fragments. Here is given, for each item, information on its first publication, the French text(s) used to prepare these translations, and previous translations consulted.

First Publication

1. "Trois Conférences faites aux Ouvriers du Val de Saint-Imier," in Michel Bakounine, *Œuvres,* 6 vols. (Paris: P.V. Stock, 1895-1913), V, 299-360.
2. "Les Endormeurs," *L'Égalité* (Geneva), nos. 23-27 (26 June and 3, 10, 17, 24 July 1869).
3. "La Montagne," *L'Égalité,* nos. 20, 25-27 (5 June and 10, 17, 24 July 1869); "Le jugement de M. Coullery," *L'Égalité,* no. 28 (31 July 1869).
4. "Politique de l'Internationale," *L'Égalité,* nos. 29-32 (7, 14, 21, 28 August 1869).
5. "L'Instruction intégrale," *L'Égalité,* nos. 28-31 (31 July and 7, 14, 21 August 1869).
6. "Rapport de la Commission sur la Question de l'Héritage, adopté par l'Assemblée générale des sections de Genève," *L'Égalité,* no. 32 (28 August 1869).
7. "Sur la Question du Droit d'Héritage," *L'Égalité,* no. 35 (18 September 1869); "Sur la Question de la Propriété foncière," *L'Égalité,* no. 37 (1 October 1869).
8. "Organisation de l'Internationale," in *Almanach du peuple pour 1872* (Saint-Imier: Propagande socialiste, 1871), pp. 11-22.
9. "La Double Grève de Genève," *L'Égalité,* no. 11 (3 April 1869); "Organisation et Grève générale," *L'Égalité,* no. 11 (3 April 1869).
10. "De la Coopération," *L'Égalité,* no. 33 (4 September 1869).
11. "Le Mouvement International des Travailleurs," *L'Égalité,* no. 18 (22 May 1869).
12. "[De la] Russie," *L'Égalité,* no. 13 (17 April 1869).
13. "Quelques paroles à mes jeunes frères en Russie," *La Liberté* (Brussels), no. 115 (5 September 1869).
14. "Aux Compagnons de l'Association Internationale des Travailleurs au Locle et à la Chaux-de-Fonds," *Le Progrès* (Le Locle), nos. 6-9, 11 (1 March and 3, 17 April and 1, 29 May 1869).

15. "Le Patriotisme physiologique ou naturel," *Le Progrès,* nos. 12, 14, 17, 19 (12 June, 10 July, 21 August, and 18 September 1869).
16. "L'Agitation du Parti de la Démocratie socialiste en Autriche," *L'Égalité,* no. 22 (19 June 1869).
17. "Le Panslavisme," *Bulletin russe* (Geneva), no. 2 (9 April 1870).

Sources Used

1. First publication; and *Archives Bakounine,* 8 vols. in 9 by 1984 (Leiden: E.J. Brill, 1961-), VI, 217-45.
2. *Œuvres,* V, 106-34; *Le Socialisme libertaire* (Paris: Denoël, 1973), pp. 93-114.
3. *Œuvres,* V, 76-108; last three installments in *Le Socialisme libertaire,* pp. 141-58.
4. *Œuvres,* V, 169-98; *Le Socialisme libertaire,* pp. 159-81.
5. *Œuvres,* V, 134-69; *Le Socialisme libertaire,* pp. 115-40.
6. *Œuvres,* V, 199-209; *Le Socialisme libertaire,* pp. 182-90.
7. *Le Socialisme libertaire,* pp. 198-203.
8. As part of "Protestation de l'Alliance," in *Œuvres,* VI, 79-97. The first publication contains some omissions and changes from this authoritative text.
9. *Œuvres,* V, 35-52; *Le Socialisme libertaire,* pp. 65-74.
10. *Œuvres,* V, 210-18; *Le Socialisme libertaire,* pp. 191-97.
11. *Œuvres,* V, 60-63; *Le Socialisme libertaire,* pp. 80-83.
12. *Œuvres,* V, 53-59; *Le Socialisme libertaire,* pp. 75-79.
13. *Archives Bakounine,* V, 11-16; *Le Socialisme libertaire,* pp. 204-11.
14. *Œuvres,* I, 207-32; first three installments in *Le Socialisme libertaire,* pp. 41-51.
15. *Œuvres,* I, 233-60; first two installments in *Le Socialisme libertaire,* pp. 51-60.
16. *Œuvres,* V, 64-75; *Le Socialisme libertaire,* pp. 84-92.
17. *Archives Bakounine,* IV, 87-89.

Previous Translations Used

Although Bakunin thought, spoke and wrote in fluent French, some Russicisms carried over from his native tongue. It was occasionally helpful to consult Russian translations of the texts, where these existed; therefore they are noted here, along with English translations consulted. The English translations listed here are not necessarily an exhaustive catalogue of previous translations of the texts.

1. Translated into English here for the first time.
2. English: G. P. Maximoff (comp. and ed.), *The Political Philosophy*

of Bakunin (Glencoe, Ill.: The Free Press of Glencoe, 1953) [hereafter *Maximoff*], pp. 82-83, 197, 199, 241, 269-70, 411.
Russian: M. A. Bakunin, *Izbrannye sochineniia,* 5 vols. (Petrograd: Golos truda, 1919-21) [hereafter *GT*], IV, 23-40.

3. Translated into English here for the first time.
4. English: *Maximoff,* pp. 189, 197-98, 214, 215-16, 278, 282-83, 311-12, 312-13, 314, 315, 315-16, 322-23, 323, 374, 375 (each reference is to a separate fragment, the entire edition being quite disorganized and hard to use); selected passages in Sam Dolgoff (ed.), *Bakunin on Anarchy* (New York: Random House, 1972), pp. 160-74.
Russian: *GT,* IV, 3-22; M.A. Bakunin, *Izbrannyia sochineniia,* ed. V. Cherkezov, 1 vol. (N.p.: F.A.K.G., 1920) [hereafter *FAKG*], I, 249-71.
5. English: *Maximoff,* pp. 82, 101-2, 102, 155, 157, 168-69, 182, 183, 271, 328, 328-29, 329, 329-30, 330, 332, 334-35, 336, 337, 382, 383, 411-12.
Russian: *GT,* IV, 41-64.
6. English: *Maximoff,* pp. 181-82, 241, 242-47.
7. Translated into English here for the first time.
8. Translated in full into English here for the first time.
9. English: *Maximoff,* pp. 321-22, 322, 372.
10. Translated into English here for the first time.
11. Translated into English here for the first time.
12. Translated into English here for the first time.
13. Translated into English here for the first time.
14. English: *Maximoff,* pp. 160, 170, 193-94, 194-95, 206, 208, 225-26, 226-27, 232, 372, 409; Albert Fried and Ronald Sanders (eds.), *Socialist Thought* (Garden City, N.Y.: Anchor Books, Doubleday & Co., 1964), pp. 332-44, for the first four installments.
Russian: *GT,* IV, 79-94; *FAKG,* I, 272-91.
15. English: *Maximoff,* pp. 227-32, 369-70.
Russian: *GT,* IV, 94-110; *FAKG,* I, 291-309.
16. Translated into English here for the first time.
17. Translated into English here for the first time.

Comment on Translating Bakunin

The three goals that Tytler enunciated some two centuries ago in his *Principles of Translation* were: (1) to give a complete transcript of the original ideas, (2) to imitate the styles of the original author, and (3) to preserve the ease of the original text.[1] Here the first of these has not been difficult to fulfill. The second presented no especial difficulties, although it required special considerations. In the case of Bakunin, the third is debatable.

Concerning the first principle, it was not hard to transcribe Bakunin's ideas, but achieving their optimal expression in English was a somewhat arduous procedure, since sentences exceeding one hundred words in the original material were not unusual. It is instructive to describe the method followed. The entire first draft of the translations was done at a typewriter, with a language dictionary on a side table. Little attention was given at this stage to precise wording; the objective was to transfer the gist of the material from one language to another. The result was a typescript in "translatorese," which then had to be transformed into regular English. That task took two, sometimes three, occasionally four revisions.

The main purpose of the first revision was to make the principal idea of the passage evident on the first reading. Previous English translations were used at this stage to suggest syntactical formulations: the previous translation was compared with the draft in translatorese, the differences in formulation was intuited, and then the draft was revised on the basis of consultation with the original French text. The focus was not on verbatim comparison; in practice, this procedure was nonverbal and structural-linguistic. Entirely new English formulations were sometimes suggested by Russian translations of the original.

The second revision was concerned with making the translated sentence flow as naturally as possible in the English language, conserving still the proper emphasis. Here entered such considerations as transposition of clauses and antecedents, and concomitant decisions on punctuation. During this second revision, alternative stylistic formulations for difficult spots were still considered, and decisions were taken on conventions for the translation of closely synonymous words. The issue of false cognates does not require comment, and anachronism was still another pitfall to be avoided (for instance, *universel,* in the nineteenth century, meant not "universal" but "worldwide"). Tertiary and still later revisions were relatively minor in scope, involving touch-ups for clarity or artistry, and the uniform application of conventions for near-synonyms.

Tytler's second point, to imitate the styles of the original author, requires a brief description of Bakunin's French. One may see in Bakunin's French a combination of two Russian styles: the "sublime" Church Slavonic and the "vulgar" popular. In the former mode, Bakunin's writing has a rhythm that carries the reader along; however, because one rarely has the opportunity for significant revisions in journalistic work such as here, Bakunin's writing in the texts translated is often more successful where it is aphoristic. This is particularly striking in the transcripts of his speeches. The sublime style is most impressive when used to discuss philosophical issues, as befits a calque of Church Slavonic.

Although this is not the place for an exhaustive study of Bakunin's style, it is worth mentioning that the five types of Russicism that Nicolaevsky discovered in Bakunin's German are present in his French as well.[2] Briefly, these are:

1. Incorrect Germanization of Russian Expressions. In Bakunin's writings translated here, there are many instances of faulty Frenchification, such as *trouver intérêt* for *prinosit' pol'zu* and *avoir la priorité du temps* for *pervenstvovat' vremeni.*
2. Russicisms in the Use of *nur* and *noch.* Similar confusions are present in Bakunin's French use of *encore, même, seulement,* etc.
3. Incorrect Verb Forms. The same problems in Bakunin's French as in his German are evident (though to a lesser degree), i.e., proper tense and mood, particularly the use of the past tenses and subjunctive mood.
4. Incorrect Prepositions and Cases. Problems with prepositions are infrequent but detectable in Bakunin's French; an example is *rejeter dans* for *rejeter sur.* Although nouns in French are not inflected, some instances of confusion over case may be found, such as the use of *rien de commun* for *rien en commun* (where the Russian genitive *nichego obshchego* suggests the French preposition *de*).
5. Incorrect Use of Articles. As in his German, Bakunin has difficulty in French with definite articles, which do not exist in Russian.

We may add here another category which Nicolaevsky omits. This is the use, in French, of participles which would be correct in Russian, where a native French-speaker would tend to use a relative clause (e.g., *ayant travaillé* for *qui a travaillé*). Such usage is not unknown in French, but it is extremely infrequent, whereas it is habitual in Russian. It is the relative frequency of this construction, and its contribution to the rhythm of the prose, which permit inference, respectively, to the native language of the author and to Bakunin personally.

It is possible to categorize systematically these six types of dysgloss.[3] The first two, mentioned by Nicolaevsky, we may call dysglosses of *idiom,* since they involve expressions peculiar to a given language. The next three that Nicolaevsky enumerates may be called dysglosses of *grammar,* since they involve inflection and localized word function. Finally, the last dysglottal feature may be called one of *syntax,* since it involves how words are put together to form global features such as clauses.

Tytler's third desideratum is that translations preserve the ease of the original text. Here the original did not always have great ease, particularly in some of the passages in French "Church Slavonic." Therefore, where a clearly new idea began in the midst of an extremely long sentence, the sentence was broken. This involved nothing more than changing a semicolon to a full stop and capitalizing the next word; but semicolons were left standing unless there were compelling reasons for such a change. Guillaume once incurred Bakunin's anger for making editorial changes too extensive, and that has been a motivating factor here for minimizing such emendations. Despite the syntactical reformulation necessary to make prolix passages comprehensible, fidelity to style was striven for through techniques that Bakunin used, such as parentheses—which were, however, more often dashed than bracketed—and tone (such as outrage or irony). Where appropriate, the style of the English translation was consciously Russified. If these translations should have more ease than the original, then Tytler's third rule has been broken only in order to fulfill his first two.

The following language dictionaries were useful: English-English (Webster), English-French (Larousse), English-Russian (Müller), French-English (Larousse), French-French (Larousse), and Russian-English (Smirnitsky). An English thesaurus (Roget) was indispensable, and a French thesis on the political vocabulary of the epoch was also helpful.[4]

The Library of Congress system of transliteration, omitting diacritical marks, has been used for Russian titles in the notes and other phrases. Where proper names figure in the English syntax, however, changes have been introduced with the nonspecialist in mind.

Part One

The Rise and Decline of the Bourgeoisie in Europe

1.

389.

~~Citoyens~~ – Compagnons

Depuis la ~~Révolution~~ grande Révolution de 1789 – 1793, aucun des événements qui ~~lui~~ ont succédé en Europe, ~~dans le monde~~ n'ont eu l'importance et la grandeur de ceux qui se déroulent à nos yeux, et dont Paris est aujourd'hui le théâtre.

Deux faits historiques, deux révolutions mémorables avaient constitué ~~le monde moderne~~ ce que nous appelons, le monde de la civilisation bourgeoise. L'une connue sous le nom de Réformation ~~religieuse~~, au commencement du XVIme siècle, avait brisé la clef de voûte de l'édifice féodal, la toute-puissance de l'Église; en détruisant cette puissance, elle prépara la ruine du pouvoir indépendant et quasi-absolu des seigneurs féodaux, qui bénis ~~par~~ protégés, consacrés par ~~cette~~ l'Église, comme les rois et souvent même contre les rois, faisaient procéder leurs droits directement de la grâce divine; et par là même elle donna un essor nouveau à l'émancipation de la classe bourgeoise, lentement préparée, à son tour, ~~pendant~~ les deux siècles qui ~~lui avaient précédé~~ avaient précédé cette révolution religieuse par le développement successif des libertés communales et par celui du commerce et de l'industrie, qui en avaient été en même temps la condition et la conséquence nécessaire.

De cette révolution sortit une nouvelle

Facsimile of the first manuscript page of "Three Lectures to Swiss Members of the International." Source: Paris, Bibliothèque nationale, Salle des Manuscrits, Nouvelles acquisitions françaises, folio 23690, p. 389.

1

Three Lectures to Swiss Members of the International

1

Comrades,

The developments [i.e., the Commune] now unfolding in Paris have the largest scale and are the most important in Europe since the Great [French] Revolution of 1789-1793.

Two historic events, two memorable revolutions created what we call the modern world, the world of bourgeois civilization. One, the Reformation, at the start of the sixteenth century, shattered that keystone of the feudal structure, the omnipotence of the Church. By destroying this empire, the Reformation prepared the overthrow of the independent and nearly absolute power of the feudal lords, who—blessed and protected like kings by the Church, and often so even in opposition to kings—claimed that their rights derived directly from divine grace; and by doing so, the Reformation gave a new push to the emancipation of the bourgeois class, itself slowly prepared over the two centuries preceding this religious Revolution by the gradual development of communal liberties, and of their necessary condition and inevitable result, commerce and industry.

From this Revolution emerged a new power, not yet that of the bourgeoisie but that of the State—an aristocratic constitutional monarchy in England, and a nobiliary, military, and bureaucratic absolute monarchy on the entire continent of Europe, except for two small republics, Switzerland and the Netherlands.

Let us leave these two republics aside out of courtesy and concern ourselves with the monarchies. Let us examine the relations of the classes and their political and social situation after the Reformation.

Giving honor where honor is due, let us begin with the priests; and by *priests* I mean not only those of the Catholic Church but also Protestant ministers—in a word, every individual who makes a living from religious worship, selling us God Almighty wholesale and retail. As for the theological differences which divide them, these are so subtle and at the same time so absurd that to concern ourselves with them would be a useless waste of time.

Before the Reformation the Church and the priests, headed by the Pope, were the true lords of the earth. According to the doctrine of the Church, the temporal authorities of every country—Emperors, kings, and the most powerful monarchs—were possessed of rights only insofar as the

Church recognized and consecrated those rights. We know that the last two centuries of the Middle Ages saw the increasingly impassioned and victorious battle of crowned sovereigns against the Pope and of the States against the Church. The Reformation put an end to this struggle by proclaiming the States independent. The sovereign's right [to rule] was recognized as proceeding immediately from God, without the interference of the Pope or any other priest; and thanks to this wholly heavenly source, it was naturally declared absolute. In this way the edifice of monarchical despotism was erected on the ruins of the Church's despotism. Having been master of the State, the Church became its servant, an instrument of government in the hands of the monarch.

The Church assumed this attitude not only in the Protestant countries where the monarch was declared the head of the Church, England and the Anglican Church in particular no exception, but also in every Catholic country, even in Spain. Shattered by the terrible blows of the Reformation, the power of the Roman Church could no longer support itself. It needed the help of the States' temporal sovereigns to continue to exist. But we know that sovereigns never give their help for nothing. They have never had any sincere religion and creed other than those of their power and of their treasury, of which the latter is at the same time the end of and the means to the former. As a result the Church, in order to buy the support of the monarchical governments, had to prove to them that it was capable and desirous of serving them. Before the Reformation it had raised the peoples up against the kings many times. After the Reformation it became the ally of the governments against the peoples in every country, even in Switzerland, a sort of black police in the hands of Statesmen and the governing classes, giving itself the mission of preaching patience, obedience, and resignation to the masses of the people. The people, said the Church, should assure themselves of heavenly treasures by abandoning earthly goods and pleasures to the prosperous and the powerful of the earth. You know that all the Christian churches, Catholic and Protestant, continue to preach this way still today. Happily they are less and less listened to, and we can foresee the time when they will be forced to close their establishments for lack of believers, or to put it another way, for lack of dupes.

Now let us see how the feudal class, the nobility, changed after the Reformation. It remained the privileged and nearly exclusive proprietor of the land but lost all its political independence. Before the Reformation the nobility had been, like the Church, the rival and enemy of the State. After that revolution it became, like the Church, a privileged servant of the State. All military and civil offices of the State, with the exception of the least important ones, were occupied by nobles. The courts of the great European monarchs, and even those of the not so great, were filled with nobles. The greatest feudal lords, once so bold and independent, became titled footmen to the sovereigns. They completely lost their boldness and independence, but they retained all their arrogance. It may even be said that this increased, since arrogance is the vice which is a flunkey's privilege. Abject, grovelling and servile in the sovereign's presence, they became more insolent toward the bourgeoisie and the people, whom they continued to plunder no longer in their own name and by divine right but with the permission of their masters and in their service, under the pretext of the greater good of the State.

This position and social station of the nobility are even now preserved nearly in full in Germany, a foreign country which seems to have the privilege of dreaming the most beautiful and noble things, only to realize the most shameful and infamous. The ignoble and atrocious barbarities of the recent Franco-Prussian War demonstrate this, as does the very recent formation of this repulsive Knouto-Germanic Empire,[1]* an incontestable menace to the liberty of every country in Europe, a challenge hurled at all humanity by the brutal despotism of an Emperor who is simultaneously police and staff sergeant, and by the stupid impudence of his nobiliary rabble.

The Reformation delivered the bourgeoisie from the tyranny and plunder of the feudal lords, acting as independent and private bandits or plunderers. But it delivered the bourgeoisie to a new tyranny and plunder—regularized under the name of ordinary and extraordinary State taxes—by these same lords, who were transformed into servants of the State, that is, brigands and legitimate plunderers. This transition from feudal plunder to a much more regular and systematic State plunder at first seemed to satisfy the middle class. We must conclude that at first it genuinely alleviated their economic and social situation. But, as the saying goes, the more one has the more one wants. State taxes, moderate enough to begin with, increased each year by a disturbing proportion, though not as formidably as they do in monarchical States nowadays. The virtually incessant wars waged by these now absolute States, under the pretext of the international balance of power, between the Reformation and the Revolution of 1789; the necessity of maintaining large standing armies, which thereafter became the principal basis of preserving these States; the growing luxury of the sovereign courts, which were transformed into permanent orgies where the nobiliary rabble, the whole titled and bedecked pack of men-servants, came to ask for pensions from their master; the need to maintain this whole privileged mob which filled the highest offices in the army, the bureaucracy, and the police: it all led to enormous expenses. Naturally, it was at first primarily the people who paid these expenses, but so did the bourgeois class, which until the [French] Revolution was also considered a milk-cow

*[Numbered notes to the texts are the editor's and appear together at the back of the volume. Those marked with an asterisk and appearing at the bottom of page are Bakunin's unless otherwise indicated.—Ed.]

(though the people were considered more of one) which had no destiny other than to support the sovereign and his innumerable throng of privileged functionaries. Moreover, the liberty which the middle class had lost through the Reformation was perhaps twice the security it had gained. Before the Reformation it had cleverly profited from its alliance with the kings, and from the indispensability of its support in their struggle against the Church and the feudal lords, in order to gain a certain degree of independence and liberty. But after the Church and the feudal lords were subordinated to the State, the kings no longer needed the services of the middle class and, little by little, they deprived it of all the freedoms which they had granted it in earlier times.

If this was where the bourgeois class found itself after the Reformation, you can imagine the situation of the popular masses, of the peasants and the workers. We know that during the Reformation, at the beginning of the sixteenth century, the peasants of central Europe, in Germany, Holland, and even part of Switzerland, formed a great movement to emancipate themselves, crying, "War on the princes and peace to the people!"[2] This movement was betrayed by the bourgeois class and cursed by the chiefs of bourgeois Protestantism, Luther and Melanchthon; it was drowned in the blood of tens of thousands of insurgent peasants. Since then the peasants have been tied to the soil more than ever, serfs in law but slaves in fact, and so they stayed until the revolution of 1789-1793 in France, until 1807 in Prussia, and until 1848 in all the rest of Germany. Serfdom still exists today in many parts of northern Germany, notably Mecklenburg, but even in Russia it has ceased to exist.

The proletariat in the towns was not much freer than the peasantry. It was divided into two categories: workers who were members of guilds, and those who were not organized at all. The activities of the former, as well as what they produced, were tied down and strangled by a multitude of rules, enslaving them to the guildmasters and the bosses. The latter were deprived of all rights, oppressed and exploited by everybody. As always, the greatest taxes inevitably fell on the people.

This ruination and general oppression of the working masses, and partly of the bourgeois class, had for its pretext and as its acknowledged goal the grandeur, power, and magnificence of the monarchical, nobiliary, bureaucratic, and military State, a State which had usurped the place of the Church and proclaimed itself a divine institution. Accordingly, there was a State morality entirely different from, or rather wholly opposed to, the private morality of men. Private morality has an everlasting basis that is more or less recognized, understood, accepted, and achieved in every human society, insofar as it is not vitiated by religious dogmas. This basis is nothing but human respect, respect for human dignity and for the right and freedom of every human individual. To respect [these principles] is a virtue; to violate them, on the contrary, is a crime. State morality is wholly opposed to this human morality. The State presents itself to its subjects as the supreme goal. Virtue consists of serving its power and grandeur, by all means possible and impossible, even contrary to all human laws and to the good of humanity. Since everything which contributes to the power and growth of the State is good, everything contrary to them is bad, be it even the noblest and most virtuous action from the human point of view. This is why Statesmen, diplomats, ministers, and all State functionaries have always availed themselves of crimes and lies and infamous treacheries to serve the State. From the moment that a villainy is committed in the service of the State, it becomes a meritorious act. That is the morality of the State. It is the very negation of human morality and of humanity.

The contradiction lies in the very idea of the State. Because the worldwide State has never been realized, every State is a limited entity comprising a limited territory and a somewhat restricted number of subjects. The vast majority of mankind hence remains outside each State, and humanity altogether remains divided among a multitude of large, medium, and small States, each of which proclaims itself to be and presents itself as the representative of the whole of humanity and as something absolute, despite the fact that it encompasses only a very limited fraction of mankind. That way each State regards everything external to it—every other State, including its subjects and their property—as deprived of all sanction and right, concluding that *it* therefore has the right to attack, conquer, massacre, and plunder so much as its resources and forces permit. You know, dear comrades, that the reason international law has never been successfully established is precisely that from the State's standpoint, everything lying outside the State is deprived of rights. Further, one State need only declare war on another in order to permit—what am I saying?—in order to *command* its subjects to commit every possible crime against the subjects of the enemy State: murder, rape, theft, destruction, arson, and plunder. And these crimes are supposed to be blessed by the God of the Christians, which each of the belligerent States regards as and proclaims to be its exclusive partisan—which naturally must put this poor Almighty God in perfect distress, in Whose name the most horrible crimes on earth have been, and still are, committed. That is why we are the enemies of God Almighty, why we call this fiction, this Divine Phantom, one of the basic sources of the evils which torment mankind.

This is why we are passionate opponents both of the State and of every State. For so long as there exist States, there will be no humanity; and so long as there exist States, war and its horrible crimes and inevitable consequences, the destruction and general misery of the peoples, will never cease.

So long as there are States, the masses of the people will be *de facto* slaves even in the most democratic republics, for they will work not with a view to their own happiness and wealth, but for the power and wealth of the

State. And what is the State? People claim that it is the expression and the realization of the common good, universal rights and freedom. Well, whoever so claims is as good a liar as someone who claims that God Almighty is everyone's protector. Ever since the fantasy of a Divine Being took shape in men's imagination, God—all gods, and among them above all the God of the Christians—has always taken the part of the strong and the rich against the ignorant and impoverished masses. Through His priests, He has blessed the most revolting privileges, the basest oppressions and exploitations.

The State is likewise nothing but the guarantor of all exploitation, to the profit of a small number of prosperous and privileged persons and to the loss of the popular masses. In order to assure the welfare, prosperity, and privileges of some, it uses everyone's collective strength and collective labor, to the detriment of everyone's human rights. In such a set-up the minority plays the role of the hammer and the majority that of the anvil.

Until the Great [French] Revolution, the bourgeois class had been part of the anvil, although less so than the popular masses. And for this reason it became revolutionary.

Yes, it was very revolutionary. It dared to revolt against all divine and human authorities, putting God, the kings, and the Pope into question. The bourgeoisie was especially mad at the nobility, which held a State position that the bourgeoisie burned with impatience to hold in its turn. But no, I don't want to be unjust, and I don't claim in the least that the bourgeoisie was impelled or guided by anything but egoistic thought in its great protests against divine and human tyranny. The force of circumstances and the very nature of its specific structure pushed it instinctively to seize power. But since it was by no means yet aware of the abyss which separates it from the masses of workers whom it exploits, and since the proletariat itself had scarcely awakened to such an awareness, the bourgeoisie, represented by its noblest and greatest personalities in this struggle against Church and State, believed in good faith that it labored impartially to emancipate everybody.

The two centuries between the battles of the religious Reformation and those of the Great [French] Revolution were the heroic age of the bourgeois class. Having acquired power as a result of its wealth and cleverness, it audaciously attacked every institution respected by Church and State. First it undermined everything by literature and philosophic criticism; later it overthrew everything in open rebellion. It was the bourgeoisie that made the revolution of 1789. To be sure, it could do so only by taking advantage of the people's might; but the bourgeoisie organized this might and directed it against the Church, the royalty, and the nobility. It was the bourgeoisie that considered [the situation] and took the initiative in every move that the people carried out. The bourgeoisie had faith in itself. It felt powerful because it knew that the people were behind it and with it.

A comparison of the giants of thought and action who emerged from the bourgeois class in the eighteenth century with the greatest celebrities, the vain and eminent dwarves who represent it now, convincingly demonstrates the decadence and the awful ruination which this class has suffered. In the eighteenth century it was intelligent, bold, and heroic. Now it appears cowardly and stupid. Then full of faith, it dared do everything and could do anything. Now it offers us the sight of the most shameful impotence, consumed by doubt and demoralized by its own injustice, resulting more from its predicament than from its own injustice.

The recent events in France prove this only too well. The bourgeoisie appears entirely incapable of saving France. It prefers the Prussian invasion to the popular revolution which can alone bring about this salvation. It has allowed the banner of human progress, of worldwide emancipation, to fall from its feeble hands. And the proletariat of Paris is today proving that from now on only the workers carry it. I shall attempt to show this at another meeting.

2

Dear Comrades,

I told you that two great historical events laid the foundation of the bourgeoisie's influence: the religious revolution of the sixteenth century, known as the Reformation, and the great political revolution [in France] of the eighteenth century. I added that the latter, accomplished of course by the people, was initiated and directed exclusively by the middle class. I want now to show you that it also benefited the middle class exclusively.

And yet, the program of this Revolution appears vast at first glance. After all, wasn't it made in the name of the Liberty, Equality, and Fraternity of humankind, three words which seem to include everything that humanity could wish for and achieve not only now but in the future as well? How is it, then, that a Revolution which had appeared to be so extensive could have resulted in the exclusive, limited, and privileged emancipation of a single class, to the detriment of the millions of workers who are today crushed by that class's impudent and unjust prosperity?

Ah! This Revolution was only a political Revolution. It audaciously overturned every obstacle and every political tyranny, but it left intact, even proclaiming sacred and inviolable, the economic bases of society which have been the eternal source and chief cause of all political and social injustices, all past and present religious absurdities. It proclaimed the freedom of each and every individual, or rather it proclaimed for each and every individual the right to be free. But really, it gave the means of realizing and enjoying this freedom only to the property-owners, the capitalists, and the rich.

"Poverty is slavery!" These are the terrible words which, in the few days I have the good fortune to spend among you, dear comrades and friends, our friend [Sylvain] Clément, in his sympathetic voice emanating from his experience and his heart, has repeated again and again.[3]

Yes, poverty is slavery—it is the need to sell one's labor, and with one's labor one's person, to the capitalist who gives you the means barely to survive. One's mind must indeed be affected by Bourgeois Gentlemen's lies to dare speak of the political freedom of the working masses. Fine freedom is this, that subjects them to the whims of capital and that shackles them through hunger to the capitalist's will! Dear friends, I surely do not have to prove to you, who have come to understand the agonies of labor through long and hard experience, that so long as capital and labor are mutually isolated, labor will be the slave of capital and workers the subjects of Bourgeois Gentlemen, who out of ridicule give you every political right and every semblance of freedom, so as to preserve its reality exclusively for themselves.

The right to freedom, without the means of achieving it, is only a ghost. And do we not love freedom too much to be satisfied with its ghost? We want its reality. But what constitutes the real basis and the positive condition of freedom? It is, for each individual, the all-round development and full enjoyment of all physical, intellectual, and moral faculties; consequently, it is all the material means necessary for each individual's human existence. It is, then, upbringing and education. A person who is dying from starvation, who is crushed by poverty, who every day is on the point of death from cold and hunger, and who sees everyone he loves suffering likewise but is unable to come to their aid, is not free; that person is a slave. A man condemned to remain a brutish creature all his life for want of a humane education, a man deprived of learning, an ignoramus, is necessarily a slave; and if he exercises any political rights, you can be sure, one way or another, that he will always exercise them against himself, for his exploiters' and masters' benefit.

The negative condition of freedom is that no person owe obedience to another; the individual is free only if his will and his own convictions, and not those of others, determine his acts. But a man compelled by hunger to sell his labor, and with his labor his own self, at the lowest possible price to the capitalist who condescends to exploit him, a man whose own brutishness and ignorance put him at the mercy of his learned exploiters, will inevitably and forever be a slave.

That is not all. The freedom of individuals is by no means an individual matter. It is a collective matter, a collective product. No individual can be free outside of human society or without its cooperation. In every Congress of the [International] Working-Men['s Association] we have fought the individualists or false-brother socialists who say that society was founded by a free contract of originally free men and who claim, along with the moralists and bourgeois economists, that man can be free, that he can be a man, outside of society.

This theory revealed by J.-J. Rousseau—the most malevolent writer of the past century, the sophist who inspired all the bourgeois revolutionaries—betokens a complete ignorance of both nature and history. It is not in the past, nor even in the present, that we should seek the freedom of the masses. It is in the future, in a future close at hand. We should seek the freedom of the masses in that historic tomorrow which we ourselves must create not only by the force of our thought and will, but also by the force of our actions. In the past there has never been a free contract. There has only been brutality, stupidity, injustice, and violence—and today still, you know only too well, this so-called free contract is a compact of hunger and of slavery for the masses, and the exploitation of hunger for the minority who oppress and destroy us.

The theory of the free contract is just as false from the standpoint of nature. Man does not voluntarily create society, he is involuntarily born into it. He is above all a social animal. Only in society can he become a human being, that is, a thinking, speaking, loving, and willful animal. Imagine a man endowed with the most inspired powers by nature, cast out from all human society into a desert since infancy. If he does not miserably perish, which is the most probable result, he will become nothing but a boor, an ape, lacking speech and thought. For thought is inseparable from speech; no one can think without words. Even if you are alone with yourself, perfectly isolated, you must use words to think. To be sure, you can have conceptions which represent things, but as soon as you want to consider something you must use words, for words alone determine thought, giving the character of thought to fleeting representations and instincts. Thought hardly exists before speech, nor does speech exist before thought. These two forms of the same activity of the human brain are born together. Thought is therefore impossible without speech. But what is speech? It is communication. It is the conversation of one human individual with many other individuals. Only through this conversation and in it can animalistic man transform himself into a human being, that is, a thinking being. His individuality as a man, his freedom, is thus the product of the collectivity.

Only through collective labor does man emancipate himself from the tyrannical pressure which the natural world exerts on each person; individual labor, impotent and sterile, can never subdue nature. Productive labor, which has created all wealth and our entire civilization, has always been social, collective labor. But until now it has been unjustly exploited by some individuals, to the detriment of the working masses. Likewise, the upbringing and education of which Bourgeois Gentlemen are so proud and which they so parsimoniously distribute to the popular masses—these are also products of the whole of society. The labor, nay, the instinctive thought of the people produced them, but up to now only some members of the bourgeoisie have benefited. It is still an exploitation of collective labor by individuals who have no right to it at all.

Everything human in man—and freedom above all—is the product of a social, collective labor. To be free in absolute isolation is an absurdity invented by theologians and metaphysicians who have replaced the society of humans by that of God, their phantom. They say that each person feels free in the presence of God, that is, in the presence of absolute emptiness, Nothingness. Freedom in isolation, then, is the freedom of Nothingness, or indeed the Nothingness of freedom: slavery. God, the figment of God, has been historically the moral source, or rather the immoral source, of all slaveries.

As for us, we want neither phantoms nor Nothingness but living human reality, and we recognize that man can feel free, be free, and therefore can achieve freedom, only among men. In order to be free, I need to see myself surrounded by free men and be recognized as such by them. I am free only when my individuality, reflected in the mirror of the equally free consciousness of every individual around me, comes back to me strengthened by everyone's recognition. The freedom of every other individual does not limit my own, as the individualists claim; on the contrary, it is the confirmation, realization, and infinite extension of my freedom. To desire the freedom and human dignity of all persons, to see and feel my freedom confirmed, sanctioned, and boundlessly expanded by universal agreement, is happiness; it is human paradise on earth.

But this freedom is possible only through equality. If there be a human being freer than I, then I inevitably become his slave. If I be freer than he, then he will be mine. Therefore, equality is an absolutely necessary condition for freedom.

The bourgeois revolutionaries of 1793 understood this logical necessity very well. The word *Equality* appears as the second term in their revolutionary formula: *Liberty, Equality, Fraternity.* But what sort of equality? Equality before the law, equality of political rights, equality of citizens within the State. Make note of this expression—the equality of citizens, not that of men—for the State does not recognize men; it recognizes only citizens. Man exists for the State only insofar as he exercises political rights—or, by pure fiction, is supposed to exercise them.[4] The man who is crushed by forced labor, by poverty and hunger, the man who is socially oppressed, economically exploited and ruined: suffering man does not exist for the State, which is ignorant of his sufferings and of his economic and social slavery, ignorant of his real servitude which hides under the cloak of a counterfeit political freedom. This is political equality, not social equality.

But, dear friends, you all know from experience how misleading is this sham political equality, which is not based on social and economic equality. For example, in a fully democratic State all men who reach the age of majority and do not find themselves criminally condemned, have the right and even the duty to exercise all their political rights and to fill every office to which they are called by the trust of their fellow-citizens. The lowest, the poorest, the most ignorant man of the people can and should exercise all these rights and fill all those offices. Can you think of a greater equality than this? He ought to do it, and he legally can do it, but in reality it is impossible for him. This power is only optional for those who make up the popular masses. It does not become real for them, and it never can, unless the economic bases of society are radically transformed—let us say it, unless there is a social revolution. These alleged political rights exercised by the people are nothing but an empty fable.

We are tired of all fables, religious and political. The people are tired of living on phantoms and fables. This diet stunts growth. Today they demand reality. Therefore, let us see whether there is anything real for them in the exercise of political rights.

To fill conscientiously the offices of the State, and above all the highest offices, it is first necessary to possess an equally large amount of education. The people totally lack this education. Is it their fault? No, the fault is institutional. The great work of all truly democratic States is to spread education plentifully among the people. Is there a single State which has done this? Let us not discuss monarchical States, which are clearly interested in spreading among the masses not education but the poison of Christian catechism. Let us discuss republican and democratic States like the United States of America and Switzerland. Certainly, it must be acknowledged that these two States have done more than all others for popular education. But have they succeeded, despite all their good will? Have they been able to give every child born in their midst an equal education? No, this is impossible. For the children of the members of the bourgeoisie, superior education; for those of the people, only primary education, and in rare occasions a little secondary education. Why this difference? For the simple reason that men of the people, workers in the fields and cities, do not have the means to support their children, that is, to feed, clothe, and lodge them for the entire duration of their studies. To obtain a scientific education, one must study until the age of twenty-one, sometimes twenty-five. I ask you, what workers are able to support their children for so long a time? This sacrifice is beyond all their means, for they have neither the funds nor the property necessary, and they live from day to day on a salary which scarcely suffices to support a large family.

And yet it must be said, dear comrades, that you workers from the mountains, in a trade which capitalist production, big capital, has not yet succeeded in absorbing—you are comparatively very prosperous. Working in small groups in your workshops, and often even working in your home, you earn much more than [you would] in large industrial establishments which employ hundreds of workers. Your [watchmaking] work is clever and artistic; it is not stupefying like the work of machines. Your competence and your skill count for something. Moreover, you have much more spare time and relative freedom; this is why you are freer, better informed, and more prosperous than others.

In the vast factories established, directed, and exploited by big capital, where not men but machines play the principal role, the workers inevitably become miserable drudges, so destitute that most often they are obliged to doom their poor small children, hardly six years old, to work twelve, fourteen, sixteen hours each day for a few miserable pennies. And they do this not out of avarice but out of need. Without it they would be wholly unable to support their families.

That is the education they can give their children. I do not believe I have to waste more words to prove to you, dear comrades, you who know so well from experience and who are already so profoundly convinced, that *so long as the people work not for themselves but to enrich those who hold property and capital,* the education which they can give their children will always be infinitely inferior to that of the children of the bourgeois class.

And so there is a considerable and disastrous social inequality which you will always find at the very foundation of the structure of every State: an inevitably ignorant mass and a privileged minority which is at least comparatively better educated, if not always more intelligent. The conclusion is easy to draw. The educated minority will rule the ignorant masses.

What is involved is not only the natural inequality of individuals; it is an inequality to which we are compelled to resign ourselves. One person's situation is more fortunate than the other's; one is born with a greater natural power of intellect and will than the other. But I hasten to add: these differences are by no means so great as may be claimed. Even from the standpoint of nature, talents and shortcomings pretty much balance out in everyone, so that [most] persons are nearly equal. There are only two exceptions to this law of natural equality: geniuses and idiots. But exceptions are not the rule, and in general it may be said that one human individual is as worthy as another; and if in present-day society enormous differences exist between individuals, their origin is not nature but the monstrous inequality in upbringing and education.

The child endowed with the greatest talents, but born into a poor family, a family of workers living from day to day on their hard labor, is doomed to an ignorance which, instead of developing his natural talents, kills them all: he will become the worker, the unskilled laborer, forced to be the bourgeoisie's man-servant and field-worker. The child of bourgeois parents, on the other hand, the child of the rich, however stupid by nature, will receive both the upbringing and the education necessary to develop his scanty talents as much as possible. He will become the exploiter of labor, the master, the property-owner, the legislator, the governor—a Gentleman. However stupid he may be, he will make laws on behalf of the people and against them, and he will rule over the popular masses.

In a democratic State, it will be said, the people will choose only the good men. But how will they recognize them? They have neither the education necessary for judging the good and the bad, nor the spare time necessary for learning the differences among those who run for election. These men, moreover, live in a society different from their own; they doff their hat to Their Majesty the sovereign people only at election-time, and once elected they turn their backs. Moreover, however excellent they may be as members of their family and their society, they will always be bad for the people, because, belonging to the privileged and exploiting class, they will quite naturally wish to preserve those privileges which constitute the very basis of their social existence and condemn the people to eternal slavery.

But why haven't the people been sending men of their own, men of the people, to the legislative assemblies and the government? First, because men of the people, who have to live by their physical labor, do not have the time to devote themselves exclusively to politics. [Second, b]eing unable to do so, being more often ignorant of the political and economic questions which are discussed in these lofty regions, they will nearly always be the dupes of lawyers and bourgeois politicians. Also, [third,] it is usually enough for these men of the people to enter the government for them to become members of the bourgeoisie in their turn, sometimes hating and scorning the people from whom they came more than do the natural-born members of the bourgeoisie.

So you see that political equality, even in the most democratic States, is an illusion. It is the same with juridical equality, equality before the law. The bourgeoisie make the law for themselves, and they practice it against the people. The State, and the law which expresses it, exist only to perpetuate the slavery of the people for the benefit of the bourgeois.

Moreover, you know, if you wish to file suit when you find your interests, your honor, or your rights wronged, you must first prove that you are able to pay the costs, that is, that you can lay aside an impossible sum; and if you cannot do so, then you cannot file suit. But do the people, the majority of the workers, have the resources to put on deposit in a court of law? Most of the time, no. Hence the rich man will be able to attack you and insult you with impunity. There is no justice at all for the people.

Political equality will be an illusion so long as economic and social equality do not exist, so long as any minority can become rich, property-owning, and capitalist through inheritance. Do you know the true definition of hereditary property? It is the hereditary ability to exploit the collective labor of the people and to enslave the masses.

That is what the greatest heroes of the Revolution of 1793 did not understand, neither Danton, Robespierre, nor Saint-Just. They wanted freedom and equality to be only political, not economic and social. And that is why the freedom and equality which they instituted merely established the domination of the people by the members of the bourgeoisie, placing it on a new foundation.

They thought they concealed this contradiction by inserting *Fraternity* as the third term of their revolutionary formula. This was again a lie! I ask you whether fraternity is possible between the exploiters and the exploited, between the oppressors and the oppressed? What is this! I make you sweat and suffer all day, and at night when I have reaped the fruit of your sufferings and your sweat, leaving you only a small portion of it so that you may survive, that is, so that you may sweat and suffer anew for my benefit again tomorrow—at night I will say to you: Let us embrace, we are brothers!

Such is the fraternity of the Bourgeois Revolution.

My dear friends, we too desire noble Liberty, wholesome Equality, blessed Fraternity. But we want these great and noble things to cease being fables and lies, we want them to become the true essence of reality!

That is the meaning and the goal of what we call Social Revolution.

The Social Revolution can be summarized in a few words: It wishes, and we wish, every individual born on this earth to be able to become human in the fullest sense of the word, to have not just the right to develop natural talents, but also the means necessary for this, to be free and prosperous in equality and through fraternity! That is what we all wish, and we are all ready to die to realize this goal.

I ask you, friends, for a third and last session in order to explain completely my thoughts to you.

3

Dear Comrades,

Last time I told you how the bourgeoisie, not completely conscious of what it was doing but at least one-quarter so, used the physical strength of the people, during the Great [French] Revolution of 1789-1793, to assert its own influence on the ruins of the feudal world. It thus became the dominant class. It is entirely incorrect to think that Robespierre and Saint-Just were overthrown and slain, their partisans guillotined or deported, by priests and *émigré* nobility who may have staged the reactionary *coup d'état* of Thermidor. Many members of these two downfallen groups doubtless took an active part in the intrigue, and they were pleased at the fall of those who had terrified them and mercilessly cut off their heads. But they were unable to do anything by themselves. Having lost their goods, they were reduced to impotence.

The principal instigators of the Thermidorean reaction were the virtuous representatives of public morality and public order who belonged to that part of the bourgeois class which had enriched itself through the purchase of national wealth, through war materiel, through the handling of public funds: those who had profited from public poverty and even bankruptcy to stuff their own pockets. They were warmly and forcefully supported by the majority of the shopkeepers, an eternally spiteful and cowardly breed which cheats the people in retail fashion, little by little corrupts them, sells them fraudulent merchandise, and has all the people's ignorance without their greatheartedness, all the vanity of the bourgeois aristocracy without their full pockets; cowards during revolutions, they turn savage under reaction. For the shopkeepers, all the ideas that make the hearts of the masses beat—the grand principles and the great concerns of humanity—do not exist. They don't even understand patriotism, seeing in it only vanity or bluster. No feelings at all can distract them from commercial preoccupations and worthless day-to-day anxieties. Everyone saw, and all sides confirm, that during that terrible siege of Paris—while the people fought and the class of the rich intrigued, preparing the treachery that delivered Paris to the Prussians, while the courageous proletariat and the women and children of the people were half-starved—the shopkeepers had but a single concern: to sell their wares, their produce, and the goods most essential to the people's survival, at the highest possible price.

The shopkeepers of all France's cities did the same thing. In towns invaded by Prussians, they opened their doors to the Prussians; in towns not invaded, they prepared to open them. They paralyzed the national defense, opposing wherever they could the insurrection and the arming of the people that alone could have saved France. The cities' shopkeepers and the countryside's peasants today compose the army of reaction. The peasants can be converted to revolution, and they must be, but the shopkeepers—never.

During the Great [French] Revolution the bourgeoisie was divided into two categories. One, forming the tiny minority, was the revolutionary bourgeoisie, known generically as the Jacobins. The Jacobins of today must not be confused with those of 1793. Those of today are only pale ghosts, ridiculously miserable specimens, caricatures of the past century's heroes. The Jacobins of 1793 were great men, they possessed the sacred fire and the creed of justice, liberty, and equality. It was not their mistake not to understand better certain words which still express all our aspirations. They considered only political appearance, not economic and social context. But I repeat, it was not their mistake, just as it is not our merit that we understand them today. The mistake and the merit are of the times. Humanity develops slowly—too slowly, alas!—and it is only by a succession of errors, mistakes, and above all the bitter experiences that inevitably result from them, that mankind gains the truth. The Jacobins of 1793 were men of good faith, men inspired by the idea, devoted to the idea. They were heroes! Had they not been so, and had they not had this sacred and great sincerity, by no means could they have accomplished the great deeds of the Revolution. We can combat the theoretical errors of the Dantons, Robespierres, and Saint-Justs, and we must do so, but while combating their false and narrow ideas, which are exclusively bourgeois in social economy, we should acknowledge their revolutionary influence. These were the last heroes of the bourgeois class, a class that used to teem with heroes.

This heroic minority aside, the other category of the bourgeoisie was the great majority of physical exploiters, for whom the ideas and the great principles of the Revolution were but words, having value and meaning only to the extent that these words could be used to stuff their large and respectable bourgeois pockets. Once the richest and accordingly the most influential of these bourgeois individuals had sufficiently used the Revolution, stuffing their pockets in its tumult, they discovered that it had gone on for too long, that the time had come to end it and to reestablish the reign of law and of public order.

They overthrew the Committee of Public Safety, killed Robespierre, Saint-Just, and their friends, and established the Directory, a true incarnation of bourgeois depravity at the end of the [eighteenth] century which marked the triumph and the reign of the wealth that a few thousand individuals had acquired by theft and collected into their pockets.

But France had not yet had time to be corrupted, it was still all throbbing with the great deeds of the Revolution, and it could not long endure this regime. There were two protests, one abortive and one victorious. The first, had it succeeded, had it been able to succeed, would have saved France and the world. The triumph of the second ushered in the kings' despotism and the peoples' slavery. I am referring to Babeuf's insurrection and the first Bonaparte's usurpation.

Babeuf's insurrection was the final revolutionary attempt of the [eighteenth] century. Babeuf and his friends had been more or less friends of Robespierre and Saint-Just. They were socialist Jacobins. They had known the creed of equality, even to the detriment of freedom. Their plan was very simple: to expropriate all holders of property and of the instruments of labor and other capital, for the benefit of the republican, democratic, and social State; the State, becoming the sole owner of all wealth, personal property as well as real estate, would as a result become society's sole employer and boss. At the same time, armed with political omnipotence, the State would make itself exclusive master of the upbringing and equal education of all children, and it would compel all adult individuals to work and live according to equality and justice. All communal autonomy and individual initiative—all freedom, in a word—would disappear, annihilated by this formidable power. Society would totally cease to exhibit anything but monotonous and forced uniformity. The government would be elected by universal suffrage, but once elected it would exercise an absolute power over all members of society so long as it remained active.

Babeuf did not invent the theory of forcibly establishing equality by the power of the State. Its first foundations were laid several centuries before Christ by Plato in his *Republic,* a work in which this great thinker of antiquity attempted to sketch the design of an egalitarian society. The first Christians undeniably fostered communism in the practice in their associations, which were persecuted by all of official society. Later, during the first quarter of the sixteenth century in Germany, at the very beginning of the religious Revolution, Thomas Münzer and his disciples made a first attempt to establish social equality on a very broad footing. The Conspiracy of Babeuf was the second practical manifestation of the egalitarian idea among the masses. All these attempts, including the last, failed for two reasons: first, because the masses were hardly sufficiently advanced to make possible the realization [of the egalitarian idea]; and second, especially, because in all these systems [Plato's, Münzer's, and Babeuf's], equality joins forces with the power and authority of the State, and the result is incompatible with freedom. For we know, dear friends, that equality is possible only with freedom and only by means of it: not by means of this freedom which is enjoyed exclusively by the Bourgeois, which is founded on the slavery of the masses, which is not freedom but privilege; but by means of a worldwide freedom of human beings, which raises each one of them to human dignity. But we also know that this freedom is possible only within [the context of] equality. Not just revolt in theory but revolt in practice, against all institutions and against all social relations created by inequality; then the establishment of economic and social equality through the freedom of everyone: that is our present program, which will succeed despite the Bismarcks, the Napoleons, the Thiers, and all the Cossacks of my august Emperor, the Tsar of All the Russias.

The Conspiracy of Babeuf brought together every citizen in Paris devoted to the Revolution who still remained after the executions and deportations of the reactionary *coup d'état* of Thermidor; of course, it included many workers. It failed; many were guillotined, but several had the good fortune to escape. Among the latter was the citizen Buonarroti, a man of iron who had an old-fashioned spirit, who so deserved respect that he knew how to make his most acute opponents respect him. For a long time he lived in Belgium, where he became the principal founder of the secret society of Carbonari-communists; and in a book which has become very rare today but which I will try to send to our friend Adhémar

[Schwitzguébel], he tells the doleful story of this last heroic protest of the Revolution against the Reaction, the Conspiracy of Babeuf.[5]

As I said, society's other protest against the bourgeois corruption which seized power under the name of the Directory was the usurpation of the first Bonaparte.

This story, a thousand times again as dismal, is known to you all. It was the first inauguration of the infamous and brutal regime of the sword, the first slap in humanity's face, imparted by an impudent upstart at the beginning of this century. Napoleon I became the hero of all the despots, whom he terrified militarily at the same time. Once he was conquered, they were left with his disastrous estate and his infamous principle: contempt for humanity and its oppression by the sword.

I will not speak to you of the Restoration. This was a ridiculous attempt to revive and return to political power two downfallen and decayed social groups: the nobility and the priests. Only under the Restoration did the bourgeoisie, threatened and attacked by the power which it thought it had conquered for all time, again, remarkably, became quasi-revolutionary. Enemy of the public order as soon as this public order is not its own, that is, as soon as it establishes and guarantees interests other than its own, the bourgeoisie conspired anew. Messrs. Guizot, Périer, Thiers and so many others, the most fanatic partisans and conspicuous defenders of an oppressive and corrupting government under Louis-Philippe, but one which was bourgeois and therefore perfect in their eyes—all these damned souls of the bourgeois reaction conspired under the Restoration.They were victorious in July 1830, and the reign of *bourgeois liberalism* was begun.

The year 1830 truly marks the exclusive domination of bourgeois politics and interests in Europe, above all in France, England, Belgium, Holland, and Switzerland. In the other countries, such as Germany, Denmark, Sweden, Italy, Spain, and Portugal, bourgeois interests entirely outweighed all others, but [there was no] political government of the Bourgeois. I do not refer to the great and unhappy Empire of All the Russias, which remains still subject to the absolute despotism of the Tsars and does not properly have any intermediary political class, no bourgeois political body at all; where in effect there is only, on the one side, the official world, an organization of military police and bureaucracy to satisfy the whims of the Tsar, and on the other side, the people, tens of millions of them destroyed by the Tsar and his functionaries. In Russia, the Revolution will come directly from the people, as I fully explained in a rather long speech which I gave a few years ago in Berne, and which I shall send to you.[6] Nor do I speak of unhappy, heroic Poland, which struggles in the talons of three infamous eagles—the Empire of Russia, the Empire of Austria, and the new Empire of Germany, represented by Prussia—always to be stifled anew but never dead. In Poland as in Russia, there is no middle class properly speaking; on the one hand there is the nobility, which in Russia is a hereditary bureaucracy and slave to the Tsar, formerly dominant but today disorganized and downfallen; on the other hand there is the enslaved peasant, overwhelmed no longer by the nobility, which has lost its power, but by the State, by its innumerable functionaries, and by the Tsar. I shall not again mention the small countries of Sweden and Denmark, which did not become really constitutional until 1848 and which have remained more or less behind the general development of Europe; nor Spain and Portugal, where the industrial movement and bourgeois politics were paralyzed for so long by the dual power of the clergy and the army. However, I ought to point out that Spain, which appeared so poorly developed to us, today offers us one of the most magnificent organizations of the International Working-Men's Association existing in the world.

I will pause for a moment on Germany. Since 1830, Germany has offered us—and still offers us—the strange sight of a country where the interests of the bourgeoisie predominate yet where political influence is not theirs, belonging rather to the absolute monarchy, under a mask of militarily and bureaucratically organized Constitutionalism which is administered exclusively by nobles.

It is in France, England, and above all Belgium that the reign of the bourgeoisie should be studied. Since the unification of Italy under the scepter of Victor-Emmanuel, Italy can also be studied. But nowhere is the bourgeoisie's reign so plainly marked as in France; it is in this country that we shall chiefly examine it.

There, the bourgeois principle has had full freedom to be expressed in literature, politics, and social economy since 1830. That principle can be summarized in a single word: *individualism*.

By *individualism* I mean that tendency which considers all members of society, the mass of individuals, to be mutually unconcerned rivals and competitors, natural enemies with whom each individual is forced to live but who block each other's way, that tendency which impels the individual to gain and erect his own well-being, prosperity, and good fortune to the disadvantage of everyone else, despite them and on their backs. It is an overland racecourse from point to point, a general headlong flight in which each individual seeks to arrive first. Woe to the weak who stop; they are passed. Woe to those who collapse on the way, tired with fatigue; they are soon crushed. Competition has neither heart nor pity. Woe to the vanquished! In this struggle, many crimes must inevitably be committed; this fratricidal struggle is moreover a continuous crime against human solidarity, which is the only basis of all morality. The State, which is said to represent justice and to deliver it, does not prevent the perpetration of these crimes. On the contrary, it eternalizes and legalizes them. What it represents and defends is not human justice but juridical justice, which is nothing but the consecration of the victory of the strong over the weak, of the rich over the poor. The State demands only one thing: that all these crimes be committed legally. I may ruin you, walk over you, and destroy you, but I must observe the laws in doing so. Otherwise I should be declared a criminal and treated as such. That is the sense of this principle, this word, individualism.

Now let us see how this principle is manifested in literature, in this literature created by the Victor Hugos, the Dumas, the Balzacs, the Jules Janins, and other authors of books and articles in the bourgeois newspapers which have inundated Europe since 1830, instilling depravity and evoking egoism in the hearts of the young people of both sexes, and unhappily even among the people themselves. Take whichever novel you like: aside from false, lofty sentiments and fine sentences, what do you find there? Always the same thing: a young man is poor, humble, and unrecognized; he is consumed by all kinds of ambitions and desires; he would like to live in a palace, eat truffles, drink champagne, live in a grand style, and sleep with some pretty marquise. While all others fail, he succeeds through heroic efforts and extraordinary adventures. That is the hero: that is pure individualism.

Let us look at politics. How is the principle expressed there? It is said that the masses need to be led and governed, that they are incapable of doing without government, as if they are also incapable of governing themselves. Who will govern them? [Under the reign of bourgeois individualism, c]lass privilege no longer exists. Everyone has the right to attain the highest social positions and offices. But to get there one must be intelligent and clever; one must be strong and wealthy; one must know how to surpass all rivals and be able to do so. It is again a race from point to point: it is the clever and strong individuals who will govern and fleece the masses.

Let us now examine this same principle in relation to the economic question, which is at bottom the basic question, one may say the only question. The bourgeois economists tell us that they are partisans of unlimited freedom for individuals and that competition is the condition necessary for this freedom. But let us see, what is this freedom? And right away, let us ask one question: Does isolated and solitary labor produce all the marvelous riches of which our age boasts, has it produced them? We know very well to the contrary. The isolated labor of individuals would hardly be able to feed and clothe a small savage tribe; a great nation becomes rich and survives only through collective labor, where the work of one person depends on that of the other. Since labor, which is the production of wealth, is collective, wouldn't it seem logical that the enjoyment of this wealth should also be collective? Well, this is what bourgeois economy does not want, what it hatefully resists. It wants individuals to enjoy [the fruits of collective labor] separately. But which individuals? All of them? Hardly! It grants this pleasure to the powerful, the intelligent, the cunning, and the wealthy. Yes, the wealthy above all. For in the social organization [which follows from bourgeois political economy], and in accordance with the law of inheritance which is [that society's] principal foundation, a minority is born richer and more successful than millions of disinherited and unsuccessful others. Then bourgeois society says to all these individuals: struggle and fight for the prize of well-being, wealth, and political influence. The winners will be the lucky ones. Does equality exist at least in this fratricidal struggle? No, not at all. A small number are able-bodied, armed from head to foot with education and inherited wealth, and millions of men of the people enter the arena almost naked, with their equally inherited ignorance and poverty. What is the inevitable result of this so-called free competition? The people yield, the bourgeoisie triumphs, and the fettered proletarian is compelled to work like a galley-slave for the individual bourgeois, who dominates him unendingly.

So long as capital opposes labor, the proletariat will never be able to defend itself against this nurturer of labor, which is the main weapon of the bourgeoisie and which has become the principal agent of industrial production in every advanced country.

Capital, as it is now organized and used, crushes not just the proletariat; it oppresses and expropriates a vast number of members of the bourgeoisie, transforming them [into proletarians]. The cause of this phenomenon, which the moyenne and petite bourgeoisie don't understand well enough and of which indeed they know nothing, is nevertheless quite simple. Thanks to this fight to the death called competition, which prevails today in commerce and industry because the people's freedom benefits the bourgeoisie, all manufacturers are forced to sell their products—or rather, the products of the workers they employ and exploit—at the lowest possible price. You know from experience that the expensive products are today more and more shut out of the market by lower-priced products, even though the latter are more poorly made than the former. Here, then, is a first disastrous result of this competition, this struggle internal to bourgeois production: it inevitably tends to replace good products with mediocre products, and skillful workers with mediocre workers; at the same time, it decreases the quality of the products and of producers.

In this competition, this struggle for the lowest price, big capital inevitably overwhelms small capital and the fat Bourgeois ruin the skinny Bourgeois.[7] For an immense factory can naturally make its products better than a small or average-sized factory, as well as give them a better price. The establishment of a large factory naturally requires great capital, but in proportion to what it can produce it costs less than a small or average-size factory: 100,000 francs is more than 10,000 francs, but 100,000 francs used in a factory will yield [a profit of] twenty to thirty percent, while 10,000 francs used in the same manner will yield [a profit of] ten percent. The large manufacturer saves on the building, on primary materials, and on machines; employing many more workers than the small or average-size manufacturer, he also gains through better organization and a greater division of labor. To put it briefly, a single manufacturer with 100,000 francs invested in an organization produces much more than ten manufacturers each using 10,000 francs; for example, if each of the latter were to realize a net profit of 2,000 francs on the 10,000-franc investment, the manufacturer who establishes and organizes a large factory costing 100,000 francs realizes 5,000 or 6,000 francs on each 10,000 francs [invested], or rather produces five or six [times as much] merchandise. Producing proportionally much more, he can naturally sell his products at a much lower price than the small or average-size manufacturer; but by selling them at a lower price he forces the small and average-size manufacturers to lower their prices, lest their products not be bought at all. But since it is much more expensive for them to produce these products than it is for the large manufacturer, they are ruined by selling them at the large manufacturer's price. In this way big capital is the death of small capital, and if big capital encounters capital bigger still, it is overwhelmed in its turn.

This is so true that there is an undisguised tendency today for big capital to agglomerate into horrendously huge capital. In the most industrialized countries—England, Belgium, and France—exploitation of commerce and industry by private companies is beginning to replace the exploitation by large unassociated capitalists. And as the civilization and national wealth of the most advanced countries increase, the wealth of the big capitalists increases but the number of capitalists decreases. Members of the moyenne bourgeoisie find themselves thrown in with the petite bourgeoisie, and a still greater number of the petite bourgeoisie are inexorably thrust into the proletariat, into poverty.

This is an incontestable fact, supported by the statistics of all countries as well as by the most precise mathematical proof. In the economic organization of present-day society, the successive impoverishment of the great bulk of the bourgeoisie, to the benefit of a limited number of monumentally huge capitalists, is an inexorable law for which the only cure is Social Revolution. If the petite bourgeoisie had enough insight and good sense to understand this, it would ally itself with the proletariat before long in order to carry out this revolution. But the petite bourgeoisie is in general very stupid; its foolish vanity and unfeeling egoism shut out the spirit [of Revolution]. Overwhelmed on one side by the grande bourgeoisie and menaced on the other by the proletariat which it despises, detests, and fears, it sees nothing, achieves nothing, and stupidly allows itself to be led into the abyss.

The consequences of this bourgeois competition are disastrous for the proletariat. The manufacturers, forced to sell their products—or the products of the workers whom they exploit—at the lowest possible price, naturally must pay their workers the lowest possible wages. Therefore they can no longer reward their workers' talent. They must seek labor which is sold, forced to be sold, at the lowest price. Since women and children are satisfied with a smaller salary, the manufacturers endeavor to employ children and women in preference to men, and mediocre workers in preference to skillful workers, unless the latter are happy with the salary of unskilled workers, children, and women. Every bourgeois economist has demonstrated and acknowledged that the size of a worker's salary is always determined by the cost of his daily living. Thus, if a worker could lodge, clothe, and feed himself on one franc a day, his salary would fall very quickly to one franc. And this [is so] for a very simple reason: workers tormented by hunger are forced to compete with each other. The manufacturer, on the other hand, is forced by bourgeois competition to sell his products at the lowest possible price and, eager to grow as quickly as possible by exploiting the workers' labor, he will naturally hire those who will offer him more hours of labor for a lower salary.

This is not just a logical deduction, it is an actual event which occurs every day in England, France, Belgium, Germany, and those parts of Switzerland where big industry, exploited in big factories by big capital, has been established. In my last lecture I told you that you were privileged workers. Although your salary is still less than the full value of your daily production, and although you are undeniably exploited by your employers, nevertheless you are better paid in comparison with workers in large industrial establishments, you have spare time, you are [relatively] free and fortunate. And I hasten to acknowledge that you deserve so much the more merit to have entered the International, becoming devoted, zealous members of this vast association of labor which will liberate the workers of the entire world. It is noble and generous of you. You prove thereby that you are thinking not just of yourselves but of the millions of your brothers who are much more oppressed and less prosperous. It is with great happiness that I bear this witness.

But let me tell you that this act of unselfish and fraternal solidarity is also an act of foresight and prudence. You perform it not only for your unhappy brothers in other industries and other countries but also, if not for yourself, then for your children. You are well-rewarded, free, and prosperous, not absolutely so but by comparison. Why is this? Simply because big capital has not yet overrun your industry. But surely you don't think that this will always be the case. Big capital is compelled, by a law inherent in it, inevitably to overrun everything. It began, naturally, by exploiting those branches of commerce and industry which promised it the greatest advantages and were the most easily exploited; and after it has sufficiently exploited them, the competition created by this exploitation will inevitably push it to assail those branches which will still then be untouched. Don't machines already make clothes, boots, and lace? Mark well these words, that sooner or later, and sooner rather than later, machines will also make watches. The springs, the escapements, the cases, the cap, the finishing, the ornamentation, and the engraving will be done by machine. The products will not be as perfect as those which come from your expert hands but they will cost much less and be sold for much less than your more perfect products, which they will eventually exclude from the market. And so you, or at least your children, will be as slavish and poor as workers in large industrial establishments now. So indeed you see that in working for your brothers, the impoverished workers of other industries and other countries, you are also working for your children if not for yourselves.[8]

You are working for humanity. The working class has today become the sole representative of the great and sacred cause of humanity. The future now belongs to the workers: those in the fields and those in the factories and cities. The classes which have always exploited the labor of the popular masses—the nobility, the clergy, the bourgeoisie, and the myriad military and civil functionaries who represent the injustice and malevolent power of the State—are corrupt classes, struck with impotence, capable neither of judging what is good nor of seeking it, influential only for evil['s sake].

The clergy and the nobility were unmasked and defeated in 1793. The Revolution of 1848 unmasked and showed the impotence and evil-doing of the bourgeoisie. During the June Days in 1848, the bourgeois class boldly renounced the religion of their fathers, this revolutionary religion whose principles and bases were liberty, equality, and fraternity. As soon as the people took equality and liberty seriously, the bourgeoisie, existing thanks only to the people's economic inequality and social bondage, retreated into reaction.

These very traitors who wish to disgrace France today once more—the Thiers, the Jules Favres, and the vast majority of the 1848 National Assembly—worked for the triumph of the most foul reaction back then, just as they do today. They began by suppressing universal suffrage, and later [using it] they raised Louis Bonaparte to the presidency. The fear of Social Revolution, the dread of equality, the awareness of its own crimes, and the fear of popular justice hurled this downfallen class, once so intelligent and heroic but now so stupid and cowardly, into the arms of the dictatorship of Napoleon III. And they had military dictatorship for the next eighteen years. We should not think that the Bourgeois Gentlemen were too inconvenienced. Those who rebelled and played at liberalism in too loud and incommodious a manner for the imperial regime were naturally isolated and repressed. But everyone else—those who left the political nonsense to the people and applied themselves earnestly and exclusively to the great concern of the bourgeoisie, the exploitation of the people—they were well protected and powerfully supported. They were even given all the appearances of liberty so that they could save their honor. Didn't a Legislative Assembly exist under the Empire, regularly elected by universal suffrage? All went well, according to the desires of the bourgeoisie. There was only one black mark. This was the ambition for conquest exhibited by the sovereign, who forcibly dragged France into ruinous expenditures which led to the destruction of his own power. But this black mark was not an accident, it was a necessity of the system. A despotic and absolute regime, even one with the semblances of freedom, must inevitably depend upon a powerful army, and every large standing army sooner or later brings foreign war, because ambition is the principal inspiration of the military hierarchy. Every lieutenant wishes to be a colonel, every colonel a general. As for the soldiers, who are systematically demoralized in their barracks, they dream of the noble pleasures of war: massacre, pillage, theft, and rape—the exploits of the Prussian army in France, for example. Well, if all these noble passions, nurtured systematically and knowingly among the officers and soldiers, remain long unsatisfied, then they grow worse, provoking the army to discontent, and from discontent to revolt. War thus becomes a necessity. So all the expeditions and wars undertaken by Napoleon III were hardly the personal caprices the Bourgeois Gentlemen claim, but a necessity of the despotic imperial system which they themselves founded out of the fear of Social Revolution. Thus the privileged classes, the cardinals and priests, the downfallen nobility, and finally this respectable, honest, and virtuous bourgeoisie above all, are as much to blame as Napoleon III himself for all the horrible misfortunes that have recently struck France.

And comrades, you all saw that to defend unhappy France there was in the entire land but a single group, the urban workers: precisely those betrayed by the bourgeoisie and delivered to the Empire, which sacrificed them to bourgeois exploitation. In the whole country, only the unselfish urban and industrial workers sought an uprising of the people for the safety of France. The rural workers, the peasants, demoralized and stupefied by the religious education which they have been given from Napoleon I to the present, took the side of the Prussians and of Reaction, against France. They could have been revolutionized. In a pamphlet which many among you have read, *Letters to a Frenchman*, I described the methods by which they could have been won over to the Revolution.[9] But for this to have happened, it was first necessary that the cities rise in insurrection and organize themselves in a revolutionary manner. The workers wanted this; they even tried it in many cities in central France, in Lyons, Marseilles, Montpelier, Saint-Étienne, and Toulouse. But everywhere they were held back and paralyzed in the name of the Republic by the bourgeois *radicals*. Yes, in the name of the Republic, the members of the bourgeoisie who had turned republican out of fear of the people—in the name of the Republic of the Gambettas, that old sinner Jules Favre, Thiers the infamous fox, and all the Picards, Ferrys, Jules Simons, Pelletans and many others—in the name of the Republic they assassinated the Republic and France.

Sentence has been passed on the bourgeoisie. It is the richest and most numerous class in France—except for the masses of the people of course—and had it wished, it could have saved France. But for that it would have had to sacrifice its money and its life and rely unreservedly on the proletariat, as did its forefathers, the bourgeoisie of 1793. Well it didn't want to sacrifice its money any more than its life, and it preferred to see France conquered by the Prussians than saved by popular revolution.

The issue between the workers in the towns and the Bourgeois was stated just as clearly. The workers said: We would sooner blow our houses up than deliver our towns to the Prussians. The Bourgeois replied: We would sooner open the doors of our towns to the Prussians than allow you to create public disorder, and we would prefer to retain our expensive houses at all cost, even if we have to kiss the behind of these Prussian Gentlemen.

And note that these same members of the bourgeoisie now dare to insult the Paris Commune, this noble Commune which is saving France's honor and, let us hope, the freedom of the world at the same time. And in the name of what do they insult the Commune? *In the name of patriotism!*

They are really brazen-faced! They have sunk to a level of infamy which has caused them to lose nearly their lowest sense of decency. They do not know shame. Before they have even died, they are already rotten to the core.

And it is not just in France, comrades, that the bourgeoisie is rotten, morally and intellectually destroyed; it is the same throughout Europe; and in all the countries of Europe, only the proletariat has kept the sacred fire. It alone is now humanity's standard-bearer.

What is its motto, its morality, its principle? *Solidarity.* All for one, one for all, and one by virtue of all. This is the motto, the fundamental principle of our great International [Working-Men's] Association which transcends the frontiers of States, thus destroying them, endeavoring to unite the workers of the entire world into a single human family on the basis of universally obligatory labor, in the name of the freedom of each and every individual. This Solidarity is collective labor and collective property in social economy; in politics, it is called the destruction of States and the freedom of every individual, which arises from the freedom of all individuals.

Yes, dear comrades, you the workers, jointly with your brothers the workers of the whole world, today you alone inherit the great mission of emancipating humanity. You have a co-inheritor; he is a worker like you, but he works under different conditions. This is the peasant. But the peasant does not yet realize the great mission of the people. He has been poisoned and is poisoned still by the priests, and he acts against himself, as an instrument of Reaction. You must teach him and save him in spite of himself, winning him over and explaining to him what Social Revolution is.

At this moment, and above all in the beginning, the workers of industry must count, can count only on themselves. But they will be all-powerful if they wish it. Only they must earnestly wish it. And there are but two ways to realize this wish. The first is by establishing, first in their own groups and then among all groups, a true fraternal solidarity, not just in words but in action, not just for holidays but in their daily life. Every member of the International must be able to feel that all other members are his brothers and be convinced of this in practice.

The other means is revolutionary organization, organization for action. If the uprisings of the people in Lyons, Marseilles, and other French towns have failed, that is because there was hardly any organization. I can speak with full knowledge of the affair, for I was there and I was pained by it.[10] And if the Paris Commune holds fast so valiantly today, this is because during the whole siege the workers are earnestly organized. Not without reason do the bourgeois newspapers accuse the International of having produced the magnificent uprising of Paris. Yes, let us say it boldly, these are our brother-members of the International, who have organized the people of Paris and whose steady efforts have made the Paris Commune possible.

Let us then be good brothers and comrades, and let us organize ourselves. Do not think that we are at the end of the Revolution, we are at its beginning. The Revolution is henceforth the order of the day, for many decades to come. It will come to find us, sooner or later. Let us therefore prepare and purify ourselves and become more genuine, let us be less talkers, less criers, less phrasemongers, less drinkers, and less rakes. Let us gird our loins[11] and properly prepare ourselves for this struggle which will save all peoples and finally emancipate humanity.

Long live the Social Revolution! Long live the Paris Commune!

Part Two

Bourgeois Socialism and Revolutionary Socialism

"Congress of Peace and Freedom at Berne." Introductory page of a contemporary collection of cartoons and caricatures concerning the Berne Congress (1868) of the League of Peace and Freedom. Bakunin is unmistakable as the figure overturning the bed labelled "peace" and holding the broom (that sweeps clean) marked "freedom." Source: Pittorino [pseud.], *Congrès de la Paix à Berne: Album* (Geneva: Braun et Cie. for Ch.T. Montaniar, [1868]). A copy of this brochure is in the Bibliothèque publique et universitaire, Geneva.

2
The Hypnotizers

1

The International Association of Bourgeois Democrats, which calls itself the "International League of Peace and Freedom," has just issued its new program, or rather, it has just uttered a cry of distress, an exceedingly touching appeal to all of Europe's bourgeois democrats, whom it begs not to let it perish for lack of funds. It needs several thousand francs to continue its newspaper, to finish the official report of its last Congress, and to enable the convocation of a new Congress—as a result of which its Central Committee, driven to extreme measures, has decided to open a subscription and is calling upon all the sympathizers and believers in this bourgeois League to demonstrate their sympathy and their faith by sending it as much money as possible, in any denomination.

Anyone who reads the new circular of the League's Central Committee may think that he hears the dying, endeavoring to awaken the dead. There is not a single living thought, only the repetition of hackneyed phrases and the impotent expression of wishes as virtuous as they are sterile, wishes condemned long ago by history precisely because of their grievous impotence.

One must, however, give this due to the League of Peace and Freedom: it assembled the most advanced, the most intelligent, the best thinking, and the most magnanimous members of the European bourgeoisie—men who (with the exception of a small group) broke every relation with the bourgeois class when they realized that life was ebbing from it, that it no longer had any reason for existing, and that it could continue to exist only by prejudicing justice and humanity; men who, despite having been born and raised in the midst of this class, turned their backs to it and sought to serve the great cause of the emancipation of the workers whom that very bourgeoisie exploits and dominates.

How, then, does it happen that this League, which counts so many intelligent, learned, and sincerely liberal individuals, now displays such poverty of thought and clear inability to will, to act, and to live? This inability and poverty are the fault not of these individuals but of the class to which they are unfortunate enough to belong. This class, the bourgeoisie, having performed outstanding services for the civilization of the modern world, is today condemned to death, as a political and social entity, by history itself. The only service that it can still perform for humanity, which it served for so long while it lived, is to die. Yet it does not want to die; and this is the only reason for its present pointless folly, for that shameful impotence which now characterizes its every political project, national as well as international.

The altogether bourgeois League of Peace and Freedom desires the impossible: that the bourgeoisie continue to exist and continue to serve the cause of progress at the same time. After long hesitations, after denying the very existence of the social question at [the meeting of] its [Central] Committee in Berne near the end of 1867, after rejecting *social and economic equality* at its last Congress by a vast majority,[12] it has finally realized that even a single step forward in history is nowadays impossible unless the social question is resolved and the principle of equality triumphs. Its circular calls on all its members to cooperate actively in "*everything that may hasten the advent of the reign of justice and equality.*" But at the same time, it poses this question: "What role can the bourgeoisie play in the social question?"[13]

We have already given our answer. If the bourgeoisie really wants to perform one last service for humanity; if its love for real, complete world-wide freedom is sincere; if it wishes, in a word, to quit being reactionary, then there is only one thing left for it to do: to die gracefully, as quickly as possible.

Understand us well. This does not mean the death of the individuals who make up the bourgeoisie, but the death of the bourgeoisie as a political and social entity economically distinct from the working class.

What is the sincere expression, the only meaning, the sole goal of the social question? It is, as the Central Committee itself finally recognizes, *the triumph and realization of equality.* But since the bourgeoisie's existence as an entity economically distinct from the mass of workers implies and inevitably produces inequality, isn't it obvious that the bourgeoisie must perish?

In vain they resort to double-talk, they complicate words and ideas, and they adulterate social science in order to benefit bourgeois exploitation. But every sensible person uninterested in self-deception now realizes that *so long as a certain number of economically privileged persons have means of existence and lead lives which are not those of the working class; so long as a rather considerable number of individuals inherit capital or land which is not the product of their own labor, while the vast majority of workers inherit nothing at all; so long as rent on land and interest on capital generally enable those privileged persons to live without working (and even if we suppose what is impossible under these conditions, that everyone in society either is obliged or prefers to work, except for one class in society which, owing to its economically and therefore socially and politically privileged position, can devote itself exclusively to labors of the intellect, while the vast majority make their living only from their physical labor); in a word, so long as every human being born into society does not discover there the same resources for personal maintenance, the same upbringing, education, labor, and leisure—then universal political, economic, and social equality will be forever unattainable.*

It was in the name of equality that the bourgeoisie once overthrew and massacred the nobility. It is in the name of equality that today we demand either the violent death or the voluntary suicide of the bourgeoisie, with this difference: being less bloodthirsty than the bourgeoisie, we wish not to kill persons, but to abolish status and its perquisites. If the Bourgeois resign themselves to this and let it happen, not a hair on their heads will be touched. But so much the worse for them if, in order to save a position which will very soon be untenable, they place themselves in opposition to both historical and popular justice and carelessly sacrifice their individual interests to the collective interests of their class, a class condemned to extinction.

2

One thing that should make the supporters of the League of Peace and Freedom stop and think is the poor financial situation in which the League now finds itself, after barely two years of existence. The present-day bourgeoisie is no doubt very distressed that Europe's most radical bourgeois democrats were unable, after meeting together, either to create an effective organization or to produce a single new and fruitful idea; but this no longer surprises us, for we have realized the main cause of this sterility and impotence. But how is it that this thoroughly bourgeois League, whose members enjoy incomparably greater freedom of movement and action than the members of the International Working-Men's Association, and who are also clearly richer—how is it that this League is now dying *for want of material means,* while the impoverished workers of the International, oppressed by a multitude of odious and restrictive laws, deprived of education and leisure, and overwhelmed by the weight of their wearisome work, have been able to establish in so short a time a formidable international organization and a host of newspapers which express their needs, their wishes, and their thoughts?

The duly established intellectual and moral bankruptcy of the League of Peace and Freedom aside, what is the root of its financial bankruptcy?

How is this! Every Swiss radical (or nearly every such), combined with the *Volkspartei* of Germany, with the Garibaldian democrats of Italy, and with France's radical democrats, plus Spain and Sweden, the former represented by Emilio Castelàr himself, the latter by the excellent colonel who appeased their souls and conquered their hearts at the recent Berne Congress—practical men, great political charlatans like Mr. Haussman and all the editors of the *Zukunft,*[14] people like Messrs. Lemonnier, Gustave

Vogt, and Barni, athletes like Messrs. Armand Goegg and Chaudey have all lent a hand in the creation of the League of Peace and Freedom, which was blessed from afar by Garibaldi, Quinet, and Jacoby of Königsberg: and now this League, having led a wretched life for two years, must perish for want of a few thousand francs! How is this! Even the symbolic, pathetic embrace of Messrs. Armand Goegg and Chaudey, who—the one representing the great Germanic homeland, the other the great [French] nation—threw themselves into each others' arms in the middle of the Congress, shouting *"Pax! Pax! Pax!"* in front of the entire perplexed assembly until little Théodore Beck of Berne was moved to weep out of enthusiasm and compassion [is not enough]. How is this! All of that has not been able to touch or to soften the hard hearts of Europe's bourgeoisie, to make them untie their moneybags—all of that has not produced a sou!

Has the bourgeoisie already gone bankrupt? Not yet. Or has it lost its taste for freedom and peace? Not at all. It continues to love freedom, of course on the condition that this freedom exist only for itself: that is, on the condition that it always retain the freedom to exploit the *de facto* slavery of the masses of the people, who under present-day constitutions have only the right to freedom but not the means to it, and who remain subjugated by force under the bourgeoisie's yoke. As for peace, the bourgeoisie has never so much as now felt the need for peace. The bourgeoisie is disturbed, paralyzed, and ruined by the armed peace which today weighs on the European world.

How is it, then, that the bourgeoisie, which on the one hand is not yet financially bankrupt and on the other hand continues to love freedom and peace, does not wish to spend a single sou to preserve the League of Peace and Freedom?

Because it has no faith in this League. And why not? Because it no longer has faith in itself. To believe is to desire passionately, and the bourgeoisie has irrevocably lost the force of desire. What could it reasonably desire today, as a separate class? Doesn't it have everything: wealth, science, and exclusive rule? It is true that the bourgeoisie does not like very much the military dictatorship which protects it a bit brutishly, but, knowing full well that it will lose everything and cease to exist the very moment this dictatorship is overthrown, it realizes that this is necessary and it prudently resigns itself. And the citizens of the League ask the bourgeoisie to donate its money and come join in the destruction of this benevolent dictatorship? Not that dumb! Endowed with a more practical mind, the bourgeoisie understands its own interests better than do [the League's members].

The latter try to convince the bourgeoisie by showing it the abyss toward which it is letting itself be led, along the path of egoistic and brutish [self-]preservation. Do they think that the bourgeoisie does not see this abyss? It too senses the approach of the catastrophe which must engulf it. But here is its reasoning: "If we preserve what exists," the bourgeois conservatives say to themselves, "we can hope to prolong our present existence some years yet, and perhaps we may die before the catastrophe arrives—and after us, the deluge![15] Whereas if we let ourselves be led down the path of radicalism, and overthrow the currently established powers, then we will die tomorrow. Therefore, it is better to preserve what exists."

The bourgeois conservatives understand the contemporary situation better than do the bourgeois radicals. Not deluding themselves, they realize that there is no compromise possible at all between the bourgeois system which is disappearing and the socialism which must take its place. That is why all the really practical members of the bourgeoisie and all their full purses are turning toward Reaction, leaving to the League of Peace and Freedom the empty purses and the less powerful minds; and as a result, this virtuous but ill-fated League is today doubly bankrupt.

If anything can demonstrate the intellectual, moral, and political death of bourgeois radicalism, this must be its present inability to create anything, an impotence already well shown in France, Germany, and Italy, and one which is now displayed more scandalously than ever in Spain. Nearly nine months ago, the Revolution in Spain exploded and triumphed. If the bourgeoisie did not have power, it at least had every means of giving itself power. What did it create? Royalty and Serrano's regency.

The modern bourgeoisie contains two categories of persons, at least some of whom—despite the depth of our antipathy toward, distrust of, and scorn for this class—we do not lose hope of converting sooner or later through socialist propaganda. The one impelled by the very force of circumstances and by the necessity of its current position, the other impelled by magnanimity, they certainly participate with us in the destruction of existing injustices and in the foundation of a new world.

We are referring [respectively] to the *petite bourgeoisie* and to the *young people in schools and universities.* We will address the question of the petite bourgeoisie in ["The International Working-Men's Movement," below]. Let us now say a few words about the bourgeois young people.

It is true that the children of the bourgeoisie usually inherit the exclusive practices, the narrow prejudices, and the egoistic instincts of their fathers. But so long as they stay young, they must not be given up for lost. In youth there is a vigor, a courage of bold yearnings, and a natural instinct of justice which are capable of counteracting many pernicious influences. Corrupted by their fathers' example as well as by their precepts, the young of the bourgeoisie are still uncorrupted by the real experience of life; their own actions have not yet excavated an abyss between themselves and justice, and their fathers' injurious traditions are little protected by the spirit of natural contradiction and protestation that has always animated youth. The young are disrespectful; they instinctively scorn tradition and the principle of authority.[16] This is their strength and salvation.

Then comes the healthy influence of education and learning: but healthy only if they are not twisted and falsified by a perverse doctrinairism to the benefit of injustice and official lies. Today, unhappily, in the vast majority of Europe's schools and universities, education and learning are to be found in precisely this state of systematic and premeditated falsification. One could even believe that these schools and universities have been established expressly for the intellectual and moral corruption of the children of the bourgeoisie. They are just so many shops for the privileged, where lies are sold retail and wholesale.

Not to mention theology, which is the science of the divine lie, nor jurisprudence, which is the science of the human lie; not to mention metaphysics or visionary philosophy either, which is the science of all the half-lies; all other sciences—history, philosophy, politics, and economic science—are essentially falsified since they are all equally founded on theology, metaphysics, and jurisprudence, and are separated from their real basis, the science of nature.

We may say without exaggeration that every young person who leaves the university and who has been steeped in these sciences, or rather in these systematized lies and half-lies which presumptuously assume the name of science, is lost unless extraordinary circumstances intervene to save him. The professors, these modern priests of patented political and social knavery, have inoculated him with a poison so corrosive that miracles are indeed necessary to cure him. He leaves the university an accomplished doctrinaire, full of respect for himself and of scorn for the popular riffraff, which he is only too glad to oppress and above all to exploit, in the name of his intellectual and moral superiority. And the younger he is, the more malevolent and hateful he is.

It is otherwise in the faculty of the exact and natural sciences. These are the true sciences! Foreign to theology and metaphysics, they are hostile to all fabrications and are founded exclusively on exact knowledge, on conscientious analysis of facts, and on pure reason, that is, on common sense as expanded by well-planned experiments. Just as the ideal sciences are authoritarian and aristocratic, so the natural sciences are democratic and entirely liberal. So what do we see? Whereas almost all the young people who study the ideal sciences rush passionately into the party of exploitative and reactionary doctrinairism, those who study the natural sciences embrace just as passionately the party of revolution. Many among them are open socialist-revolutionaries like ourselves. These are the young people on whom we count.

The demonstrations at the last Liège Congress[17] make us hope that we will very soon see the whole intelligent and courageous segment of the young people in the universities form new sections of the International Working-Men's Association. Their cooperation will be valuable only if they understand that the mission of science today is no longer to rule over labor but to serve it, and that they will have many more things to learn from the workers than to teach them. The workers, if they make a good match with the bourgeois youth, today constitute the youth of humanity;

they carry its entire future in themselves. During the events which will soon be upon us, the workers will then be senior, and the well-intentioned bourgeois students will be junior.

But let us return to the poor League of Peace and Freedom. Why is it that in the League's Congresses the bourgeois youth is distinguished only by its absence? Ah! This is because for the doctrinaires the youth is already too advanced, and for the socialist minority it is not far enough advanced. After these young people come the great bulk of students, young people who have sunk into nullity and who are indifferent toward everything which is not today's trivial amusement or tomorrow's lucrative job. They are ignorant of the very existence of the League of Peace and Freedom.

When Lincoln was elected President of the United States, the defeated Colonel Douglas, who was then one of the principal leaders of the defeated party, exclaimed: "Our party is lost, the young are no longer with us!"[18] Well, this poor League never had the young with it. It was born old, and it will die without having lived.

Such will also be the fate of the whole party of the radical bourgeoisie in Europe. Its existence has never been but a handsome dream. During the Restoration and the July Monarchy, it dreamt. In 1848, showing itself unable to establish anything substantial, it took a great fall, and its consciousness of this inability and impotence pushed it into [the party of] Reaction. After 1848, it had the misfortune to survive. It still dreams, but no longer of the future; it dreams, rather, the retrospective dream of an old man who has never really lived. And while it persists in its stupid dreams, it senses around itself a new world in movement, the potency of the future being born. This is the potency, and the world, of workers.

The noise made by the workers has finally half-awakened the radical bourgeoisie, which, after having long ignored and disavowed the workers, has finally come to recognize their real strength. It sees them full of the life which it has always lacked, and wishing to save itself by identifying with them, it now tries to transform itself. It no longer calls itself radical democracy, but *bourgeois socialism.*

Under this new name, it has existed only one year. In [our next] article, we will describe what it has done during this year.*

3

Since we view the League of Peace and Freedom as a dying entity whose days are numbered, our readers may wonder why we bother with it and why we do not let it die peacefully, as befits one who no longer has anything to do in this world. Ah! We would ask nothing better than to let it end its days quietly without speaking of it at all, if it did not threaten before

*[See also "*La Montagne* and Mr. Coullery," below.—Ed.]

dying to leave us a very unpleasant heir named *bourgeois socialism.*

And we would not bother even with this illegitimate child of the bourgeoisie, unpleasant as it is, if only it did not give itself the mission of converting the members of the bourgeoisie to socialism; and, not having the least confidence in the success of its exertions, we could even admire its magnanimity if it did not simultaneously pursue a diametrically opposite goal, which seems to us particularly immoral: the propagation of bourgeois theories among the working classes.

Bourgeois socialism is a sort of hybrid, located between two irreconcilable worlds, the bourgeois world and the workers' world; and while on the one hand its harmful and ambiguous activity hastens the death of the bourgeoisie, on the other hand, it simultaneously corrupts the proletariat from birth. It corrupts the proletariat doubly: first, by adulterating and distorting its principle and program; second, by impregnating it with impossible hopes accompanied by a ridiculous faith in the bourgeoisie's approaching conversion, thereby trying to draw it into bourgeois politics and to make it an instrument thereof.

As for the principle which it professes, the position of bourgeois socialism is as embarrassing as it is ridiculous. Too lax or corrupt to stick to a single well developed principle, it aspires to marry together two absolutely incompatible principles which it has the singular pretension to reconcile. For example, it wishes to preserve personal property in capital and land for the bourgeoisie and it simultaneously declares its magnanimous intention to assure the well-being of the worker. It even promises him the full benefits of the fruits of his labor; but since interest and rent are levied only on the fruits of labor, this cannot be realized until capital ceases to collect interest and property in land ceases to produce rent.

Bourgeois socialism likewise wishes to preserve the freedom currently enjoyed by the members of the bourgeoisie, a freedom which is only the ability to exploit and which exists only thanks to the power of capital and property (which are the workers' labor); and simultaneously it promises the fullest economic and social equality of the exploited with their exploiters!

It upholds the right of inheritance, that is, the privilege of the children of the rich to be born into wealth and that of the children of the poor to be born into poverty; meanwhile, it promises to all children the equality of upbringing and education that justice demands.

It upholds, in favor of the Bourgeois, the inequality of means that follows directly from the right of inheritance, and it promises to the proletarians that everyone will work under its system, the work being determined only by the individual's natural capabilities and inclinations. This would be possible only under two conditions, each equally absurd: either that the State, whose power the bourgeois socialists detest as much as we do, compel the children of the rich to work just like those of the poor, which would lead us directly to despotic State communism; or that all the children of the rich, impelled by magnanimous intention and a miracle of self-denial, freely put themselves to work the same hours at the same jobs filled by those whose poverty and hunger compel them so, and this without being forced to do so out of necessity. And even under this supposition, basing ourselves on the psychological and natural sociological law that two actions with different causes can never be alike, we can still predict with certainty that the worker who is forced to work would inevitably be the inferior and dependent one, the slave of the worker who works by the grace of his will.

The bourgeois socialist can be recognized by one sign above all: he is a *rabid individualist* and feels a hidden fury every time he hears a mention of collective property. As an enemy of collective property, he is naturally also an enemy of collective labor; and being unable to eliminate collective labor entirely from the socialist program, he reserves, in the name of this freedom which he so poorly understands, a large place in that program for individual labor.

But what is individual labor? In every undertaking where a person's strength or physical ability is immediately involved (that is, in all material production), it is impotence. The isolated labor of a single person, however strong and capable, is never enough to counteract the collective labor of the many who are associated and well-organized. What is called individual labor in industry today is nothing but the exploitation of the collective labor of the workers by individuals who are privileged holders either of capital or of learning. But from the moment that this exploitation ceases—and the bourgeois socialists affirm, at least, that they wish it to end as much as we do—there will no longer be any labor in industry other than collective labor nor, as a result, any property other than collective property.

Individual labor will therefore remain possible only in intellectual production, in the works of the mind. And yet, is the mind of the world's greatest genius ever anything but the product of the collective intellectual and industrial labor of all past and present generations? To be convinced of this, let one imagine this same genius conveyed to a desert island since earliest infancy. Supposing that he not die of starvation, what will he become? A stupid and unreasoning creature who will not even know how to utter one word and who consequently will never have reflected. Convey him thereto at the age of ten years, and what will he be several years later? Still an unreasoning beast who will have lost the habit of speech and who will have preserved but a vague instinct of his past human nature. Convey him there finally at the age of twenty or thirty years, and ten, fifteen, or twenty years later, he will be a blockhead. Perhaps he will invent some new religion!

What does this demonstrate? That the man best endowed by nature receives only mental abilities from nature, but that these abilities remain dead unless they are fertilized by the potent and beneficial activity of the collectivity. We shall say more: the more endowed by nature an individual is, the more that person takes from the collectivity; from which it follows, in all justice, that more must be repaid.

We willingly recognize, however, that although a large number of intellectual labors could be performed better and more quickly collectively than individually, there are others which require solitary labor. But what can one claim to conclude from this? That isolated works of genius or talent, because they are rarer, more precious, and more useful than those of ordinary workers, should be better remunerated than these latter? On what basis, I ask you? Are these works more painful than manual labors? On the contrary, the latter are incomparably more exhausting. Intellectual labor is an attractive labor which brings its own reward and which needs no other repayment. The intellectual worker also is remunerated by the esteem and recognition of his contemporaries, by the wisdom he imparts to them, and by the good which he does for them. You Bourgeois-Socialist Gentlemen who are so strongly devoted to the ideal, do you find this repayment less worthy than some other, or would you prefer more substantial reward, in hard cash?

And further, you would be quite embarrassed if you had to establish a tax on the intellectual products of genius. These are, as Proudhon well observed, of incomparable value: they cost nothing, or they cost millions.[19] But do you realize that under such a system you would have to hurry and abolish the law of inheritance as quickly as possible? For if you did not, you would have children of men of genius and talent who would inherit millions or hundreds of millions of francs; and add that these children are, as a result either of a still unknown natural law or of the privileged position which they have attained through their fathers' labors, ordinarily very ordinary intellects and often even quite stupid. But what would then become of this distributive justice, which you like so much to talk about and in the name of which you oppose us? How will this equality which you promise us be realized?

To us the clear result of all this is that the isolated works of the individual intellect, and every work of the mind, should be, as an invention and not as an application, free of charge. But how will the men of talent and genius make their living? Oh, my God! They will live by their collective, manual labor, like everyone else. What! You wish to compel great intellects to do manual labor, just like the lowest intellects? Yes, for two reasons. First, we are convinced that the great intellects, far from losing anything by this, will on the contrary gain much in health of body and vigor of mind, and above all in the spirit of solidarity and justice. Second, it is the only way to elevate and humanize manual labor, and thus to establish real equality among human beings.[20]

4

We are now going to consider the three great ways to emancipate the working class which *bourgeois socialism* advises, and it will be easy for us to show that each of these ways, outwardly very respectable, conceals an impossibility, an hypocrisy, or a lie. They are: 1) *popular education,* 2) *cooperation* and 3) *political revolution.*

We will examine [here] what they mean by popular education.

We hasten to state first of all that this is a point on which we agree perfectly with them: *The people must have education.* Only those who wish to perpetuate the slavery of the masses of the people can at present question or deny this. We are so convinced that education is the standard for measuring the degree of freedom, prosperity, and humanity that a class or an individual can attain, that we call not just for *some* education for the proletariat but for *full* education, all-round education, and complete education, so that no class may exist above them superior by its knowledge, so that no aristocracy of the intellect may protect and direct them—that is, exploit them.

We say that this so-called aristocracy of the intellect is the most hateful, scornful, insolent, and oppressive of all the aristocracies that have, each in its turn and sometimes all at once, oppressed human society. The aristocracy of the nobility tells you: "You are a very gallant man, but you were not born noble!" This is a bearable insult. The aristocrat of capital acknowledges that you have all kinds of merits. "But," he adds, "you haven't a sou!" This is equally bearable, for at bottom it is nothing but the statement of a fact, which in most cases (like the first) even benefits him to whom the taunt is addressed. But the aristocrat of the intellect tells you: "You know nothing, you understand nothing, you are an ass, and I, an intelligent man, can load a pack-saddle on you and lead you." This is insufferable.

The aristocracy of the intellect, this dear child of modern doctrinairism and last refuge of the spirit of domination which has afflicted the world since the beginning of history, which has sanctioned every State and been its essence, is a pretentious and ridiculous cult of licensed intellect which could quicken only in the womb of the bourgeoisie. The aristocracy of the nobility did not need science to prove its right [to rule]. They rested their power on two irresistible arguments: for its basis, violence and physical force; for its sanction, the grace of God. The aristocracy committed violence and the Church gave its blessings—such was the nature of their right. This intimate union of triumphant brutality with divine sanction conferred great prestige on the aristocracy and brought forth in it a sort of *chivalrous* virtue which took all hearts by storm.

The bourgeoisie, bereft of all virtue and grace, can base its right [to rule] on only one argument: the very real but very prosaic power of money. This is the cynical negation of every virtue: if you have money then you possess every right, however stupid you are and whatever riffraff you may be; if you haven't a sou, then you count for nothing, no matter what your personal merits. That is the fundamental principle of the bourgeoisie in its unpolished candor. It is understood that such an argument, however powerful it may be, could not suffice to establish and, above all, to consolidate bourgeois power. Human society is so constituted that only with the aid of respectable appearances can the worst things establish themselves. Hence the proverb that hypocrisy is the respect that vice pays to virtue.[21] Even the mightiest violence needs consecration.

We have seen that the nobility put its own violence under the protection of divine grace. The bourgeoisie could not resort to this protection. First of all, Almighty God and his representative the Church had over-compromised themselves over the centuries by protecting exclusively the monarchy and the nobility, this mortal enemy of the bourgeoisie. Second, the bourgeoisie, regardless of what it says and does, is atheist at the bottom of its heart; it speaks of Almighty God for the people but has no need of Him itself; it pursues its interests not in the temples dedicated to the Savior, but in those dedicated to Mammon,[22] at the Stock Exchange, in the counting-houses of commerce and banking, and in large industrial establishments. The bourgeoisie had to seek sanction outside of God and Church. It found sanction among licensed intellectuals.

The bourgeoisie knows very well that the principal base of its present political power, one could say its only base, is its wealth; but, neither wishing to affirm this nor being able to do so, it seeks to explain its power by the superiority not of its natural ability but of its scientific ability. It claims that one must be aware of many things to govern men, and that at present only it has such knowledge. It is a fact in every European State that only the exploiting and dominating class—the bourgeoisie, which includes a nobility that today exists in name only—receives a somewhat serious education. Further, there appears in its bosom a naturally less numerous class of men who dedicate themselves exclusively to the study of the greatest problems of philosophy, social science, and politics, men who properly constitute the new aristocracy of licensed and privileged intellectuals. This is the quintessence, the scientific expression, of the spirit and interests of the bourgeoisie.

The modern universities of Europe, which form a sort of scientific republic, currently perform for the bourgeois class the same services that the Catholic Church once rendered to the aristocracy of nobles; and just as Catholicism then sanctioned the violences perpetrated by the nobility on the people, so does the university, this church of bourgeois learning, now explain and legitimize the exploitation of these same people by bourgeois capital. Is it any wonder that in the great struggle of socialism against bourgeois political economy, licensed learning has taken, and continues to take so resolutely, the side of the members of the bourgeoisie?

Let us not seize upon the effects, but always attack the causes: the science of the schools is a product of the bourgeois spirit, and the men who represent this science have been born, raised, and educated in the bosom of the bourgeoisie, under the influence of its spirit and its exclusive interests, all of which are by nature opposed to the full, genuine emancipation of the proletariat; all their economic, philosophical, political, and social theories have been worked out one after the other along these lines and have at bottom no goal other than to demonstrate the ultimate inability of the working masses [to manage their own affairs], as well as the mission of the bourgeoisie (which is educated because it is wealthy and which can always make itself wealthier because it possesses education) to govern the workers until the end of time.

What must we recommend to the world of the workers in order to break this fatal circle? Naturally, acquire learning and seize knowledge, this powerful weapon without which the workers may make revolutions but without which the equality, justice, and liberty that form the very basis of their political and social yearnings, could never establish themselves on the ruins of bourgeois privileges. Here we agree with the bourgeois socialists.

But there are two other very important points on which we entirely differ with them:

(1) The bourgeois socialists ask only a little more education for the workers than they receive today, and they reserve the privileges of superior education only for a very limited group of wealthy men—men from the property-owning class, from the bourgeoisie, or just men who by a lucky accident have been embraced and welcomed into this class. The bourgeois socialists claim that it is useless for everyone to receive the same amount of education because, if everyone wished to devote himself to science, no one would be left to do the manual labor without which even science itself would not exist.

(2) On the other hand they declare that, in order to emancipate the working masses, one must start first of all by giving them education, and that they should not consider a radical change in their economic and social position until they become more educated.

We shall return to these two points in ["All-Round Education," below].

3

La Montagne and Mr. Coullery

1

La Montagne is a newspaper published in La Chaux-de-Fonds, managed by Mr. Jeanrenaud, whom every worker of this area knows for his remarkable devotion to and indefatigable propaganda of the religious ideas of the Protestant sect to which he belongs.[23]

Our readers are all familiar with the movement that has appeared in Neuchâtel canton; every one of them knows that the conservatives in this canton have allied themselves with socialists from elsewhere, and that they have formed a political party rather like the one that flourished in Geneva some years ago. *La Montagne* is the organ of this party, with which the workers' movement has nothing in common. This newspaper nevertheless dares to call itself the "organ of social democracy."

At the meeting on 30 May [1869] held in Crêt-du-Locle,[24] this organ was with great reason unanimously disavowed, for insofar as social questions are concerned it deals with petty questions of local politics and Protestant propaganda. It professes a socialism to which all reactionaries would eagerly subscribe, it propagates the false news about our strikes and the general calumnies about the workers' movement that the *Journal de Genève* invents. In a word, it misleads the working class of La Chaux-de-Fonds, seeking to separate them from the International [Working-Men's] Association, the resolutions and principles of which it condemns and distorts.

Also *La Montagne*'s clumsy friend, the *Journal de Genève* has just given it good marks (see its issue of 2 July [1869]),[25] which is an eye-opening sign to workers who know what this approval means.

We sincerely regret that men who have made so many sacrifices for the people's cause, men whose nobility of heart we are happy to recognize, are letting themselves be fooled by self-love, persisting in holding a false position that completely separates them from their former friends. But regardless of the distress this separation causes, we would be lax in our obligation [if we did not] signal to the workers of all Europe that these persons have deserted their great cause and become the intimate friends of bourgeois reaction.

Workers of La Chaux-de-Fonds, beware! *La Montagne* is an organ of bourgeois reaction, and if the words "organ of social democracy" appear on its masthead, this is only a mask with which to trick you!

2

La Montagne, a Chaux-de-Fonds newspaper founded and edited by Dr. Coullery, which calls itself an organ of social democracy (note well the contrast with socialist democracy!), has the indisputable honor of having invented a new kind of socialism. Up to now we have had various types of hybrid socialism: doctrinaire or scholastic socialism, which prepares Procrustean beds for future humankind; authoritarian socialism, which makes the State a sort of God Almighty on earth, bestowing and regulating human life and liberty; the hypnotic socialism of the bourgeoisie, which attempts to show the workers, who are exploited so harshly by bourgeois capital, that they need only count upon their bosses' forbearance; finally, we have the socialism of radicals who would like to use the *subversive passions* of the working masses as tongs to draw power to themselves. Mr. Coullery has the distinguished honor of adding to *bourgeois socialism,* of which he has always been a most fervent apostle, a new invention of his brain: JESUITIC OR PROTESTANT SOCIALISM.

To demonstrate this, we refer to the speech he recently gave at the Chaux-de-Fonds section of the International, which he reproduced in No. 18 of *La Montagne.* But to explicate this speech we must refer to some previous events, particularly to the charges made not against Mr. Coullery personally but against his clearly reactionary and bourgeois tendencies, at the Crêt-du-Locle meeting of 30 May 1869, and to the verdict against them which was pronounced unanimously, save for three votes, by an assembly which convoked more than one hundred fifty delegates from the [International's] Jura sections, among whom were nearly a hundred delegates from La Chaux-de-Fonds; then, we must recount the facts on which the charges and the verdict were based.

Whoever has followed the development of socialist ideas in the International['s sections] in French-speaking Switzerland knows very well that all of Mr. Coullery's propaganda has been, from the beginning, the purest sort of bourgeois socialism. As the editor of *La Voix de l'Avenir,* he always championed the principles on which the omnipotence of the bourgeois world is chiefly founded and from which the slavery of the proletariat naturally and inevitably springs: individual property, the law of inheritance, unrestrained competition in industry and commerce, and above all—*freedom!*

As a pupil, admirer, and worshipper of Bastiat, whom he considers the greatest revolutionary and who, from the standpoint of socialism, is the greatest reactionary that has ever lived, Mr. Coullery fanatically worships this sacred and divine freedom. This is a fine passion, which we would dearly love to share with him and for which we would praise him greatly, if we did not know that *this freedom,* whose knight he has exclusively made himself, is in reality only the privilege of the few and the slavery of the many. It is the freedom of the *Journal de Genève,* the freedom extolled by every member of the bourgeoisie who asks the police to supervise his workers' labor.

Ah! We also want freedom! But we want it whole, not just religious, or civil, or political, or economic, but human—expansive, like the world. We want it unencumbered by all the chains of the present religious, political, juridical, and economic institutions that ruin it. We want complete freedom for every individual, manifesting itself in the all-round cultivation of all natural abilities, based on the solidarity and equality of everyone! Unfortunately for Mr. Coullery, this freedom will be the death of his as surely as the emancipation of the workers will be the death of all economic and political privileges enjoyed by the members of the bourgeoisie.

One often wonders whether these preachers of bourgeois freedom who appear so ardent and sincere, are hoaxers or dupes. Are their lies to the workers the fault of their heart or of their mind?

Let us see, Mr. Coullery, tell us, hand over your heart, where do you find the courage to speak of freedom to workers who are slaves of capital, and simultaneously to preach respect for the foundation of their slavery, the economic and political organization of society? Is it really possible that you have not realized that the worker's freedom must destroy the bases of that organization, lest it be destroyed by them?

Whatever be the motives that have inspired Mr. Coullery, it is certain that nearly all his articles in *La Voix de l'Avenir* have been suggested by the socialism of the Bourgeois, a socialism so fraternal in form but so hopeless and unfeeling in the end. Have the various sections of the International in French-speaking Switzerland at all hesitated to protest repeatedly against this newspaper's tendencies? It was tolerated only for want of something better, and only as long as possible. The crisis broke out in October 1868, after the Brussels Congress [of the International].

This is a memorable year in the history of militant and practical workers' socialism. Three extremely important events occurred. First, the International Working-Men's Association concluded that so long as the bourgeoisie has a separate existence, based on individual and hereditary property in land and capital, any serious and sincere reconciliation between it and the millions of workers whom it exploits is impossible; and the International refused the alliance that the members of the bourgeoisie proposed. Meeting in congress in Brussels, the International Working-Men's Association declared that, from the standpoint of honest socialism or of the all-round emancipation of the workers, the entirely bourgeois League of Peace and Freedom had no reason for existing.

[Second, t]he League of Peace and Freedom, meeting in congress in Berne two weeks later, agreeing with the insight of the Brussels Congress, eliminated the principle of *economic and social equality* from its program, by a vast majority; in this way, it definitively asserted itself as a bourgeois league, therefore hostile to the workers' program.[26] The break was thus clarified and openly proclaimed by each side almost simultaneously. The impossibility of any reconciliation became obvious to everybody, and everyone who was not so broad-minded as to hold simultaneously two mutually destructive principles was forced to take one of the two sides, to the exclusion of the other.

To these two events we add a third, still more important and above all more explicit than the first two: the adoption of the great principle of *collective property* by the Congress of Workers in Brussels, and the entirely natural and logical support of individual and hereditary property by the Congress of Bourgeois in Berne.

Collective property and *individual property!* These are the two banners under which the great battles of the future will be fought. This open way of posing the question did not please Mr. Coullery. Broken-hearted at no longer being able to remain the friend of both parties, he finally allowed himself to follow freely his bourgeois instincts and turned furiously against both the Brussels Congress and the dissenters at the Berne Congress. By contrast, he proved himself to be full of enthusiasm for the socialism of Messrs. Goegg and Chaudey.

This was too much for the International Working-Men's Association in French-speaking Switzerland. Mr. Coullery had to quit *La Voix de l'Avenir,* which then ceased to appear. On the ruins of this paper, *L'Égalité* was later founded.

3

Whatever our opponents say, we have the greatest respect, not for all opinions, but for the right of all individuals to hold their own opinions; and the more honesty and openness a person brings to them, the more esteem we have for that person.

Mr. Coullery, having been a fiery radical, parted company with radicalism. That is his right. This sorry radicalism, which has rendered indisputable services to the world, is now being abandoned by living persons. Mr. Coullery, who is alive at least in his imagining if not in his thinking, has left it like the others. The point, then, is to know what road he has taken since leaving it. He had to choose between two paths.

In one direction was the great road of the future, of universal, unique, full freedom, of the complete emancipation of the proletariat by the economic and social equalization of everyone on earth. It was the new world, a limitless ocean. It was Social Revolution.

In the other direction were the romanesque and picturesque ruts of a past both mystical and brutal. There was the Church, there were the monarchy and aristocracy that had been blessed and consecrated by the Church; there were bourgeois privileges and the separation of the working masses as a body from the professions. There were many small well-restricted freedoms, and the absence of *freedom.* There was the reign of violence, a quite indecent reality enveloped in a cloud of divine mysticism which partly concealed its daily monstrosities and which lent it a false appearance of grandeur. [In this direction, i]n a word, was the world of brutality, triumphant but cheerful brutality, which sought self-consolation in the silly stories of religion and other pleasant fables: a world which still remains the ideal homeland of every romanesque and sentimental soul, of every spirit warped and corrupted by spiritualism.

Can we be angry with Mr. Coullery for not having chosen the other path? We do not think so; it would be unjust, for in the end one's own nature determines one's path. In siding with Reaction against Revolution, Mr. Coullery has only obeyed his own nature.

Our criticism, then, is not directed at the decision which Mr. Coullery, in his innermost heart, believed he had to take by leaving the radical party—this does not concern us—but to the totally ambiguous position in which he later placed himself with respect to the party of socialist democracy, the International Working-Men's Association. We reproach him for a great lack of sincerity and candor. Like most religious persons, he doubtless believes that it can often be useful to mislead people for their own good, and that only God deserves the whole and undisguised truth. This can still be a legitimate conviction by itself. It has long been professed and practiced by Jesuits as well as by Protestants, and we would not have attacked it in the person of Mr. Coullery if he had not wished to make it a weapon for perverting the International.

What we oppose in Mr. Coullery is his enormous pretension to be the friend of and most intimate collaborator in an openly reactionary party, and simultaneously to pass as an honest socialist and devoted partisan of the emancipation of the working masses. He would like to convince us that he has become more worthy of our sympathy and confidence since rallying to the politics of the aristocrats and Protestants, that he has drawn closer to the very spirit of the International.

We would not stop to address this question if it lived [only] in Mr. Coullery's heart or mind. But it appears absolutely necessary for us to fight the notion, for if it succeeds in being accepted by any number of workers, it would inevitably pervert their hearts as well as their minds, leading them directly into slavery.

To be sure, Mr. Coullery has had a thousand excellent reasons to part company with radicalism. Perhaps the radical party erred in not having left enough space for this personage so profoundly preoccupied with himself. Mr. Coullery's nature is in large degree whimsical and sentimental; it requires warmth, real or feigned, a great deal of dramatic movement, and above all much personal exposure. He naively identifies his precious person with his principles, and he so loves the world's attention that when the world forgets or ignores him, Mr. Coullery willingly concludes that his principles have been forgotten. Need we be amazed that, in such a frame of mind, he felt constrained in the prosaic world of bourgeois radicalism, and that he let himself be converted to religious and political Protestantism? Doesn't everyone naturally seek, and hasn't everyone the right to adopt, the most appropriate arena?

Mr. Coullery made only one mistake, which ultimately we would prefer to attribute to his head rather than to his heart. He imagined that he made progress by retreating into the camp of reaction! This mistaken view has certainly not allowed him to realize that if the socialists fight bourgeois radicalism, then this is done hardly from the standpoint of the past but rather from that of the future. No person possessed of heart and mind would dare hesitate in the choice between the present and the past; for in short, contemporary radicalism, with all its imperfections and contradictions, is still a thousand times better than the sordid past, which Revolution has smashed and which equivocal, vain, and confused persons would like to revive.

If socialism disputes radicalism, this is hardly in order to reverse it but rather to advance it. Socialism criticizes radicalism not for being what it is but, on the contrary, for not being enough so, for having stopped in midstream and thus having put itself in contradiction with the revolutionary principle, which we share with it. Revolutionary radicalism proclaimed the Rights of Man, for example, human rights. This will be its everlasting honor, but it dishonors itself today by resisting the great economic revolution without which every right is but an empty phrase and a trick. Revolutionary socialism, a legitimate child of radicalism, scorns its father's hesitations, accuses it of inconsistency and cowardice, and goes further [than it]. But at the same time, revolutionary socialism gladly recognizes the solidarity between itself and radicalism, and never will Dr. Coullery succeed in leading us into the camp of aristocratic and Protestant reaction.

Mr. Coullery would like to deny his alliance with the party of the old royalists, who now call themselves *democrats* in Neuchâtel canton. But he cannot. These reactionaries, these old political tricksters, are naturally more clever and more practical than he, and you need give them but the tip of your finger for them to seize your whole person. They know how to entangle and swallow up in their snares even the most resistant individuals. Mr. Coullery perhaps imagines, in his naive self-conceit, that he will fool them, and they have already fooled him; he pretends to lead them, and he follows them. He now serves them acting as a weapon against the International Working-Men's Association, whose doors he tries to open to their corrupting propaganda.[27]

Here is how he recommends these reactionaries to the workers of the International, in the 3 July [1869] issue of his newspaper *La Montagne*:*

*Note that the principal editors of this newspaper are, in addition to Dr. Coullery: Mr. Louis Jeanrenaud (a Protestant who differs from many others in that he never hid the fact of being

"Doesn't the conservative or liberal party share many of our opinions? Don't its newspapers, speakers, and writers ask, with us, the separation of Church and State? In the Grand Conseil haven't they supported Mr. Coullery in the suppression of privileges,[28] as well as in the idea of separation? Haven't they warmly defended just, honest, equitable, and proportional representation? Isn't one of their most influential members** passionately concerned with social problems, with cooperation?" And later he adds: "What matters the past of those who share our ideas? (Mr. Coullery should have said: of those whose ideas we now share.) We do not ask them: What were you? (But they have not changed, they remain what they were. It is Mr. Coullery who has joined them.) We ask instead: What are you, what do you wish, do you march with us?" (If Mr. Coullery wished to be honest, he should have said: "Will you suffer us to walk with you?")

These are the how-do-you-do's and proofs of socialism that Mr. Coullery has [offered] in his sad obligation to address the old aristocrats of Neuchâtel republic, the very persons who have fought this republic to benefit the King of Prussia. These are the new allies whom he attempts to smuggle into the International [Working-Men's] Association, doubtless so that they may later impose themselves on it by violence. Isn't this the way Jesuits and Protestants operate?

In the 13 July [1869] issue of *La Montagne* we read: "For what reason does *L'Égalité* take to task the editor of *La Montagne,* Mr. Louis Jeanrenaud? And to what end does it make his religious convictions a crime? Is it an accident that one must have a badge of rationalism or atheism to be a member of the International? *Up to now we thought that a person's political and religious opinions did not affect his standing as a member of the International; as for us, we maintain that point of view.*"

This time the confession is complete. Impelled by his eloquence, or perhaps by the necessity of giving reactionary proofs to his dear allies and collaborators, Mr. Coullery confesses to us: *first,* that *according to him* even the most fanatical reactionary who is concerned in any way with the social question, even from a wholly retrogressive standpoint like Mr. Henri Dupasquier or Dr. Coullery, has the right to enter the International; and second, he unmasks for us his forethought, and his hereafter clear

---

one, whom everyone in La Chaux-de-Fonds, Neuchâtel, and Le Locle knows to be one of the most zealous and fanatical members of that anti-rational, anti-liberal, anti-socialist, and anti-humanitarian community), and Messrs. Edouard Perrochet and Henri Dupasquier, both representatives of the old royalist party. One imagines that Mr. Coullery, in such an entourage, with all his love of freedom, is not free. These latter, who know very well what they want, would not have accepted Mr. Coullery had he not given them proofs of his fidelity and were they not hoping to use him to attain their goal. So Mr. Coullery is obliged to make his acts conform to their desires and to write in the newspaper only what they wish to let him write. To them will accrue the utility, to him the glory.

**Mr. Henri Dupasquier, one of the editors of *La Montagne,* the same one whose reactionary speech aroused unanimous indignation at the 1867 Congress of [the League of] Peace [and Freedom] in Geneva.[29]

intention, to open wide the gates of the International to aristocrats, Jesuits, and Protestants, doubtless in the hope that they will sooner or later plant the banner of reaction there.

La Montagne does not yet dare call itself an organ of the International. But it clearly aspires to this masthead, and Mr. Coullery's last speech, at the 5 July [1869] meeting of the Chaux-de-Fonds section [of the International], demonstrates his formal intention to make this section solidaristic with his reactionary policy. What follows from this? That Mr. Coullery is not so preoccupied with the International Working-Men's Association, and that he has troubled himself to form new sections of it in the Jura only so as to make them simultaneously a pedestal for his own person and an instrument of reaction.

Mr. Coullery is fooling himself. The International is stronger than him and all his aristocratic and Protestant friends taken together. Their intrigues may well be able to disturb a very small part of it, on the surface, for an instant. But the day after, no trace will remain.

Mr. Coullery's Verdict[30]

The International Working-Men's Association has a fundamental law that each section and each member must obey, under penalty of expulsion. This law is set forth in the General Rules proposed by the General Council of the Association in 1866 to the Geneva Congress, discussed and unanimously approved by this Congress, and at last ultimately approved through their unanimous acceptance by the sections of every country. Thus, it is the fundamental law of our great Association.

The Preamble at the head of these General Rules defines clearly the basis and goal of the Association, and it establishes above all:[31]

That the emancipation of the workers must be accomplished by the workers themselves;

That the efforts of the workers must strive to establish the same rights and the same obligations for everyone—that is, political, *economic,* and social equality;

That the subjection of the worker to capital is the source of all political, moral, and material servitude;

That, for this reason, *the economic emancipation of the workers is the great goal to which every political movement should be subordinated;*

That the emancipation of the workers *is not a simply local or national problem*—but INTERNATIONAL.

As a result of these principles, the International Working-Men's Association admits all workers' societies, as well as all separate individuals, whatever their origin and without regard to *color, belief, or nationality,* with the special clause, however, that they adhere *to these principles openly, completely, without second thoughts,* and *that they undertake to observe them.*

Let us see, then, what obligations follow from these principles, that each workers' society and each individual assumes upon entering the International [Working-Men's] Association.

The first obligation, which we find at the head of the Preamble, is to strive with every effort for the triumph of EQUALITY; not just of political equality, which would be pure radicalism, but of simultaneously political, *economic,* and social equality, through the abolition of all possible privileges, economic as well as political, so that for all persons on earth, without regard to color, nationality, or sex, there may henceforth be only a single social way of life: "*the same obligations, the same rights.*"

This is the whole program of revolutionary socialism, of which *equality* is the first condition and first word, admitting freedom only after equality, in equality, and through equality; for every freedom extraneous to equality constitutes a privilege, which is to say, domination by a small number and slavery for the vast majority.

Better to establish the revolutionarily socialist character of the program of the International, the Preamble follows this first declaration with a second and no less important one: "*That the subjection of labor to capital is the source of all political, moral, and material servitude,* and that *for this reason,* THE ECONOMIC EMANCIPATION OF THE WORKER is the great goal to which every political movement must be subordinated."[32]

This is the reversal of all bourgeois politics, the point where socialist democracy is absolutely and definitively separated from the exclusively political democracy of the Bourgeois, separated from both Mr. Coullery and the radicals, and from Mr. Coullery even more than from the radicals.

From the moment when the International recognized the great goal to which every political movement must be subordinated, it rejected all politics which do not strive to attain this goal directly. Thus it rejected all bourgeois, monarchical, liberal, or even radical democratic politics; for we know both that bourgeois politics neither has nor can have any goal other than the consolidation and extension of bourgeois power, and that this power is founded exclusively on the dependence of the worker and on the exploitation of the worker's labor. So that no uncertainty may remain on this point, the Preamble adds: "*That the subjection of the laborer to capital is the source of all political, moral, and material servitude.*" Which is to say, that to attain the great goal of the International—the economic emancipation of labor—the tyranny of capital must be broken, and all the power and life of the bourgeoisie must be smashed.

How to smash the tyranny of capital? Destroy capital? But that would be to destroy all the riches accumulated on earth, all primary materials, all the instruments of labor, all the means of labor. That would be to condemn all humanity—which is infinitely too numerous today to exist like savages on the simple gifts of nature, and which therefore can exist henceforth only with the help of this capital—to the most terrible death, death by starvation. Thus capital cannot and must not be destroyed. It must be preserved. But if it is preserved and if it continues to stay separate from labor and superior to it, then there is no human force that can stop it from oppressing and enslaving labor.

Capital which exists isolated from labor and superior to it: this is the constitution, the economic, political, and social power of the bourgeoisie. Labor remaining isolated from capital and inferior to it: this is the *proletariat.* So long as they remain separate from one another, can they be reconciled? Can a political constitution be invented which prohibits capital from oppressing and exploiting labor? This is impossible. All the arrangements one could make would result only in a new exploitation of labor by capital, inevitably detrimental to the workers and advantageous to the members of the bourgeoisie; for political institutions exercise power only so long as they are not in contradiction with the economic force of circumstances; from which it follows that so long as capital remains in the hands of the members of the bourgeoisie, the latter cannot be prevented from exploiting and enslaving the proletariat.

Since capital is indestructible and destined not to remain concentrated in the hands of a separate, exploiting class, there is but a single solution—*the intimate and complete union of capital and labor;* the members of the bourgeoisie must be compelled to become workers and the workers must obtain not individual but *collective* property in capital: for if they tried to divide among themselves the capital that exists, they would first of all reduce it, reduce to a large degree its productive power, and with the help of the law of inheritance they would very soon reconstitute a new bourgeoisie—a new exploitation of labor by capital.

Here is the clear result of the principles contained in the General Rules. This result has moreover been decidedly established by the Brussels Congress, which proclaimed *collective property in land* and *free credit,* that is, the collective property of capital, as the absolutely necessary conditions of the emancipation *of labor and of the workers.*[33] These are the two very resolutions of the Brussels Congress that horrified all Mr. Coullery's bourgeois instincts and that made him understand that he could have nothing in common with the International Working-Men's Association.

This Association poses a vast goal: *equality.* The means it proposes as the only effective and real ones, are no less formidable: *the overthrow of the power of the members of the bourgeoisie and the destruction of their existence as a separate class.* It is understood that the International Working-Men's Association, being willing and obliged to strive by these *means* to this *goal,* declares *open war* on the bourgeosie. Compromise between the bourgeoisie and the proletariat is no longer possible, the proletariat desiring only equality and the bourgeoisie existing only through inequality. For the bourgeoisie, as a separate class, equality is death; for the proletariat, the least inequality is slavery. The proletariat is tired of being the slave, and the bourgeoisie naturally does not wish to die. Thus it is irreconcilable war, and one must be either crazy or a traitor to advise and preach conciliation to the working classes. May Mr. Coullery take it as read.

The International [Working-Men's] Association, in undertaking this formidable war against the bourgeoisie, does not in the least delude itself about the vast difficulties awaiting it. It is unaware neither of its adversary's influence nor of the colossal efforts which it will have to make in order to be victorious. It knows that all defensive and offensive arms, capital and credit, all the organized military, bureaucratic, and diplomatic powers of these vast, oppressive, centralized entities which call themselves States, all the corrupting effects of religion, and all the practical applications of science are on the side of our enemies; and to oppose it all, we have only justice, the already aroused instinct of the masses of the people and the vast number of the proletariat. And still the International has hardly despaired of victory, nor does it so despair.

It has realized that with the help of the political and moral corruption and dissolution of the enemy camp, a formidable force can be created by unifying and organizing in a very real and solid manner these millions of proletarians who are tired of suffering and who are now impatient for emancipation across all Europe: a force able to struggle against and triumph over the coalition of all privileged classes and all States. At the same time, it has realized that for this organization to be effective and substantial, rejecting every compromise and every equivocation, it must above all conform and remain faithful to its principle. And in the Preamble to the General Rules, we find this statement: *That the emancipation of the workers must be accomplished by the workers themselves*—which, added to subsequent statements, signifies that the International Working-Men's Association absolutely excludes from its midst all those who wish to pursue any goal other than the all-round and definitive emancipation of the workers, that is to say, equality; and that, if it makes exception to receive members of the bourgeoisie, this is only on the condition that they adhere fully, sincerely, and wholeheartedly to the workers' program, that they henceforth pursue only the unique and grand policy of the International and have absolutely no goal other than this emancipation of labor in the world, renouncing all personal and local policies.

To make this meaning clearer still, the Preamble adds this other statement: "*That the emancipation of the workers is not a simply local or national problem,*" that it is eminently *international;* from which it follows that the entire policy of the Association can only be an *international policy,* excluding absolutely all patriotic conceits which always interest the members of the bourgeoisie, excluding every exclusively national policy.

The homeland of the worker, the homeland of the member of the International, is henceforth the great federation of the workers of the whole world, in the struggle against bourgeois capital. The worker can henceforth have no compatriots or brothers other than workers, regardless of their country, and no foreigners other than the members of the bourgeoisie, unless these latter break all solidarity with the bourgeois world and openly embrace the cause of labor against capital.

That is the program of the International Working-Men's Association. *Equality* is its goal; *the organization of the might of the workers,* the unification of the proletariat of the entire world across State frontiers and on the ruins of all patriotic and national narrowness, is its weapon, its great and only policy, to the exclusion of all others. Whoever adopts this program can with good reason be called a worthy member of the International Working-Men's Association.

In ["The Policy of the International," below], we shall show how Dr. Coullery, by his acts as well as by all his writings and speeches, has put himself in flagrant contradiction with all the basic principles of this program.

Part Three

The Program of Revolutionary Socialism

Samedi 7 Août 1869 — PAS DE DROITS SANS DEVOIRS, PAS DE DEVOIRS SANS DROITS — Première année. N° 29

L'ÉGALITÉ

Journal de l'Association internationale des Travailleurs de la Suisse romande

PARAISSANT A GENEVE LE SAMEDI MATIN

AVERTISSEMENT

La Rédaction.

AUX SECTIONS ROMANDES

Au nom du Comité Fédéral romand:

H. PERRET.

GENEVE, 6 AOUT

Politique de l'Internationale

I

Facsimile of the first installment of "The Policy of the International," in *L'Égalité,* no. 29 (7 August 1869).

4

The Policy of the International

1

"Up to now," says [the 13 July 1869 issue of] *La Montagne,* "we thought that a person's political and religious opinions did not affect his standing as a member of the International; as for us, we maintain that point of view."

At first glance, we might think Mr. Coullery to be correct. For indeed, when the International welcomes a new member into its bosom, it does not ask him whether he is an atheist or a believer, or whether he belongs to any particular political party. It asks him only: Are you a worker? If not, do you wish, do you feel the need, have you the strength, to embrace the workers' cause totally and unreservedly, and are you willing to identify yourself with it, to the exclusion of all opposing causes?

Do you feel that the workers, who produce all the wealth of the world, who are the creators of civilization, and who have won every bourgeois freedom, are today condemned to poverty, ignorance, and slavery? Have you realized that the chief cause of all the ills afflicting the worker is poverty, and that this poverty, the fate of all workers of the world, results inevitably from the present economic organization of society, especially from the subjugation of labor—i.e., the proletariat—to the yoke of capital—i.e., the bourgeoisie?

Have you realized that there is, between the proletariat and the bourgeoisie, an irreconcilable antagonism which results inevitably from their respective stations in life? That the prosperity of the bourgeois class is incompatible with the prosperity and freedom of the workers because this exclusive prosperity [of the former] is based on the exploitation and subjugation of the latter's labor; and that, for the same reason, the prosperity and human dignity of the masses of workers absolutely require the abolition of the bourgeoisie as a distinct class? That as a result, war between the proletariat and the bourgeoisie is unavoidable, and that its only outcome can be the destruction of the latter?

Have you realized that no worker, however intelligent and strong, can struggle alone against the influence that the members of the bourgeoisie organize so well, an influence epitomized and chiefly supported by each and every State? That in order to become strong you must unite not with members of the bourgeoisie—this would be a folly or a crime, for every member of the bourgeoisie is, as a member of the bourgeoisie, our irreconcilable enemy—nor with traitorous workers who are so base as to curry favor with the members of the bourgeoisie, but with strong and virtuous workers who honestly want what you do?

Have you realized that an isolated local or national workers' association will never be victorious against the formidable coalition of all the privileged classes, property-owners, capitalists and States throughout the world—even if it belongs to one of Europe's largest countries; and that to resist this coalition and win this victory, nothing less is needed than the union of all local and national workers' associations into a worldwide association, *the great International Working-Men's Association of all countries*?

If you feel, if you have indeed realized and really want all this, then join us, regardless of your political and religious beliefs. But for us to welcome you, you must pledge: (1) to subordinate henceforth your personal interests and even those of your family, as well as your political and religious convictions and their manifestations, to the supreme concern of our association—the struggle of labor against capital, of the workers against the bourgeoisie in the economic field; (2) never to compromise with members of the bourgeoisie for personal gain; (3) never to strive to rise above the working masses as an individual for your personal advantage, for this would immediately make you a member of the bourgeoisie, an enemy and an exploiter of the proletariat, since the whole difference between the two is that a member of the bourgeoisie always seeks his own good outside the collectivity, while the worker seeks his and intends to claim it only in solidarity with all [others] who work and are exploited by bourgeois capital; (4) to remain always faithful to the solidarity of the workers, for the International considers the least betrayal of this solidarity to be the greatest crime and most infamous deed of which a worker is capable. In a word, you must accept our General Rules fully and unreservedly, taking a solemn oath to adhere to them henceforth in your life and in your acts.

We think that the founders of the International were very wise to eliminate all political and religious questions from its program. To be sure, they lacked neither political views nor well defined anti-religious views. But they refrained from expressing those views in their program because their main purpose, before all else, was to unite the working masses of the civilized world in a common movement. Inevitably they had to seek a common basis, a set of elementary principles on which all workers should agree, regardless of their political and religious delusions, simply so that they might show themselves to be earnest workers, that is, harshly exploited and long-suffering.

Had they unfurled the flag of some political or anti-religious system, they hardly would have united the workers of Europe but instead would have divided them even more; for the priests, the governments, and even the reddest bourgeois political parties, aided by the workers' ignorance, have disseminated a horde of false ideas among the working masses through their own self-interested and highly corrupting propaganda. And these blinded masses are still, unfortunately, too often taken in by lies, the only purpose of which is to make them serve, voluntarily and stupidly, the interests of the privileged classes, to the detriment of their own.

Moreover, there is still too great a difference in the level of industrial, political, intellectual, and moral development among the working masses in various countries for it to be possible today to unite them around a single political, anti-religious program. To suggest such a program for the International and to make it an absolute condition for admission to that Association, would be to establish a sect, not a worldwide association, and it would destroy the International.

There was yet another reason for eliminating from the start all political tendencies from the program of the International, at least in appearance, *and only in appearance.*

From the beginning of history until today, there has never been a politics of the people, and by "the people" we mean the common people, the *working rabble* whose labor is the world's pabulum. There has only been the politics of the privileged classes, and these classes have used the physical force of the people to dethrone each other and to take one another's place. The people, in turn, have supported or opposed them only in the vague hope that at least one of these political revolutions—none of which could have been made without their help but none of which has been made for their sake—might alleviate somewhat their poverty and their age-old slavery. They have always been deceived. Even the Great French Revolution betrayed them. It eliminated the aristocratic nobility and replaced it with the bourgeoisie. The people are no longer called slaves or serfs; the law proclaims them free-born. But their slavery and their poverty remain unchanged.

And these will remain unchanged so long as the masses of the people continue to be used as the tool of bourgeois politics, whether this is called conservative, liberal, progressive, or radical politics, even if it gives itself the most revolutionary airs in the world. Because all bourgeois politics, regardless of its color and its label, has at bottom but a single aim: *to preserve bourgeois rule; and bourgeois rule is proletarian slavery.*

So what did the International have to do? First of all, it had to separate the working masses from all bourgeois politics and eliminate from its program all bourgeois political schemes. But when the International was founded, the only political programs in the world were those of the Church, the monarchy, the aristocracy, and the bourgeoisie. The program of the bourgeoisie, especially that of the radical bourgeoisie, was certainly more liberal and more humane than those of the others, but they were all based on the exploitation of the working masses, and none of them actually had any purpose other than to contend over who should monopolize this exploitation. The International therefore had to begin by clearing the ground. And since, from the standpoint of labor's emancipation, all politics was tarnished with reactionary elements, the International first had to cast out from its bosom all known political systems so that it could establish, upon the ruins of the bourgeois world, a genuine workers' program—the policy of the International.

2

The founders of the International Working-Men's Association acted wisely in establishing, as the basis of this Association, the exclusively economic struggle of labor and capital, rather than political and philosophical principles. With such a basis, they could be sure that a worker, as soon as he set foot on its ground, would inevitably discover, through the very force of circumstances and through the development of this struggle, the political, socialist, and philosophical principles of the International—principles, indeed, which are but the legitimate expression of its point of departure and of its goal. They could be sure that the worker would become imbued with confidence, both from his sense of being right and from the numerical strength he gains by uniting in solidarity, in the struggle against bourgeois exploitation, with his comrades-in-labor.

We have explained these principles in ["*La Montagne* and Mr. Coullery," above]. From the political and social standpoint, they inevitably result in the abolition of classes (and hence of the bourgeoisie, which is the dominant class today), the abolition of all territorial States and political fatherlands, and the foundation, upon their ruins, of the great international federation of all national and local productive groups. Since the principles of the International, from the philosophical standpoint, aim at nothing less than the realization on earth of the human ideal, of human well-being, of equality, justice, and freedom, these principles strive to render hopes for a "better world" in heaven totally pointless, and they will also result inevitably in the abolition of all cults and religious systems.

But if you start by announcing these two goals to unlearned workers crushed by their daily labor, workers who are demoralized and corrupted (by design, one might say) by the perverse doctrines liberally dispensed by governments in concert with every privileged caste—the priests, the nobility, the bourgeoisie—then you will alarm the workers. They may resist you without suspecting that these ideas are only the most faithful expression of their own interests, that these goals carry in themselves the realization of their dearest wishes, and that the religious and political prejudices in the name of which they may resist these ideas and goals are on the contrary the direct cause of their continued slavery and poverty.

We must distinguish clearly the prejudices of the masses of the people from those of the privileged class. As we have just said, the masses' prejudices are based only on their ignorance and totally oppose their very interests, while the bourgeoisie's are based precisely on its class interests and resist counteraction by bourgeois science itself only because of the collective egoism of its members. The people want but do not know; the bourgeoisie knows but does not want. Which of the two is incurable? The bourgeoisie, to be sure.

General rule: Only those who feel the need to be converted, who have already received through their outward privations or inward instincts everything you want to give them, can be converted. You will never convert those who do not feel the need to change, or even those who are discontent with their situation and want to change it but who, because of the nature of their moral, intellectual, and social habits, seek that situation in a world which is not the world you envision.

I ask whether you can convert to socialism a noble who covets riches, a member of the bourgeoisie who would like to be a noble, or even a worker who in his soul strives only to become a member of the bourgeoisie! You might as soon convert a real or imaginary aristocrat of the intellect, a scientist, a half-scientist, a quarter-, tenth-, or hundredth-part scientist who is full of scientific ostentation and of arrogant scorn for the illiterate masses—often just because he has been lucky enough somehow to understand a few books—and who thinks he is called, with others of his kind, to establish a new ruling, i.e., exploiting, caste.

No argument or propaganda will ever convert these miserable persons. There is only one way to convince them: by acting, by destroying the very possibility for privileged positions to exist, by destroying all domination and exploitation; by social revolution, which in sweeping away every basis of inequality in the world will moralize those persons by forcing them to seek their welfare through equality and solidarity.

The case is different with earnest workers. By "earnest" workers we mean all those who are really overwhelmed by the burden of labor, all those who are in so destitute and precarious a situation that none of them, save in the most extraordinary circumstances, could consider gaining a better situation for *himself,* and only for himself, under present economic conditions and in the present social environment—becoming in his turn, for example, a manager or a State counselor. To be sure, we also include in this category those rare and magnanimous workers who could rise individually above the working class but who do not wish to take advantage of the possibility, workers who would prefer to be exploited by the members of the bourgeoisie a bit longer, in solidarity with their comrades-in-poverty, rather than become exploiters in their turn. These workers do not have to be converted; they are pure socialists.

We are referring to the great mass of workers who, exhausted by their daily labor, are poor and unlearned. These workers, regardless of the political and religious prejudices implanted in their mind, are *socialist without knowing it;* their most basic instinct and their social situation makes them more earnestly and truly socialist than all the scientific and bourgeois socialists taken together. They are socialist because of all the conditions of their material existence and all the needs of their being, whereas others are socialist only by virtue of their intellectual needs. And in real life the needs of the being are always stronger than those of the intellect, since the intellect is never the source of being but is always and everywhere its expression, reflecting its successive development.

The workers lack neither the potential for socialist aspirations nor their actuality; they lack only socialist thought. Each worker demands, from the bottom of his heart, a fully human existence in terms of material well-being and intellectual development, an existence founded on justice, that is, on the equality and freedom of each and every individual through labor. This is the instinctive ideal of everyone who lives only from his own labor. Clearly, this ideal cannot be realized in the present social and political world, which is founded on injustice and on the indecent exploitation of the labor of the working masses. Thus, every earnest worker is inevitably a socialist revolutionary, since he can be emancipated only by the overthrow of all things now existing. Either this structure of injustice must disappear along with its showy display of unjust laws and privileged institutions, or the working masses will be condemned to eternal slavery.

This is socialist thought, the germs of which will be found in the instinct of every earnest worker. The goal, then, is to make the worker fully aware of what he wants, to unjam within him a stream of thought corresponding to his instinct, for as soon as the thought of the working masses reaches the level of their instinct, their will becomes unshakable and their influence irresistible.

What impedes the swifter development of this salutary thought among the working masses? Their ignorance to be sure, that is, for the most part the political and religious prejudices with which self-interested classes still try to obscure their conscious and their natural instinct. How can we dispel this ignorance and destroy these harmful prejudices? By education and propaganda?

To be sure, these are excellent means. But, given the present plight of the working masses, they are insufficient. The isolated worker is too overwhelmed by his daily grind and his daily cares to have much time to devote to education. Moreover, who will conduct this propaganda? Will it be the few sincere socialists who come from the bourgeoisie and who certainly are magnanimous enough but who, on the one hand, are too few in number to propagandize as widely as necessary and, on the other hand, do not adequately understand the workers' world because their [social] situation puts them in a different world, and whom therefore the workers rather legitimately distrust?

"The emancipation of the workers must be accomplished by the workers themselves," says the Preamble to our General Rules. And it is a thousand times right to say so. This is the principal basis of our great Association. But the workers' world is in general unlearned, and it totally lacks theory. Accordingly, it is left with but a single path, that of *emancipation through practical action.* What does this mean?

It has only one meaning. It means workers' solidarity in their struggle against the bosses. It means *trade-unions, organization, and the federation of resistance funds.*[34]

3

If the International at first tolerated the subversively reactionary political and religious ideas of the workers who joined it, this was hardly because the International was indifferent to those ideas. The International cannot be accused of being indifferent because it detests and rejects those ideas with all the strength of its being, for as we have already shown, every reactionary idea is the inversion of the basis of the International.

This tolerance, we repeat, is prompted by a far-seeing wisdom. The International knows full well that every earnest worker is socialist because of all the wants intrinsic to his wretched station in life, and that any reactionary ideas he has can result only from his ignorance. To deliver him from that ignorance, the International relies on the collective experience he gains in its bosom, especially on the progress of the collective struggle of the workers against the bosses.

And indeed, as soon as a worker believes that the economic state of affairs can be radically transformed in the near future, he begins to fight, in association with his comrades, for the reduction of his working hours and for an increase in his salary. And as soon as he begins to take an active part in this wholly material struggle, we may be certain that he will very soon abandon every preoccupation with heaven, voluntarily renounce divine assistance, and become increasingly accustomed to relying on the collective strength of the workers. Socialism replaces religion in his mind.

The same thing will happen to the worker's reactionary politics, the chief prop of which will disappear as his consciousness is delivered from religious oppression. On the other hand, through practice and collective experience, which is naturally always more broadening and instructive than any isolated experience, the progressive expansion and development of the economic struggle will bring him more and more to recognize his true enemies: the privileged classes, including the clergy, the bourgeoisie, and the nobility; and the State, which exists only to safeguard all the privileges of those classes, inevitably taking their side against the proletariat in every case.

The worker thus enlisted in the struggle will necessarily come to realize that there is an irreconcilable antagonism between the henchmen of Reaction and his own dearest human concerns. Having reached this point, he will recognize himself to be a revolutionary socialist, and he will act like one.

This is not the case with the members of the bourgeoisie. All their interests are opposed to the economic transformation of society. And if their ideas are also opposed to it; if these ideas are reactionary or, as they are now politely called, moderate; if their heart and mind detest this great act of justice and liberation that we call the Social Revolution; if they are horrified of real social equality, that is, of simultaneously political, social, and economic equality; if at the bottom of their soul they desire, as many bourgeois socialists now do, to preserve a single privilege—even just their intellect—for themselves, their class, or their children; if they do not abhor the present order of things, with both mental logic and impassioned strength: then we may be sure that they will remain reactionaries and enemies of the workers' cause all their life. They must be kept far from the International.

They must be kept very far away, because their admission would only demoralize the International and divert it from its true path. There is, moreover, an unmistakable sign by which the workers can tell whether a member of the bourgeoisie who seeks admittance to their ranks comes to them straightforwardly, unhesitatingly, and without subversive hidden motives. This sign is the relations he maintains with the bourgeois world.

The antagonism between the world of the workers and that of the bourgeoisie is becoming more and more pronounced. Every serious-thinking person whose opinions and ideas are not distorted by the often unconscious influence of self-interested sophists must now realize that there is no reconciliation possible. The workers want equality and the bourgeoisie wants to maintain inequality. The one obviously destroys the other. Thus the vast majority of bourgeois capitalists and property-owners—the ones who have the courage honestly to admit what they want—are also bold enough to show just as honestly the horror that the present labor movement evokes in them. These are our resolute and sincere enemies. We know who they are, and this is good.

But there are other members of the bourgeoisie who are of a different kind; they have neither the same candor nor the same courage. They are enemies of social liquidation, which we call, with all the force of our souls, a great act of justice, the necessary point of departure and the indispensable basis for an egalitarian and rational organization of society. Like all other members of the bourgeoisie, they wish to preserve economic inequality, the everlasting source of all other inequalities; and at the same time they claim to want what we want, the all-round emancipation of the worker and of labor. With a passion worthy of the most reactionary members of the bourgeoisie, they support the very source of the proletariat's slavery, the separation of labor from landed property and capital, which are now represented by two different classes; and they nevertheless pose as apostles who will deliver the working class from the yoke of property and capital!

Are they fooling themselves or are they just fooling? Some, in good faith, fool themselves, but many are impostors; most fool both themselves and others. They all belong to the radical bourgeoisie and the category of bourgeois socialists who founded the *League of Peace and Freedom.*

Is this League socialist? As we have already noted, it rejected socialism with horror in the beginning, during the first year of its existence. This past year, it triumphantly rejected the principle of economic equality at its Berne Congress. Now, sensing that it is dying and wishing to live still a bit longer, but finally realizing that the social question is now the crux of political life, it calls itself socialist. It has become bourgeois-socialist and wants to decide all social questions on the basis of *economic inequality.* It wishes to preserve rent and interest, as it must, but it pretends to emancipate the workers with them. It tries to give nonsense some substance.

Why does it do this? What makes it attempt so unseemly and unproductive a task? This is not difficult to understand.

A large part of the bourgeoisie is tired of the reign of *Caesarism* and *militarism* which it itself founded, out of fear of the proletariat, in 1848. Just remember the June Days, those precursors of the December Days; remember the National Assembly that unanimously offered nothing but curses and insults after the June Days, unanimously but for a single voice, the voice of the illustrious and heroic socialist Proudhon, who alone had the courage to throw down the challenge to this rabid bourgeois herd of conservatives, liberals, and radicals. Nor should we forget that some of those citizens who reviled Proudhon are still alive and more militant than ever, [while others] have since become martyrs to liberty, beatified by the December persecutions.[35]

There is therefore absolutely no doubt that the entire bourgeoisie, including the radical bourgeoisie, was the creator of the Caesarean and military despotism, the effects of which it now deplores. Having used this despotism against the proletariat, the bourgeoisie now wants to be rescued from it. Nothing is more natural; this regime ruins and humiliates the bourgeoisie. But how to get rid of it? In the past the bourgeoisie was daring and strong, and its triumphs gave it strength. Now it is cowardly and weak, troubled by the impotence that accompanies age. It recognizes its weakness only too well and senses that it can do nothing by itself. Therefore it needs help, and only the proletariat can provide this; consequently, the bourgeoisie needs to win over the proletariat.

But how to win it over? By promises of freedom and political equality? These words no longer touch the workers. They have learned at their own expense, and they have realized through harsh experience, that these words mean nothing to them but the preservation of their economic slavery, often harsher than before. If you want to touch the hearts of these wretched millions of labor's slaves, speak to them of their economic emancipation. Every worker knows that this is the only real, serious foundation of every other emancipation. Accordingly, the workers must be approached on the ground of economic reforms of society.

Well, said the Leaguers of Peace and Freedom to themselves, let us do that, and let us call ourselves socialists as well. Let us promise them economic and social reforms, but always on the condition that they fully respect the bases of civilization and of bourgeois omnipotence: individual and hereditary property, interest on capital, and rent on land. Let us convince them that the worker can be emancipated only under these conditions, which guarantee our domination and their slavery.

Let us even convince them that the achievement of all these social reforms requires that they first make a good political revolution, but an exclusively political one, as red as they like politically and with much head-chopping if that becomes necessary, but with the greatest respect for the inviolability of property: in short, a wholly Jacobin revolution that will make us masters of the situation. And once we become the masters, we will give the workers, well, what we can give them and what we want to give them.

Here is an infallible sign by which the workers can recognize a false socialist, a bourgeois socialist: if, speaking of revolution, or if you like of social transformation, he says that political transformation *must precede* economic transformation; if he denies that they must be accomplished together and simultaneously, or if he denies even that political revolution is something other than the immediate and direct implementation of full and complete social liquidation, let the workers turn their backs on him, for he is either a fool or a hypocritical exploiter.

4

If the International Working-Men's Association is to be faithful to its principle and if it is to remain on the only path that can bring it success, then it must above all counteract the influences of two kinds of bourgeois socialists: the partisans of *bourgeois politics, including even bourgeois revolutionaries;* and the so-called *practical men,* who advocate *bourgeois cooperation.*

Let us first consider the former.

We have said that economic emancipation is the basis of all other emancipations. This summarizes the entire policy of the International.

Indeed, the following statement appears in the Preamble to our General Rules:

"*That the subjection of labor to capital is the source of all political, moral, and material servitude,* and that for this reason the economic emancipation of the workers is the great goal to which every political movement should be subordinated."[36]

Of course, every political movement which does not have the *full and definitive* economic emancipation of the workers for its immediate and direct goal, which does not have written clearly on its standard the principle of *economic equality,* that is, the *full restitution of capital to labor* or *Social Liquidation*—every such political movement is bourgeois and, as such, must be ruled out of the International.

As a result, the policy of bourgeois democrats or bourgeois socialists, which declares that political freedom is the *prior* condition for economic emancipation, must be mercilessly ruled out. These words mean nothing but that political reforms or political revolution must *precede* economic reforms or economic revolution, and that the workers must therefore unite with the somewhat radical members of the bourgeoisie in order first to carry out political changes with them, but without later carrying out economic changes against them.

We strongly dispute this pernicious theory, which can only make the workers once more a tool of their own exploitation by the bourgeoisie. To gain political freedom *first* can only mean to gain it by itself, leaving economic and social relations as before, that is, the property-owners and capitalists with their impudent riches and the workers with their poverty.

But, they say, once this freedom is won, it will give the workers a means of later gaining *equality or economic justice.*

Freedom, indeed, is a splendid and powerful tool. The question is whether the workers will really be able to use it and whether it will really be theirs, or whether, as has always been the case until now, their *political freedom* will be but a false front and a fraud.

Wouldn't a worker who, in his present economic predicament, is told of political freedom, respond with the refrain of a well-known song:[37]

Do not speak of freedom:
Poverty is slavery!

Indeed, one would have to be in love with illusions to imagine that a worker, under present economic and social circumstances, can really and truly make use of his political freedom or fully profit from it. For this he lacks two little things: spare time and material resources.

Furthermore, didn't we see precisely this in France on the day after the Revolution of 1848, the most radical revolution desirable from the political standpoint? The French workers were certainly neither indifferent nor unintelligent, and despite the most far-reaching universal suffrage they had to let the members of the bourgeoisie do as they pleased. Why? Because they lacked the material resources necessary to make political freedom a reality, because hunger forced them to remain slaves to hard labor, while radical, liberal, and even conservative members of the bourgeoisie—republicans of recent vintage, some converted the day before the revolution, some the day after—came and went, agitated, spoke, took action and conspired freely, some able to do so because of their annuity or other lucrative bourgeois situation, and others able because of the State budget, which they naturally preserved and made stronger than ever.

We know what happened: first the June Days; later, their inevitable result, the December Days.[38]

But, someone will say, the workers have become wiser by their very experience, and they will send common workers, rather than members of the bourgeoisie, to Constituent or Legislative Assemblies. As poor as they are, they will somehow manage to give their parliamentary deputies something to live on. Do you know what the result of this will be? The worker-deputies, transplanted into a bourgeois environment, into an atmosphere of purely bourgeois political ideas, will in fact cease to be workers and, becoming Statesmen, they will become bourgeois, and perhaps even more bourgeois than the Bourgeois themselves. For men do not make their situations; on the contrary, men are made by them. And we know from experience that *bourgeois[ified] workers* are frequently no less egoistic than bourgeois exploiters, no less pernicious to the International than bourgeois socialists, and no less vain and ridiculous than bourgeois nobles.

Regardless of what is said and done, the workers will have no freedom so long as they remain in their present predicament, and whoever advises them to gain political freedoms without first mentioning the boiling questions of socialism, without saying the words that cause the members of the bourgeoisie to pale—*social liquidation*—that person simply says: First win this freedom for us, so that we can later use it against you.

But, someone will say, these bourgeois radicals mean well and they are sincere. [We reply that n]o good intentions nor any sincerity can counteract the influence of one's [social] standing; and since we have said that the very workers thrust into this situation inevitably become bourgeois, that is all the more reason for those who remain in this situation to remain bourgeois.

If a member of the bourgeoisie, motivated by a great passion for justice, equality, and humanity, earnestly wishes to work for the emancipation of the proletariat, let him begin first by breaking all political and social ties with the bourgeoisie, all connections between the bourgeoisie and his interests, his mind, his vanity, and his heart. Let him understand before all else that no reconciliation is possible between the proletariat and the bourgeoisie, which lives only by exploiting others and which is the proletariat's natural enemy.

After he has turned his back on the bourgeois world for good, let him fall in under the workers' standard, on which are written the words: "Justice, Equality, and Liberty for all. Abolition of classes through worldwide economic equalization. Social liquidation." He will be welcome.

We have only one piece of advice to give the workers about the bourgeois socialists and the bourgeois[ified] workers who will tell us about compromise between bourgeois politics and workers' socialism: turn your backs on them.

Since bourgeois socialists are now trying, *with socialism as bait,* to agitate a great workers' unrest in order to gain political freedom, a freedom which we have seen would profit only the bourgeoisie; since the masses of workers, enlightened and set in motion by the International, have reached a clear understanding of their predicament and are in fact organizing themselves and becoming really strong, not along national lines but internationally, and not for the bourgeoisie's designs but for their own; since a revolution is necessary even to achieve the bourgeoisie's ideal of complete political freedom with republican institutions; and since revolutions can succeed only thanks to the people's might—for all these reasons, this strength must stop being used to pull chestnuts out of the fire for Bourgeois Gentlemen. It must from now on contribute only to the victory of the people's cause, the cause of everyone who labors against everyone who exploits labor.

The International Working-Men's Association, true to its basic principle, will never lend a hand in any political agitation that has any immediate and direct purpose other than the *complete economic emancipation of the worker*—that is, the abolition of the bourgeoisie as an economic class isolated from the bulk of the population—or in any revolution which, from the first day, from the first hour, does not have written on its standard the words *Social Liquidation.*

But revolutions are not improvised. They are not made arbitrarily either by individuals or even by the most powerful associations. They occur independently of all volition and conspiracy and are always brought about by the force of circumstances. They can be foreseen and their approach can sometimes be sensed, but their outbreak can never be hastened.

Convinced of this truth, we ask: What policy should the International follow during this somewhat extended time period that separates us from this terrible social revolution which is so universally anticipated?

Paying no attention to any local or national politics, as its articles require, the International will give labor unrest in all countries an *essentially economic* character, with the aim of reducing working hours and increasing salary, by means of the *association of the working masses* and the accumulation of *resistance funds.*

It will propagandize its principles because these principles, which are the purest expression of the collective interests of the workers of the entire world, are the soul and the whole vital force of the Association. It will propagandize widely without regard for bourgeois sensibilities, so that each worker who emerges from the intellectual and moral torpor that has been used to restrain him may understand his predicament, understand exactly what he must do, and know under what conditions he can gain his human rights.

The International will propagandize so much more vigorously and whole heartedly that we shall often encounter influences in the International itself that will attempt to portray the latter's principles as a useless theory and affect disdain for them, trying to restore the workers to the political, economic, and religious catechism of the bourgeoisie.

Lastly, the International will expand and organize across the frontiers of all countries, so that when the revolution—brought about by the force of circumstances—breaks out, the International will be a real force and will know what it has to do. Then it will be able to take the revolution into its own hands and give it a direction that will benefit the people: an earnest international organization of workers' associations from all countries, capable of replacing this departing political world of States and bourgeoisie.

We conclude this faithful statement of the policy of the International by quoting the last paragraph of the Preamble to our General Rules:

"The movement occurring among the workers of Europe's most industrialized countries, in giving rise to new hopes, gives solemn warning not to fall back into old errors."

5

All-Round Education

1

The first question we must now consider is whether the working masses can be fully emancipated so long as the education that they receive is inferior to that given to the members of the bourgeoisie, or, in general, so long as any class of any size enjoys, because of its birth, the privileges of a better upbringing and a fuller education. Doesn't this question answer itself? Isn't it obvious that of two persons endowed with nearly equal natural intelligence, the one who knows more, who is broader-minded thanks to scientific learning, who grasps more easily and fully the nature of his surroundings because he better understands those facts which are called the laws of nature and society and which interconnect natural and social events—that that person will feel freer in nature and society, and that he will also in fact be the cleverer and stronger of the two? The one who knows more will naturally rule over the one who knows less; and if between two classes just this one difference in education and upbringing existed, it would be enough to produce all the others in short order, and the human world would find itself in its present state, divided anew into a large number of slaves and a small number of rulers, the former working for the latter, as is the case now.

Now you understand why bourgeois socialists call for only *some* education for the people, a little more than they have now, and why we socialist-democrats call for *all-round education* for them, *total* education as full as the intellectual development of the times allows, so that in the future no *class* can rule over the working masses, exploiting them, superior to them because it knows more. The bourgeois socialists wish to preserve classes, each of which, according to them, should fulfill a different social function—one that of learning, for example, and another that of manual labor. We, on the contrary, desire the full and definitive abolition of classes, the unification of society, the economic and social equalization of all human beings on earth. They want to lessen, mitigate, and prettify inequality and injustice, preserving all the while these historical bases of contemporary society; but we wish to destroy them. From this it clearly follows that no understanding nor conciliation, nor even coalition, is possible between the bourgeois socialists and us.

But, they will say (and this argument they advance most often against us, for Doctrinaire Gentlemen of every color consider it irresistible), it is impossible for all humanity to devote itself to scientific learning; it would die of hunger. While some study, accordingly, the others must work to produce the vital necessities, first of all for themselves and then also for those persons who have consecrated themselves exclusively to labors of the intellect. For these latter work not just for themselves: don't their scientific discoveries, through application to industry and agriculture as well as to political and social life generally, both broaden human understanding and improve the situation of every human being without exception? Don't artistic creations ennoble everyone's life?

No, not at all. And our greatest criticism of science and the arts is precisely that they spread their good deeds and exercise their beneficial influence only over a very small portion of society, to the exclusion of the vast majority and hence also to their detriment. We may now say of the progress of science and the arts what has already quite correctly been said of the stupendous development of industry, commerce, credit—social wealth, in a word—in the most civilized countries of the modern world. This wealth, concentrated in an ever smaller number of hands and sloughing off the lower strata of the middle class, the petite bourgeoisie, into the proletariat, is wholly exclusive and becomes moreso every day, growing in direct proportion to the increasing poverty of the working masses. From this it follows that the abyss which already divides the wealthy and privileged minority from the millions of workers whose physical labor supports them, is always widening, and that the wealthier the exploiters of the people's labor get, the poorer the workers get. Simply juxtapose the extraordinary affluence of the great aristocratic, financial, commercial, and industrial world of England to the wretched predicament of the workers of that country. Simply read once more the unpretentious, heartrending letter recently written by an intelligent, honest London goldsmith, Walter Dugan, who *voluntarily* poisoned himself, his wife, and his six children just to escape the humiliations, the poverty, and the tortures of hunger. You will have to acknowledge that from the material standpoint this vaunted civilization means only oppression and ruination to the people.[39]

The situation is the same with respect to the modern progress of science and the arts. There has been vast progress, yes. But the greater the progress, the more it becomes a cause of intellectual and hence material slavery, a cause of the people's poverty and inferiority; for this progress always widens the abyss that already divides the insight of the people from that of the privileged classes. From the standpoint of natural ability, the insight of the people today is clearly less jaded, less depleted, less affected, and less corrupted by the need to defend unjust interests, and as a result it is naturally more cogent than bourgeois insight. But on the other hand, the privileged classes are fully armed, formidably armed, with knowledge. It happens quite often that a very bright worker must stand silent while a stupid scholar gets the better of him, not because the latter has any sense but because of the education denied to the worker, which the other has been able to get because the labor of the worker clothed him, lodged him, fed him, and provided him with tutors, books, and everything else he needed for his education while his stupidity was being scientifically developed in the schools.

We know perfectly well that the amount of learning each individual acquires is hardly the same even within the bourgeois class. Within the bourgeoisie too, there is a scale which depends not on the individuals' abilities but on the relative wealth of the social stratum in which they were born. For example, the education received by the children of the lowest stratum of the bourgeoisie is scarcely more than that which the workers manage to give themselves, and it is almost no education when compared to what society distributes so generously to the grande and moyenne bourgeoisie. So what do we see? The petite bourgeoisie, which now counts itself among the middle class only out of foolish vanity on the one hand and out of its dependence on the big capitalists on the other, is most of the time in a poorer and much more humiliating predicament than even the proletariat. So when we speak of the privileged classes, we never mean the poor petite bourgeoisie. If it had a bit more insight and courage, it would not hesitate to join us in battle against the grande and moyenne bourgeoisie which crush it now no less than they crush the proletariat. And if the economic development of society were to continue in this direction for yet another decade, which to us seems nevertheless impossible, we would see the majority of the moyenne bourgeoisie sink first into the present predicament of the petite bourgeoisie and disappear a little later into the proletariat, thanks always to the inevitable concentration of [social wealth in an] always fewer number of hands. The unfailing result of this will be eventually to divide the social world into a small, excessively affluent, learned, ruling minority and a vast majority of wretched, ignorant, slavish proletarians.

Every honest person, everyone who has human dignity and justice at heart, everyone who believes in the freedom of each individual through the equality of every individual and in that context, must be astounded that all inventions of the human mind and all the great applications of science to industry, to commerce, and to social life in general, have until now redounded only to the benefit of the privileged classes and never to the benefit of the masses of the people, extending the influence of those eternal protectors of every political and social injustice. We need only name these machines for every worker and every sincere partisan of the emancipation of labor to acknowledge this fact. Whose strength still now maintains the privileged classes in their positions, with all their arrogant prosperity and unjust delights, against the legitimate indignation of the masses of the people? Is this strength inherent in these privileged classes? No, [their positions are preserved] by the strength of the State alone, of which moreover every ruling office—and even middle and lower offices, save those of workers and soldiers—is now filled by their children, as they always have been. And what is now the basis of all the influence exerted by the States? It is science.

Yes, science. The science of government, the science of administration, and financial science; the science of fleecing the people without making them complain too much and, when they begin to complain, the science of imposing silence, forbearance, and obedience on them by scientifically organized violence; the science of tricking and dividing the masses of the people, of keeping them eternally and advantageously ignorant so that they may never, by helping each other and through unifying their efforts, constitute a force able to overturn the States; above all, military science, with all its improved weapons, its formidable tools of destruction which "perform wonders";[40] finally, the inventors' science, which has produced steamboats, railroads, and telegraphs—railroads which, as used by military strategy, increase tenfold the defensive and offensive force of States, and telegraphs which have created the most formidable politically centralized entities ever in the world, transforming each government into a hundred- or thousand-armed Briareus[41] and allowing it to be present, to act, and to strike everywhere.

Who, then, can deny that every scientific advance, without exception, has until now resulted only in increasing the wealth of the privileged classes and the influence of the States, to the detriment of the welfare and freedom of the popular masses and the proletariat? Someone will object: Don't the working masses also benefit from scientific progress? Aren't they much more advanced now than heretofore?

We reply with the words of Lassalle, the famous German socialist. To assess the progress of the working masses from the standpoint of their political and social empancipation, we should not compare their current intellectual level with their past intellectual level.[42] Having determined the difference between them and the privileged classes at a given time, we should examine whether they have advanced at the same rate as the latter. For if they have advanced at an equal rate, then the intellectual distance separating them from the privileged world will be the same. If the proletariat advances further and at a faster rate than do the privileged, this distance necessarily will have decreased. But if, on the contrary, the workers' progress is slower and therefore less than that of the dominant classes, then the distance between them will have grown over the same period of time; the abyss separating them will have become larger, the privileged will have become more powerful, and the worker will have become more dependent, more of a slave than in the beginning. If you and I leave simultaneously from two different spots, and if you begin 100 paces ahead of me and make 60 paces a minute while I make only 30, then at the end of an hour the distance separating us will no longer be 100 paces, but 280 [*sic* for 1,900].

This example gives an entirely fair idea of the progress of the bourgeoisie and of the proletariat respectively until now. The members of the bourgeoisie have trodden the path of civilization faster than have the proletarians, not because their intellect is naturally more powerful (we might with good reason say the exact opposite today) but because until now the economic and political organization of society has been such that only they could educate themselves, such that learning existed only for them, and such that the proletariat has been condemned to forced ignorance, with the result that even if the proletariat makes progress—and its progress is certain—this has occurred not thanks to society, but in spite of it.

We summarize. Under the present organization of society the advance of science has caused the *relative* ignorance of the proletariat, just as the advance of industry and commerce has caused its *relative* impoverishment. Intellectual and material advances alike have thus tended to increase its slavery. What follows from this? It follows that we must repudiate and fight *this* bourgeois science, just as we must repudiate and fight bourgeois wealth. To repudiate and fight them means destroying the social order that makes them the patrimony of one class or several classes; and for this we must lay claim to them as the common property of everyone.

2

We have shown that so long as the various strata of society have more than one level of education, there will inevitably be classes, that is, economic and political privileges for the small number of the wealthy, and slavery and poverty for the vast number of others.

As members of the International Working-Men's Association, we want Equality, and because we want it, we also must want the same all-round education for everyone.

Someone will ask: If everybody is educated, who will want to work? Our answer is simple: *Everyone shall work and everyone shall be educated.* A frequent objection to this reply is that such a combination of industrial and intellectual labor can only hurt both, that workers will be poor scholars and scholars will be poor workers. Yes, [this is true] in present-day society, where both manual and mental labor are distorted by the wholly artificial separation to which they have both been condemned. But we are convinced that well-rounded living persons must develop muscular and mental activities equally and that these activities, far from harming each other, not only will not impede each other but instead will support, broaden, and reinforce each other; the scholar's science will become more fertile, more useful, and broader in scope when the scholar ceases being a stranger to manual labor, and the educated worker will work more intelligently and therefore more productively than the unlearned worker.[43]

From this it follows, in the interest of both labor and science, that there should no longer be either workers or scholars but only human beings.

As a result, those who are now preoccupied with the intolerant world of science because of their greater intellect, those who submit to the requirements for being bourgeois once they are established in the bourgeois world, those who place all their inventions at the exclusive disposal of the privileged class to which they themselves belong—once these persons really share solidarity with everybody, not in their imagination nor just in words but in fact, through their own labor, then they will just as inevitably place the discoveries and applications of science at everyone's disposal, to facilitate and above all to ennoble labor, which is the only legitimate and real basis of human society.

It is possible and even quite probable that the most esteemed sciences will fall considerably below their present level [of esteem] during the rather extended transitional period that will naturally follow the great social crisis. Doubtless too, luxury and all the refinements of life will have to disappear from society for a long time, and they will not be able to reappear until society finds the necessities of life for everyone, when luxuries no longer will be exclusive delights but will ennoble everyone's life. But will this temporary eclipse of higher science be so great a misfortune? Won't science gain what it loses in lofty exaltation by getting a broader base? Certainly, there will be fewer illustrious scholars, but at the same time there will be infinitely fewer ignorant people. No longer will there be a few who touch the skies, but millions who are now crushed and degraded will walk on the earth as human beings. There will be no demigods, but neither will there be any slaves. The demigods and slaves will be humanized to an identical intellectual level, the former coming down a little, the latter rising quite a bit. Then neither deification nor scorn will have any place. Everyone will join together, and once united, they will march with a new spirit to new conquests, in science as well as in life.

Rather than dread this very momentary eclipse of science, we invoke it, for we see that it will humanize scientists and workers together, reconciling science and life. And we are convinced that after this new basis is established, the progress of humanity in both science and life will very quickly surpass everything we have seen until now and everything we can now imagine.

But here another question appears: *Are all individuals equally capable of rising to the same level of education?* Let us imagine a society organized in the most egalitarian way, in which all children will have, from birth, the same start in life, economically, socially, and politically—absolutely the same care, upbringing, and education; among those millions of little individuals, will we not discover endless differences in energy, natural ability, and aptitude?

That is the great argument of our opponents, both the bourgeois socialists and the pure Bourgeois. They believe it is irresistible. Let us try to prove the opposite. First of all, by what right do they cite the principle of individual capabilities? Can these capabilities develop in existing society? Can they develop in a society which continues to be based economically on the right of inheritance? Clearly not, for as soon as [the right of] inheritance exists, children's careers will never be the result of their capabilities and their individual energy; before all that, it will be the result of the financial state, the wealth or poverty, of their families. Rich but stupid heirs will receive a superior education; the most intelligent children of the proletariat will continue to inherit ignorance, just like now. Isn't it only hypocrisy and filthy fraud to speak of individual rights based on individual capabilities in present-day society, or even to do so with a view to a reformed society still based on individual property and the right of inheritance?

Individual freedom is much talked about today, but what prevails is hardly the multifaceted individual but the individual defined by the privileges of social standing; what prevails, then, is social class. Just let an intelligent member of the bourgeoisie rise up against the economic privileges of this respectable class, and you will see how much the other members of this class, who now speak of individual freedom, will respect his! And they speak to us of individual abilities! Do we not see the ablest members of the working class and bourgeoisie forced every day to yield and even kowtow to the stupid heirs of the golden calf?[44] Only under total equality will actual abilities of individuals be fully developed and individual liberty be human rather than privileged. Only when there exists, for all persons on earth, *equality from the beginning* which still safeguards the higher rights of that solidarity which has always produced material goods and human intellect—in a word, social life—only then can it be said that every individual is the child of his labors more than today. From this we conclude that for a single individual's abilities to thrive and bear full fruit, every political and economic privilege, that is, every class, must be abolished. Individual property and the right of inheritance must disappear, and economic, political, and social Equality must triumph.

But once equality has triumphed and is well established, will various individuals' abilities and their levels of energy cease to differ? Some will exist, perhaps not so many as now, but certainly some will always exist. It is proverbial that the same tree never bears two identical leaves, and this will probably always be true. And it is even truer with regard to human beings, who are much more complex than leaves. But this diversity is hardly an evil. On the contrary, as the German philosopher Feuerbach rightly observed, it is a resource of the human race.[45] Thanks to this diversity, humanity is a collective whole in which the one individual complements all the others and needs them. As a result, this infinite diversity of human individuals is the fundamental cause and the very basis of their solidarity. It is an all-powerful argument for equality.

Even in modern society, if we disregard the differences artificially created by a thousand social causes, such as upbringing, education, and economic and political standing—which differ not only among social strata but nearly from family to family—we will see that from the standpoint of intellectual abilities and moral strength, excluding geniuses and idiots, the vast majority of individuals either are quite similar or at least balance each other out (since one who is weaker in a given respect nearly always makes up the difference by being equivalently stronger in another respect), with the result that it becomes impossible to say whether one individual from this mass rises much above or sinks much below another. The vast majority of human individuals are not identical, but they are equivalent and hence equal. Only the cases of geniuses and idiots therefore remain to support our opponents' reasoning.

We know that idiocy is a physiological and social illness. It ought to be treated as such, not in schools but in hospitals, and we have the right to expect that the introduction of a social hygiene that is more rational and especially concerned with the physical and moral health of individuals will lead to the disappearance of this affliction, which so degrades the human race. As for geniuses, we must first of all observe, happily or unhappily as you wish, that they have appeared in history only as very rare exceptions to all known rules; and exceptions cannot be categorized. In any case, we may hope that society, through the genuinely democratic and popular organization of its collective strength, will find a way to make these great geniuses less necessary, less overpowering, and more truly beneficial to everyone. For we must never forget the profound saying about Voltaire: "There is someone who has greater sense than the greatest geniuses, and that is everyman."[46] The task, then, is only to organize this *everyman* in accordance with the greatest freedom, based on the fullest economic, political, and social equality, so that we may have nothing left to fear from the dictatorial whims and despotic ambition of geniuses.

As for producing geniuses through upbringing, this need not be considered. Moreover, no celebrated geniuses, or almost none of them, have manifested their talent in infancy, in adolescence, or even in early adulthood. Their genius was demonstrated only when they had reached a mature age, and many were not recognized until after their death, while many who had been proclaimed superior in their youth ended their careers in complete obscurity. Thus, neither the relative superiorities and inferiorities of individuals, nor the extent of their abilities, nor their natural proclivities can be determined in their infancy or even in their adolescence. All these things become clear and are resolved only by the individuals' development; and since some individuals are precocious and others very slow although not inferior (they are often even superior), it is clear that no single professor or schoolmaster can predict the career and the sort of occupation that a child will choose after having become an adult.

From this it follows that society has no way to determine and no right to determine any child's future career, and that it owes everyone, without exception and without regard for real or imagined differences in inclination or ability, *an absolutely equal upbringing and education.*

3

Education ought to be equal for everyone in all respects. It must therefore be all-round education, that is, it should prepare every child of each sex for the life of thought as well as for the life of labor. This way, all children are equally able to become full human beings.

Positive philosophy,[47] which has dethroned religious myths and metaphysical dreams in people's minds, already allows us to glimpse what scientific education should be in the future. It will be based on the knowledge of nature and be crowned by sociology. Ideals will cease having dominion over life and violating it, as they always do in every metaphysical and religious system. They will become nothing but the final, finest expression of the real world. Ceasing to be dreams, they will themselves become realities.

Since, on the one hand, no mind however powerful can encompass every specialty of every science, and since, on the other hand, a general knowledge of all sciences is absolutely necessary for the mind to be fully developed, instruction will naturally be divided into two parts: the general part, which will furnish both the basic elements of every science without exception and a very real, not superficial, knowledge of the whole that they form together; and the special[ized] part, which will be divided of necessity into several groups or faculties, each of which will cover in full the particular aspects of a given number of sciences that are intrinsically very complementary.

The first or general part will be obligatory for all children. It will constitute, if we may put it this way, the humane instruction of their mind. It will replace completely metaphysics and theology and at the same time give the children a perspective broad enough for them to be fully aware in choosing, once they have reached adolescence, the particular ability which best suits their individual aptitude and tastes.

Undoubtedly some adolescents, influenced by either their own or someone else's secondary interest, will be mistaken in the choice of their scientific specialty, initially choosing a faculty and career not quite best suited to their aptitudes. But since we are sincere, unhypocritical partisans of *individual freedom;* since we detest with all our heart, in the name of this freedom, the principle of authority[48] and every possible manifestation of that divine, anti-human principle; since we detest and condemn, from the full depth of our love for freedom, the authority both of the father and of the schoolmaster; since we find them equally demoralizing and disastrous (for daily experience shows us that the head of the family and the schoolmaster, in spite of and even as a result of their acknowledged and proverbial wisdom, are worse [judges] of their children's abilities than are the children themselves, because they follow an indisputable, irrevocable, and entirely human law that leads every domineering person astray, leading every schoolmaster and family head to give much greater weight to their own tastes than to the natural aptitudes of the child in their arbitrary determination of their children's future); finally, since the mistakes of despotism are always more disastrous and less rectifiable than those of freedom: [for all these reasons] we support fully and completely, against every official, semi-official, paternal, and pedantic tutor in the world, the freedom of children to choose and decide their own career.

If they err, the error itself will be an effective lesson for the future, and the general education which they will have received will help them guide themselves back onto the path indicated to them by their own nature. Like mature persons, children become wise only through experiences of their own, and never through those of others.

Along with *scientific or theoretical* instruction, in all-round education there must inevitably be *industrial or practical instruction.* This is the only way to train the full human being, the worker who understands what he is doing.

Industrial instruction will parallel scientific instruction in being divided into two parts: general instruction, which should give children the general idea of all trades without exception and their first practical familiarity with them, as well as the idea of their aggregate, which is the essence of the material aspect of civilization and the totality of human labor; and the special[ized] part, divided into groups of trades which are more closely interrelated.

General instruction should prepare adolescents to choose freely the special group of trades, and from this group the specific trade which suits their taste. Once they have entered this second phase of industrial instruction, they will serve their first apprenticeship in serious work under the guidance of their teachers.

Alongside scientific and industrial instruction there will have to be practical instruction as well, or rather, a series of experiments in morality, not divine morality but human morality. Divine morality is based on two immoral principles: respect for authority and contempt for humanity. Human morality, on the contrary, is founded on contempt for authority and respect for the freedom of humanity. Divine morality considers labor to be a degradation and a punishment. Human morality sees in it the highest condition of human happiness and human dignity. Divine morality inevitably results in a policy that acknowledges only the rights of those who can live without working because of their economically privileged position. Human morality concedes rights only to those who live by working; it acknowledges that human beings become human only through labor.

The upbringing of children, the starting-point of which is authority, should lead afterwards to the fullest freedom. By freedom we mean, from the positive point of view, the full independence of the will of the individual with respect to the will of others.

Man is not and will never be free of natural and social laws. Laws may be divided into [these] two categories to facilitate the acquisition of knowledge, but in reality they belong to one and the same category, for they are all natural laws without exception, irrevocable laws which are the basis and the necessary condition of all existence. As a result, for any living being to rebel against them is to commit suicide.

But these natural laws must be distinguished from the authoritarian, arbitrary, political, religious, criminal, and civil laws that the privileged classes have established over the course of history, always for the sole purpose of exploiting the labor of the working masses and muzzling their freedom—laws which have, under the pretext of a fictitious morality, always been the source of the lowest immorality. Obedience to the laws that constitute, independently of all human volition, the very life of nature and of society is involuntary and inevitable. But this obedience [should be] as independent as possible of every dictatorial claim, of every collective and individual human will that would impose its [own artificial] law rather than its natural influence.

The natural influence which human beings exert on each other is only one of the conditions of social life against which revolt would be impossible and useless. This influence is the very material, intellectual, and moral basis of human solidarity. The human individual is a product of solidarity, i.e., of society, and can, while still obeying society's natural laws, react against this solidarity to a certain extent under the influence of outside feelings, especially when they come from a foreign society. But the individual could not leave that society without entering another sphere of solidarity and experiencing new influences there. Life outside all society and outside all human influences—absolute isolation—is intellectual, moral, and material death to a human being. Solidarity is not the product of individuality but its mother, and the human individual can be born and develop only in human society.

The sum of the dominant social influences, as expressed by the common or general awareness of a more or less outspread human group, is called *public opinion.* And who is unaware of the all-powerful influence of public opinion on every individual? Compared to it, the effect of the most draconian and restrictive laws is nothing. Public opinion is thus the pre-eminent educator of human beings. From this it follows that for individuals to be moralized, society itself must be moralized before all else; its public opinion, its conscience must be humanized.

4

To moralize human beings, we have said, we must moralize the social environment.

Socialism, which is founded on positive science, rejects absolutely the doctrine of *free will.* It recognizes that every so-called human vice and virtue is only the product of the combined action of nature, properly so called, and society. Through its ethnographic, physiological, and pathological processes, nature gives rise to so-called natural abilities and inclinations, and social organization develops them or halts or warps their development. All individuals, at every moment of their life, are, without exception, what nature and society have made them.

A science of statistics is possible only because of this natural and social *inevitability.* This science is not satisfied with ascertaining and enumerating social facts but looks for their links to and correlations with the organization of society. Criminal statistics show, for example, that in a given country, in a given town, over a period of ten, twenty, thirty, or more years, the same crime or misdemeanor occurs every year in the same proportion [to the total], if the fabric of society has not been altered by political and social crises. Even more remarkably, a given *modus operandi* recurs from year to year in the same proportion; for example, the number of poisonings, knifings, and shootings, as well as the number of suicides committed one way or another, are almost always the same. This led the famous Belgian statistician Quetelet to utter the following memorable words: "Society prepares the crimes while individuals only carry them out."[49]

This periodic recurrence of the same events in society would not take place if the acts and the intellectual and moral inclinations of individuals depended on free will. Either the term "free will" has no meaning or it means that human individuals make up their minds by themselves, spontaneously, with no outside influence of nature or society. But if this latter were the case, and if all individuals conducted themselves as they wished, then the world would be wholly anarchic; all solidarity among individuals would be impossible. These millions of wholly mutually independent wills would clash with one another and tend inevitably toward mutual destruction, succeeding in this if there did not exist above them the despotic will of divine providence, "guiding their actions" and simultaneously annihilating them, imposing divine order on this human confusion.

Now we understand why every partisan of the principle of free will is compelled by logic to recognize the existence and the influence of divine providence. This is the basis of all theological and metaphysical doctrines. It is a magnificent system which has pleased the people's minds for quite a while and which, seen from afar, from the standpoint of abstract reflection and poetic imagination, actually appears extremely harmonious and noble.

The historical reality that corresponds to this system has unfortunately always been horrifying, and the system itself cannot withstand scientific criticism.

Indeed, we know that so long as divine right reigned on earth, the vast majority of individuals were brutally and pitilessly exploited, tormented, oppressed, and slaughtered. We know that when [a small number of privileged individuals] now try to keep the masses of the people enslaved, it is still always in the name of the theological or metaphysical divinity. It cannot be otherwise, because as soon as a divine will begins to rule the world—both nature and human society—then human freedom is totally abolished. Human volition is necessarily impotent in the presence of divine will. What follows from this? That it is necessary to deny the real freedom of human beings in order to defend their metaphysical, abstract, or imaginary freedom, called "free will." In the presence of divine omnipotence and divine omnipresence, man is a slave. Since human freedom is annihilated by divine providence, only privilege remains, that is, special rights accorded by divine grace to some individual, hierarchy, dynasty, or class.[50]

Divine providence likewise makes all science impossible, which is to say very simply that it is the negation of human reason, or that acknowledging it requires one to renounce his own good sense. As soon as the divine will begins to rule the world, the natural connections among events become nothing but a series of manifestations of the supreme will, the orders of which—as the holy Scripture says—can never be understood by human reason, lest they lose their divine character. Divine providence is not only the negation of all human logic, but of logic in general, because all logic implies natural causality, and this contradicts divine freedom. Divine providence is, from the human standpoint, the triumph of nonsense. Those who wish to believe in it must therefore renounce both freedom and science and, while they allow themselves to be exploited and negated by the privileges of God Almighty, they should repeat with Tertullian, *"I believe in the absurd,"*[51] adding to that declaration another, equally logical one: *"And I desire injustice."*

As for us, humbly confessing that we understand nothing through divine logic, and contenting ourselves with human logic which is based on experience and on the knowledge of how events in nature and society are interrelated, we voluntarily surrender all claims to the bliss of another world and instead lay claim to the full triumph of humanity on this earth.

The accumulated, coordinated, considered experience that we call science shows us that *free will* is an untenable fiction, contrary to the very nature of things; that what we call volition is only the manifestation of a certain neural activity, just as our physical power is only the result of muscular activity; and that both, as a result, are equally products of natural and social life, that is, of the physical and social conditions in which each individual is born and grows up—from which clearly follows the truthfulness of what we stated [above]: that for human beings to be moralized, their social environment must be moralized.

There is only one way for this to happen, and that is for justice to triumph: the fullest freedom* of every individual through the fullest equality of each. The inequality of conditions and laws and its unavoidable result, the absence of individual freedom, is the great collective injustice which gives birth to all individual injustices. Abolish it, and all the others will disappear.

In view of the reluctance of persons of privilege to let themselves be moralized, i.e., equalized, we greatly fear that this triumph of justice can take place only through social revolution. We shall not discuss this now; we shall limit ourselves to announcing the obvious truth that the morality of individuals will be impossible so long as the social environment is not moralized.

For individuals to be moralized and become fully human, three things are necessary: a hygienic birth; rational, all-round education, accompanied by an upbringing based on respect for labor, reason, equality, and freedom; and a social environment wherein each human individual will enjoy full freedom and really be, *de jure* and *de facto,* the equal of every other.

Does this environment exist? No. Therefore it must be established. If, in the existing social environment, we cannot even successfully establish schools which would give their students an education and upbringing as perfect as we might imagine, could we successfully create just, free, moral persons? No, because on leaving school they would enter a society governed by totally opposite principles, and, because society is always stronger than individuals, it would soon prevail over them, that is, demoralize them. What is more, the very foundation of such schools is impossible in the present social environment. For social life embraces everything, pervading the schools as well as the life of families and individuals who are a part of it.

Instructors, professors, and parents are all members of this society, all more or less stultified or demoralized by it. How would they give students what they themselves lack? One can preach morality successfully only by example; and since a socialist morality is entirely the opposite of current morality, the schoolmasters, who are inevitably more or less dominated by the latter morality, will act in front of their pupils in a manner wholly contrary to what they preach. As a result, a socialist upbringing is impossible not only in modern families but in the schools as well.

But all-round education is equally impossible under present conditions:

*We have already said that by freedom we mean, on the one hand, the fullest possible development of every individual's natural faculties and, on the other hand, that of his independence: not with respect to natural and social laws, but with respect to all laws that other human wills—collective and isolated [from the collectivity]—impose.

the members of the bourgeoisie will hear nothing of their children becoming workers, and workers are deprived of every resource for giving their children a scientific education.

I am quite amused by those good bourgeois socialists who always tell us, "Let us first educate the people, and then we shall emancipate them." We say, on the contrary: Let them first emancipate themselves, and then they will educate themselves. Who will educate the people? You [bourgeois socialists]? But you do not educate them, you poison them by trying to inculcate in them all those religious, historical, political, juridical, and economic prejudices which guarantee your own separate existence, destroy their intelligence, and weaken their legitimate indignation and will. You let them be crushed by their labor and their poverty, and you say to them, "Study, get educated!" We should like to see all of you, with your children, take to study after thirteen, fourteen, or sixteen hours of brutalizing labor, with your payment entirely in poverty and with uncertainty about what tomorrow will bring.

No, Gentlemen, despite our respect for the great question of all-round education, we declare that right now it is hardly the greatest question confronting the people. The first question concerns their economic emancipation, which necessarily entails their simultaneous political emancipation, and soon thereafter their intellectual and moral emancipation.

Therefore, we thoroughly endorse the resolution passed by the Brussels Congress:

"Recognizing that it is for the moment *impossible to organize a rational* [*system of*] *instruction,* the Congress calls upon the various sections [of the International] to establish public courses following a program of scientific, professional, and productive instruction, that is, all-round instruction, in order to remedy as much as possible the insufficient education that workers currently receive. *It is correctly understood that the reduction in the hours of labor is considered to be an indispensable preliminary condition.*"[52]

Yes, certainly, the workers do everything possible to obtain all the education they can in the material circumstances in which they currently find themselves. But without being led astray by the Sirens' song of the bourgeois socialists and the members of the bourgeoisie,[53] they will above all concentrate their efforts on the great question of their economic emancipation, which is the mother of all their other emancipations.

6

Report of the Committee on the Question of Inheritance[54]

Citizens,

This question, which will be discussed at the Basle Congress, is divided into two parts, the first being the *principle,* and the second being the *practical application of the principle.*

The question of the principle itself should be considered from two standpoints: *expedience* and *justice.*

From the standpoint of the emancipation of labor, is it expedient, is it necessary, to abolish the right of inheritance? In our opinion, to ask this question is to answer it. What can the emancipation of labor mean, if not its deliverance from the yoke of property and capital? And how can property and capital be prevented from dominating labor and exploiting it so long as they are divorced from labor, monopolized by the members of a class who need not work in order to live because of their exclusive enjoyment of the fruits of that monopoly, who will continue to exist and to keep labor down by levying on it land's rent and capital's interest, who are made strong by this state of affairs, and who thus secure for themselves all the profits of industrial and commercial enterprises as is the case now everywhere, leaving to the workers, who are themselves crushed by the mutual competition into which they are forced, only what is absolutely necessary to keep them from starving to death?

No political or juridical law, however severe, will be able to prevent this domination and exploitation, no law can prevail against the force of circumstances, no law can prevent a given situation from producing all of its natural results. From this it clearly follows that, so long as property and capital remain on one side and labor remains on the other, the former constituting the bourgeois class and the latter the proletariat, the workers will be the slaves and the members of the bourgeoisie will be the masters.

But what separates property and capital from labor? What distinguishes the classes economically and politically from one another, what destroys equality and perpetuates inequality, the privilege of the few and the slavery of the many? It is the *right of inheritance.*

Need we demonstrate how the right of inheritance gives rise to every economic, political, and social privilege? Plainly, it alone maintains class differences. Through the right of inheritance, both natural and passing differences among individuals, of fortune or prosperity, differences that should not outlive the individuals themselves, are eternalized, one may say petrified. Becoming traditional differences, they create privileges of birth, they establish classes, they become a permanent source of the exploitation of millions of workers by mere thousands of the wellborn.

So long as the right of inheritance is in effect, there can be no economic, social, and political equality in the world; and so long as inequality exists, there will be oppression and exploitation. In principle, then, from the standpoint of the all-round emancipation of labor and laborers, we must desire the *abolition of the right of inheritance.*

It is understood that we do not intend to abolish physiological heredity, that is, the natural transmission of physical and intellectual abilities, or to be more precise, that of muscular and neural abilities from parents to their children. This transmission is often unfortunate, for it causes the physical and moral maladies of past generations to be passed on to present generations. But the disastrous effects of this transmission may be fought only by applications of science to individual and collective social hygiene, and by a rational and egalitarian organization of society.

What we want to abolish, what we must abolish, is the *right of inheritance,* which was established by jurisprudence and which constitutes the very basis of the *juridical family* and the *State.*

It is also understood that we do not intend to abolish *sentimental inheritance.* By this we mean the passing on, to children or friends, of objects of slight value which belonged to their friends or deceased parents, and which, because of their long use, have personal meaning. Substantial inheritance is what guarantees to heirs, either in full or in part, the possibility of living without working, by levying upon collective labor either land's rent or capital's interest.

We intend that both capital and land—in a word all the raw materials of labor—should cease being transferable through the right of inheritance, becoming forever the collective property of all productive associations. Equality, and hence the emancipation of labor and of the workers, can be obtained only at this price.

Few are the workers who do not realize that the abolition of the right of inheritance will in the future be the ultimate condition of equality. But some fear that if it is abolished now, before a new social organization has guaranteed the lot of all children regardless of the conditions under which they are born, then their children will find themselves in financial difficulties after their death.

"What!" they say. "From the sweat of my brow and through great privation, I have amassed two or three or four hundred francs, and my children will be denied them!" Yes, these will be denied them, but in return they will be cared for by society, without prejudice to the natural rights of the mother and father, and they will receive an upbringing and an education which you could not guarantee them even with thirty or forty thousand francs. For it is clear that as soon as the right of inheritance is abolished, society will have to take responsibility for all costs of the physical, moral, and intellectual development of all children of both sexes born in its midst. It will become their supreme guardian.

We shall stop here, because at this point the question joins that of all-round education, on which another committee should report to you.[55] But there is another point we should clarify.

Many persons hold that if the right of inheritance is abolished, then the greatest stimulus that impels them to work will be destroyed. Those who so believe still consider labor a necessary evil or, to speak theologically, the result of Jehovah's curse, which he angrily hurled at the unhappy human race and in which, by a singular caprice, he included the whole of creation.

Rather than enter into this solemn theological discussion, we shall base ourselves on the simple study of human nature, answering those who disparage labor, by saying that for every person who possesses human capabilities, labor, far from being an evil or a painful necessity, is a need. To be convinced of this, you may conduct a simple experiment on yourself: force yourself to be absolutely inactive for only a few days, or to do sterile, unproductive, and stupid work, and see whether at the end you do not feel most unhappy and degraded! Man's very nature compels him to work, just as it compels him to eat, drink, think, and speak.

If labor is hated today, this is because it is excessive, brutalizing, and forced, because it is the death of leisure, because it deprives one of the possibility of enjoying life fully, and because nearly everyone is compelled to apply his productive energy to that type of labor which least fits his natural inclinations. Labor is hated, finally, because in this society, which is founded on theology and jurisprudence, the possibility of living without working is considered an honor and a privilege, and the need to work for a living is regarded as a sign of degradation, a punishment and a disgrace.

When the labor of body and mind, manual and intellectual together, is considered the greatest honor, the sign of virility and humanity, then society will be saved. But that day will never arrive so long as inequality reigns, so long as the right of inheritance has not been abolished.

[Examining the principle of the abolition of inheritance from the second standpoint, we ask:] Will this abolition be *just*? But if it is in everyone's interest, in the interest of humanity, how could it be unjust? We must distinguish historical, political, and juridical justice from rational or simply human justice. The first has ruled the world until now, making it a repository of bloody oppressions and injustices. The second will emancipate us. Therefore let us examine the right of inheritance from the standpoint of human justice.

A man, we are told, has acquired through his labor several tens or hundreds of thousands of francs, a million, and he will not have the right to leave them as an inheritance to his children! Is this not an attack on natural right, is this not unjust plunder?

First, it has been proven a thousand times that an isolated worker cannot produce very much more than what he consumes. We challenge any real worker, any worker who does not enjoy a single privilege, to amass tens or hundreds of thousands of francs, or millions! That would be quite impossible. Therefore, if some individuals in present-day society do acquire such great sums, it is not by their labor that they do so but by their privilege, that is, by a juridically legalized injustice. And since a person inevitably takes from the labor of others whatever he does not gain from his own, we have the right to say that all such profits are thefts of collective labor, committed by a few privileged individuals with the sanction of the State and under its protection.

Let us proceed.

The thief who is protected by law dies. With or without a testament, he leaves his land or his capital to his children or to his parents. This, we are told, is a necessary result of his individual freedom and his right; his desires must be respected. But a dead man is dead for good. Outside of the altogether moral and sentimental existence created either by the pious memories of his children, parents, or friends (if he deserved such memories) or by public recognition (if he rendered some real service to the public), he no longer exists at all. He therefore can have neither freedom nor right nor personal will. Ghosts should not rule and oppress this world, which belongs only to the living.

So that he may continue to will and to act after his death, a juridical fiction or political lie is necessary, and as he is henceforth incapable of acting by himself, some power—the State—must take responsibility for acting in his name and for him. The State must execute the will of a man who can have no will because he no longer exists.

And what is the influence of the State, if it is not everyone's influence organized to everyone's disadvantage and to the advantage of the privileged classes. Before all else, it is the production and the collective strength of the workers. So do the masses of workers have to guarantee the principal source of their poverty, the transfer of inheritances, to the privileged classes? Must they forge with their own hands the chains that shackle them?

For the right of inheritance, which is exclusively political and juridical and hence contrary to human right, to collapse by itself, the proletariat need only declare that it no longer wishes to support the State, which sanctions its slavery. The abolition of the right of inheritance is enough to abolish the juridical family and the State.

Moreover, all social progress has proceeded from successive abolitions of rights of inheritance. First, the right of divine inheritance was abolished, the traditional privileges or punishments which were long considered the result of either divine benediction or divine malediction. Then the right of political inheritance was abolished, resulting in the recognition of the sovereignty of the people and the equality of citizens before the law. At present, in order to emancipate the worker, the human being, and to establish the reign of justice on the ruins of all the political and theological injustices of the present and the past, we must abolish economic inheritance.

The last question to be resolved addresses the practical measures we must take to abolish the right of inheritance. The right of inheritance may be abolished in two ways: either by *successive reforms* or by *social revolution.*

It can be abolished by *reforms* in those fortunate countries, which are very few in number if they exist at all, where the class of property owners and capitalists, the members of the bourgeoisie, inspired by a spirit and a wisdom that they now lack, finally realize the imminence of social revolution and earnestly desire to come to terms with the world of the workers. In this case, but only in this case, the path of peaceful reforms will be possible. By a series of successive, prudently planned modifications, mutually agreed between the workers and the members of the bourgeoisie, the law of inheritance could be abolished completely in twenty or thirty years, replacing the present customs of property, labor, and education with collective labor, collective property and all-round upbringing and education. It is impossible for us to determine further the character of these reforms, for they must necessarily be adapted to the particular situation in each country. But in all countries the goal remains the same: the establishment of collective property, collective labor, and individual freedom, through universal equality.

The way of revolution will naturally be shorter and simpler. Revolutions are never made either by individuals or by associations. They are brought on by the force of circumstances. The International by no means has as its goal the making of the revolution, but it ought to take advantage of [the spirit of R]evolution, organizing it as soon as it appears as the result of the increasingly clear injustice and ineptitude of the privileged classes. We must understand that on the first day of the revolution the right of the inheritance will simply be abolished, along with the State and juridical law, so that on the ruins of these injustices the new international world may then appear, the world of labor, science, freedom, and equality, organizing itself from the bottom up, by the free association of all productive associations, across all political and national frontiers.

The Committee proposes the following resolutions:

Whereas the right of inheritance is one of the principal causes of the economic, social, and political inequality which governs the world;

Whereas, so long as there is no equality, there can be neither freedom nor justice but only oppression and exploitation—slavery and the labor of the people;

Therefore, the Congress recognizes the need to abolish fully and completely the right of inheritance.

This abolition will be accomplished as events require, either by reforms or by revolution.

7

Speeches to the Basle Congress

On the Question of Landed Property

The absence of representatives of agriculture is no reason to dispute the right of the Congress to take a position on the question of property.[56] The Congress is only a minority, but there has in every age been a minority which represents the interests of all humanity. In 1789, the bourgeois minority represented the interests of France and the world; it signalled the emergence of the bourgeoisie. Babeuf's protest was made in the name of the proletariat; we are his continuators, and our small minority will soon be a majority.

Contrary to what has been said, the collectivity is the basis of the individual. It is society that makes man; an isolated human being would not even learn to speak or think. Do not mention men of genius and their discoveries, Arago, Galileo, etc. They would have invented nothing were it not for the labor of previous generations. He who has greater intellect than Voltaire—is everyman.[57] If the greatest genius lived on a desert isle from the time he was five years old, he would produce nothing; the individual is nothing without the collectivity. Individual property has been and is nothing but the exploitation of collective labor. We can do away with this exploitation only by establishing collective property. I therefore ask the Congress to consider the following conclusions:

I vote for collectivity, especially of land and in general of all social wealth, in the sense of social liquidation.

By social liquidation I mean expropriation *de jure* of all current property-owners by the *abolition of the political and juridical State,* which is the protector and sole guarantor of present property and of all so-called juridical law; and expropriation *de facto,* by the very force of events and circumstances, wherever and to whatever extent possible.

As for the subsequent organization: whereas all productive labor is inevitably collective, including the misnamed "individual labor," which is possible only thanks to the collective labor of past and present generations, I am resolved on the *formation of interassociated communes* [la solidarisation des communes] which the majority of the committee has proposed, all the more willingly because such solidarity implies the organization of society from the bottom up, while the minority's proposal speaks to us of the State.[58]

I am a resolute opponent of the State and of all bourgeois State politics. I call for the destruction of all national and territorial States, and the foundation upon their ruins of the International Working-Men's State.

On the Question of the Right of Inheritance

There is but a simple difference between the standpoint of those collectivists who believe that it is useless to vote to abolish the right of inheritance after having voted for collective property, and that of those collectivists who think, as do we, that it is useful and even necessary to do so.

They place themselves entirely in the future and, taking collective property as their point of departure, discover that there is no longer any good reason to be concerned with the right of inheritance.

We on the contrary take our departure from the present, where we are under the system of individual property triumphant, and we encounter an obstacle in our advance toward collective property: the right of inheritance. We therefore believe that it must be overthrown and abolished.

The report of the General Council [of the International] says that since the juridical reality is only the result of economic realities, the transformation of the latter suffices to destroy the former. It is indisputable that everything called a juridical or political right in history has only been the expression or the result of an established fact. But it is also indisputable that the right, being an effect of previously established facts or events, becomes in turn the cause of future events, itself a very real, very powerful fact that must be overthrown if we wish to arrive at an order of things different from what now exists.

Thus, the right of inheritance, once the natural result of the violent appropriation of natural and social riches, became the basis of the political State and the juridical family, which guarantee and sanction individual property. We must therefore vote to abolish the right of inheritance.

We have been much spoken to of practice. Well, it is in the name of practice that I urge you to vote to abolish the right of inheritance.

It has been said today that the transformation of individual property into collective property will meet with grave obstacles among the peasants, the small landowners. And indeed, if we tried to expropriate these millions of small farmers by decree after proclaiming the social liquidation, we would inevitably cast them into reaction, and we would have to use force against them to submit them to the revolution, that is, we would have to use reaction against them in order to bring them under the revolution.

Then it would be well to leave them the possessors *de facto* of these parcels which they now own. But if you do not abolish the right of inheritance, what will happen then? They will leave these parcels to their children, with the State sanctioning their property rights.

You will preserve and perpetuate the individual property which you have voted to abolish and transform into collective property.

On the contrary, if you carry out social liquidation at the same time that you proclaim the political and juridical liquidation of the State, if you abolish the right of inheritance, what will be left to the peasants? Nothing but possession *de facto,* and this possession, deprived of all legal sanction, will be no longer shielded under the State's powerful protection and will be transformed easily under the pressure of revolutionary events and forces.

Part Four

The Tactics of Revolutionary Socialism

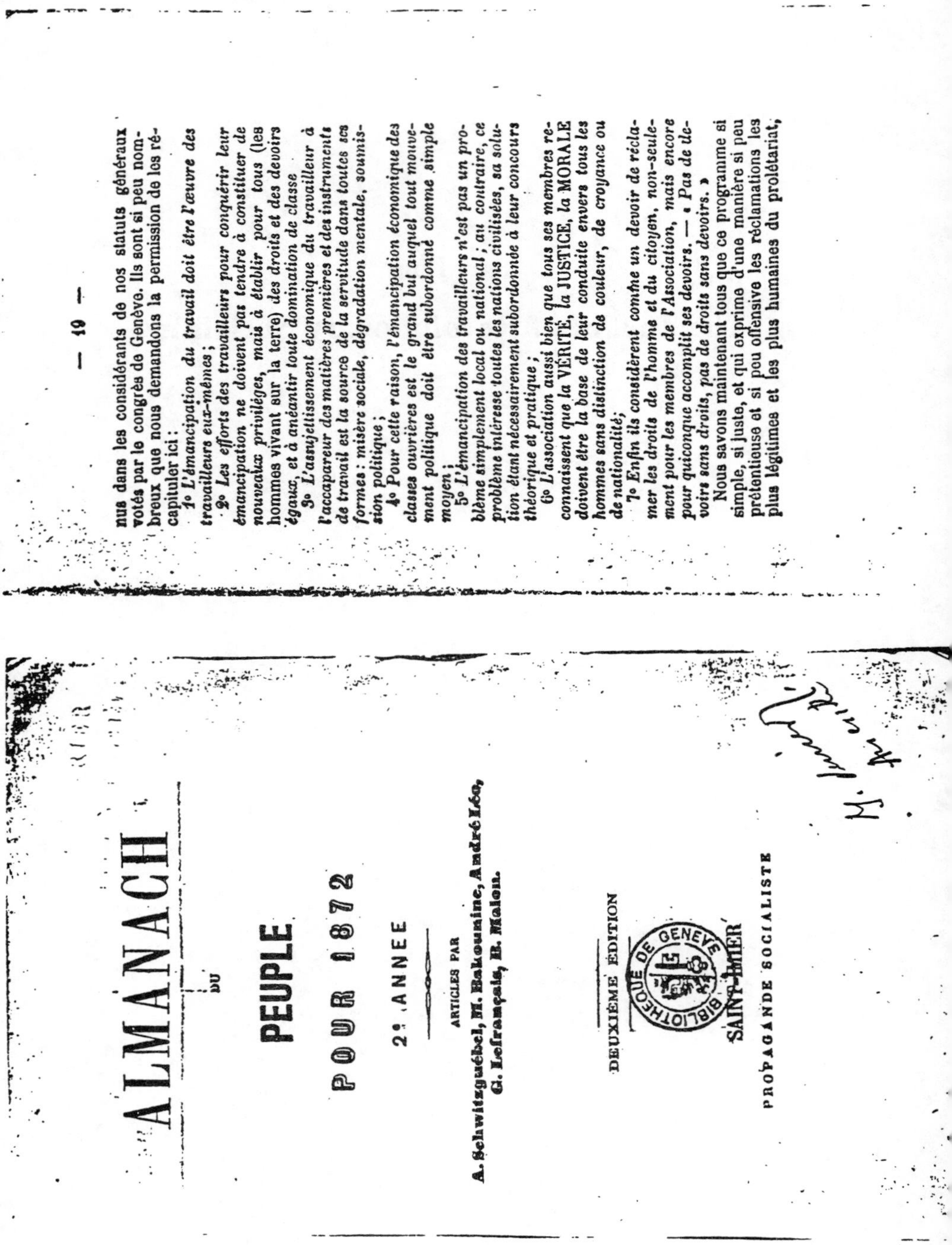

ALMANACH

DU

PEUPLE

POUR 1872

2e ANNEE

ARTICLES PAR

A. Schwitzguébel, M. Bakounine, André Léo, G. Lefrançais, B. Malon.

DEUXIÈME ÉDITION

SAINT-IMIER

PROPAGANDE SOCIALISTE

nus dans les considérants de nos statuts généraux votés par le congrès de Genève. Ils sont si peu nombreux que nous demandons la permission de les récapituler ici :

1° *L'émancipation du travail doit être l'œuvre des travailleurs eux-mêmes ;*

2° *Les efforts des travailleurs pour conquérir leur émancipation ne doivent pas tendre à constituer de nouveaux privilèges, mais à établir pour tous* (les hommes vivant sur la terre) *des droits et des devoirs égaux, et à anéantir toute domination de classe*

3° *L'assujettissement économique du travailleur à l'accapareur des matières premières et des instruments de travail est la source de la servitude dans toutes ses formes : misère sociale, dégradation mentale, soumission politique ;*

4° *Pour cette raison, l'émancipation économique des classes ouvrières est le grand but auquel tout mouvement politique doit être subordonné comme simple moyen ;*

5° *L'émancipation des travailleurs n'est pas un problème simplement local ou national ; au contraire, ce problème intéresse toutes les nations civilisées, sa solution étant nécessairement subordonnée à leur concours théorique et pratique ;*

6° *L'association aussi bien que tous ses membres reconnaissent que la* VÉRITÉ, *la* JUSTICE, *la* MORALE *doivent être la base de leur conduite envers tous les hommes sans distinction de couleur, de croyance ou de nationalité;*

7° *Enfin ils considèrent comme un devoir de réclamer les droits de l'homme et du citoyen, non-seulement pour les membres de l'Association, mais encore pour quiconque accomplit ses devoirs. — « Pas de devoirs sans droits, pas de droits sans devoirs. »*

Nous savons maintenant tous que ce programme si simple, si juste, et qui exprime d'une manière si peu prétentieuse et si peu offensive les réclamations les plus légitimes et les plus humaines du prolétariat,

Title page of the workers' vademecum wherein "The Organization of the International" was published for the first time, along with page 19 of the booklet, where Bakunin summarizes the General Rules of the International.

8

The Organization of the International

The huge task undertaken by the International Working-Men's Association—to emancipate the workers and to free the people's labor definitively and completely from the yoke of all its exploiters, from the bosses and from those who hold raw materials and the instruments of production (in a word, from all the representatives of capital)—is not just an economic or simply material project. It is at the same time and to the same degree a social, philosophical, and moral project. It is also, if you wish, highly political, but only in the sense of destroying all politics by abolishing States.

We think we need not prove that it is impossible economically to emancipate the workers within the existing political, juridicial, religious, and social structure of the most advanced countries; or that it will therefore be necessary, in order to attain this goal and to realize it fully, to destroy all existing institutions—State, Church, Court of Law, Bank, University, Administration, Army, and Police—which are in fact only so many fortresses erected by privilege against the proletariat. Nor is it enough to overturn those institutions in a single country. They must be overthrown in all countries because, since the foundation of modern States in the seventeenth and eighteenth centuries, there has existed, across the frontiers of all countries, a solidarity and a very strong international alliance among all these institutions.

The task that the International Working-Men's Association has undertaken is thus nothing less than the total liquidation of the presently existing political, religious, juridical, and social world and its replacement by a new economic, philosophic, and social world. But an undertaking as gigantic as this could never succeed without the use of two equally gigantic and forceful levers, which are mutually complementary: first, the ever growing intensity of the masses' suffering, of their needs and their economic claims; second, the new social philosophy, a highly realistic philosophy of the people, inspired by nothing but real knowledge, that is, simultaneously experimental and theoretical knowledge based only on those principles which express the masses' timeless claims, the human principles of equality, liberty and worldwide solidarity.

Driven by those needs, the people must win in the name of these principles. These principles are not foreign to the people nor are they even new to them, insofar as the people have always carried them *instinctively* in their hearts. The people have always longed for their emancipation from every yoke that has enslaved them; and since the worker, who fosters society and creates all the riches of civilization, is the last slave and the most slavish of all slaves, since he can emancipate himself only by emancipating the whole world with him, he has always longed for universal emancipation and for worldwide freedom. He has always dreamt passionately of equality, which is the highest form of freedom. Again and again crushed by the [poverty of the] individual lives of each of his hapless children, he has always sought his well-being in solidarity; for up to now good fortune has been uncommon and unshared, meaning an egoistic life lived at the expense of others by exploiting and subjugating them. Only the unfortunate, hence the masses of the people, have felt fraternity and made it come true.

Because of this, social science, acting as a moral doctrine, only develops and formulates the instincts of the people. Between these instincts and this knowledge [which that science represents], however, there is an abyss to fill. For if just instincts were enough to deliver the peoples, they would long ago have been delivered. These instincts have not prevented the masses from accepting every religious, political, economic, and social absurdity which has ever victimized them over the melancholic and tragic course of their history.

It is true that these cruel experiences, which the masses have been condemned to undergo, have not been all lost on them. These experiences have created among them a sort of historic awareness, a traditional and practical science which serves them as theoretical knowledge. For example, we can be certain today that no western people will let themselves be led astray by a new religious or messianic charlatan or by any political swindler. We can also say that the masses of the people in Europe, even the less advanced ones, keenly feel the need for an economic and social revolution; for had the masses not expressed this instinct so clearly, deeply, and resolutely, no socialists in the world, not even men of the greatest genius, would have been able to stir them.

The people are ready, they suffer greatly, and what is more they are beginning to understand that they do not have to suffer. Tired of turning their hopes drunkenly toward heaven, they are no longer disposed to display much patience on earth. Independent of all propaganda the masses have, in a word, become consciously socialist. The deep worldwide sympathy elicited by the Paris Commune among the proletariat of every country, is a proof of this.

The masses are mighty, they are the basic element of all might. What, then, do they require to overturn this order of things which they detest? They require two things: organization and science, precisely those things on which every government has always based its own might.

Thus: organization first, which, let us add, can never be worked out separately from science. Thanks to military organization a battalion, a thousand armed men, can and effectively do keep in awe a million who are armed but disorganized. Thanks to bureaucratic organization the State, with several hundred thousand employees, keeps vast countries in chains. So to make the people's might strong enough to be able to eradicate the State's military and civil might, it is necessary to organize the proletariat.

That is precisely what the International Working-Men's Association does, and by the time it has come to include a half, a third, a quarter, or only a tenth of the European proletariat, organizing them, the State—nay, every State—will have ceased to exist. Since the goal of the organization of the International is not the creation of new States or new despotisms but rather the radical destruction of all private dominions, its character and its organization must be essentially different from those of the States. So much as the latter are authoritarian, artificial, and violent, foreign and hostile of the natural development of the instincts and interests of the people, that much must the organization of the International be free and natural, conforming in every way to those interests and instincts. But what is the natural organization of the masses? It is organization based on the various ways that their various types of work define their actual day-to-day life; it is organization by trade association. From the moment that every occupation—including the various agricultural trades—is represented within the International, its organization, the organization of the masses of the people, will be complete.

For in fact it is only necessary that one worker in ten join the [International Working-Men's] Association *earnestly* and *with full understanding of the cause* for the nine-tenths remaining outside its organization nevertheless to be influenced invisibly by it, and insofar as the well-being of the proletariat requires them at critical moments to follow the International's lead, they will do so without doubting themselves.

It may be objected that this manner of organizing the International's influence on the popular masses suggests the establishment of a system of authority and a new government on the ruins of old authorities and existing governments. Such a belief would be a serious blunder. The organized effect of the International on the masses, which will be its only "government," will always differ from that of all States and governments because of this essential characteristic: it is nothing but the entirely natural organization—neither official nor clothed in any authority or political force whatsoever—of the effect of a rather numerous group of individuals who are inspired by the same thought and headed toward the same goal, first of all on the opinion of the masses and only then, by the intermediary of this opinion (restated by the International's propaganda), on their will and their deeds. But the governments—armed with an authority, a power, a material strength which some say come from God, others say come from their superior intelligence, and still others say come from the people's will itself (ascertained and expressed by the conjuring trick called universal suffrage)—impose themselves violently on the masses, who are forced to obey them and to execute their decrees, usually without even the appearance of their own wishes, needs, or desires having been consulted. The difference between the State's influence and the International's influence is the same as that between the official effect of the State and the natural effect of a club. The International's influence has never been and will never be anything but one of opinion, and the International will never be anything but the organization of the natural effect of individuals on the masses. But the State and all its institutions—Church, University, Court of Law, Bureaucracy, Treasury, Police, and Army—not only require their subjects passively to recognize and obey their doubtless very elastic laws, but also corrupt as much as they can the [natural] effect of the State's subjects [on each other and their situation] as well as their will to act [to change that situation].

The State is authority, domination, and force, organized by the property-owning and so-called enlightened classes against the masses; the International is the release of the masses therefrom. The State, never seeking nor ever being able to seek anything but the subjugation of the masses, calls upon them to submit; the International, seeking only their complete freedom, calls upon them to revolt. But for this revolt in turn to be powerful and able to overturn the State's domination, and that of the privileged classes whom it solely represents, the International must organize itself. To reach this goal it uses only two methods which, although they are hardly legal (since legality is usually nothing but the juridical consecration of privilege, that is, of injustice), are legitimate from the standpoint of human rights. As we have said, these two methods are, first the propagation of its ideas, and second, the organization of its members' natural effect on the masses.

To anyone who supposes an effect thus organized is still an attack on the freedom of the masses, an attempt to create a new authoritarian force, we reply that he is either a sophist or a drunkard. So much the worse for those who are so unaware of the natural and social law of human solidarity, that they imagine the mutual and absolute independence of individuals and masses to be possible or even desirable. To desire such a thing is to desire the very destruction of society, for all social life is only this never ceasing mutual dependence of individuals and masses. At every moment, every individual, even the most intelligent or the strongest, and above all the strong *and* intelligent, [contributes to] the production of the will of the masses as well as to their effect, and is simultaneously the product of them. The very freedom of every individual results from this great number of material, intellectual, and moral influences which every individual around him and which society—in whose midst he is born, grows up, and dies—continually exercise on him. To wish to escape this influence in the name of a transcendent, divine, absolutely egoistic and self-sufficient freedom is to condemn oneself to non-existence; to wish to cease exercising it over others is to cease [producing] every social effect, it is to cease expressing thoughts and feelings, and so again it leads to non-existence. The independence so exalted by idealists and metaphysicians, and individual freedom conceived in that sense, is hence nothingness.

In nature as in human society, which is still nothing but this same nature, everything alive lives only on the condition that it intervene in the most positive manner, and as influentially as its own nature allows, in the life of others. To abolish this mutual influence would be to die. And when we reclaim the freedom of the masses, we hardly wish to abolish the effect of any individual's or any group of individuals' natural influence upon the masses. What we wish is to abolish artificial, privileged, legal, and official influences. If the Church and the State could be private institutions, we would oppose them but we would not contest their right to exist. They are private institutions in the sense that they exist only for the particular interests of the privileged classes, but we contest them because they nevertheless impose themselves authoritatively, officially, and violently upon the masses by using the collective strength of the organized masses. If the International were able to organize itself into a State, we—its convinced and passionate partisans—would become its most bitter enemies.

But the fact is precisely that it cannot organize itself into a State; it cannot do so, first of all, because it abolishes all borders, as its name sufficiently suggests; and no State exists without borders, history having shown that the worldwide State—a dream of peoples who conquer and of the world's greatest despots—is impossible to realize. So whoever speaks of a State thus necessarily is speaking of more than one State—oppressive and exploitative internally, mutually hostile if not seeking conquest externally—and so is negating humanity. The worldwide State, or rather the People's State of which the German communists speak, can therefore mean only one thing: *the abolition of the State.*

The International Working-Men's Association would make absolutely no sense unless it led invincibly to the abolition of the State. Only in order to destroy every State does it organize the masses of the people. And how does it organize them? Not from the top down like the States do, imposing an artificial unity and order upon the natural life of the masses, upon the social diversity produced among them by the diversity of their labor; but from the bottom up, taking, on the contrary, the social existence of the masses and their real aspirations as the point of departure, inducing the masses to group, harmonize, and equilibrate themselves in conformity with this natural diversity of occupations and stations in life, and helping them to do so. This is the very goal of the organization of the trade sections.

We have said that in order to organize the masses and to instill in them the beneficial effect of the International Working-Men's Association it would be enough for one worker in ten in a given trade to join the [proper trade] section [of the International]. This is quite possible. In moments of great political or economic crises, when the instinct of the masses, red-hot, is open to every favorable suggestion, when these troops of slavish, bent, downtrodden but never resigned men finally revolt against their yoke but feel disoriented and powerless because they are totally disorganized, then ten, twenty, or thirty well-informed and well-organized men among them, who know where they are going and what they want, will easily rally a hundred, two hundred, three hundred or even more. We saw this recently in the Paris Commune. There the organization [of the masses] was in earnest barely started during the siege, and it was neither very complete nor very strong; nevertheless, it was enough to create a formidably strong resistance.

What will happen when the International [Working-Men's] Association is better organized, when it comprises a much larger number of sections—above all, more agricultural sections—and, in each section, counts double and treble the number of members presently there? Above all, what will happen when each of its members understands still better than at present the ultimate goal of the International, its true principles, and the means to realize its victory? The influence of the International will become irresistible.

But for the International really to acquire this influence, for a tenth of the proletariat, organized by this Association, to be able to rally the other nine tenths, each member of each section must be penetrated much more thoroughly by the principles of the International than is now the case. Only on this condition will he be able effectively to discharge the mission of propagandist and apostle in time of peace and calm, and that of a revolutionary principal in time of struggle.

When we speak of the International's bases, we mean none other than those in the Preamble to our General Rules, voted by the Geneva Congress (1866). They are so few that we ask permission to review them here:

1. The emancipation of labor should be the work of the laborers themselves;

2. The efforts of the workers to emancipate themselves should lend themselves to the establishment not of new privileges but of equal rights and equal obligations for everyone, and to the abolition of all class domination;

3. The economic subjection of the worker to the monopolizers of primary materials and of the instruments of labor is the origin of all forms of slavery: social poverty, mental degradation, and political submission;

4. For this reason, the economic emancipation of the working classes is the great goal to which every political movement should be subordinated as a simple means;

5. The emancipation of the workers is not a simply local or national problem; on the contrary, this problem is of interest to all civilized nations, depending for its solution upon their theoretical and practical circumstances;

6. The Association and all its members recognize that Truth, Justice, and Morality must be the basis of their conduct toward all men, without regard to color, creed or nationality;

7. Finally the Association considers itself obliged to demand human and civil rights not only for its members but also for whoever fulfills his obligations: "No obligations without rights, no rights without obligations."[59]

All of us now know that this program, so simple and so just, which expresses so unpretentiously and inoffensively the most legitimate, human demands of the proletariat, contains, precisely because it is exclusively a humane program, all the seeds of a vast social revolution: the overthrow of everything now existing and the creation of a new world.

That is what now must be explained to all members of the International and made entirely clear to them. This program includes a new science, a new social philosophy that should replace all the old religions with an altogether new and international policy which, we hasten to say, can, as such, have no goal other than the destruction of all States. For each member of the International to be able to fulfill with full awareness his double duty among the masses as propagandist and natural principal [in the Revolution], he must himself be penetrated as thoroughly as possible by [the knowledge represented in] this science, this philosophy, and this policy. It is not enough to know and to say that the workers should be economically emancipated, that everyone should benefit fully from the objects he produces, that classes as well as political subjection should be abolished, that human rights should be fully realized, that everyone should be perfectly equal in his duties and his rights—that human fraternity, in a word, should be fulfilled. All of that is doubtless very good and very just, but if the workers of the International stop there and do not examine thoroughly the conditions necessary for these great truths to be realized, and their consequences and spirit as well—if they are satisfied to repeat those truths for ever and ever in this general form—then they run a high risk of turning those truths very soon into hollow and sterile words, ties which are held common but not understood.

But, someone will say, even though every worker may become a member of the International, they cannot all have learning. And is it not enough for the International to contain a group of men who possess the knowledge, the philosophy, and the policy of socialism—insofar as is currently possible—in order for the majority, the people of the International, faithfully obeying [the former's] *fraternal command* (in the style of that Jacobin dictator *par excellence,* Mr. Gambetta),[60] to be sure of following the path leading to the full emancipation of the proletariat?

That is an argument which the nowadays triumphant authoritarian party within the International has often expressed, not openly—they are neither sincere nor courageous enough—but clandestinely, developed with all kinds of rather clever qualifications and demagogic compliments addressed to the supreme wisdom and omnipotence of the sovereign people. We have always fought this view passionately, for we are convinced that the moment the International [Working-Men's] Association is divided into two groups—one comprising the vast majority and composed of members whose only knowledge will be a blind faith in the theoretical and practical wisdom of their commanders, and the other composed only of a few score individual directors—from that moment this institution which should emancipate humanity would turn into a type of *oligarchic State,* the worst of all States. What is more, this learned, clairvoyant, and cunning minority, carefully hiding its despotism behind the appearance of obsequious respect for the will of the sovereign people and for its resolutions, would yield to the necessities and requirements of its privileged position, thus assuming along with all its responsibilities, all the rights of government, a government all the more absolute because it would always urge those resolutions itself upon the so-called will of the people, thereby very soon becoming increasingly despotic, malevolent, and reactionary.

The International [Working-Men's] Association will become an instrument of humanity's emancipation only when it is first itself freed, and that will happen only when it ceases to be divided into two groups, the majority blind tools and the minority skilled manipulators: when each of its members has considered, reflected on, and been penetrated by the knowledge, the philosophy, and the policy of socialism.

9

Geneva's Double Strike[61]

The Bourgeois are inciting us. They are striving in every way to provoke us beyond endurance, thinking not too unreasonably that their interests would be very well served if we were compelled today to engage them in battle.

They calumniate and insult us in their newspapers. Counting on the sympathies of their public, which will forgive them everything so long as the Bourgeois and the bosses are whitewashed and the workers blackened, they invent, misrepresent, and water down the facts. Confident of impunity and sympathy, the devout prevaricator *Journal de Genève* especially outdoes itself in lies.

They are not satisfied to incite and provoke us with what they write; impatient to make us lose our patience, they resort to the deed. Their unhappy children, these golden youths who in their depraved and shameful idleness abhor work and workers, these university students who know everything about theology and nothing about science—these liberals from the rich bourgeoisie descend upon the streets and gather in crowds in the cafes, like just last year, armed with poorly hidden revolvers in their pockets. They would say that they fear an attack by the workers which they believe themselves compelled to repulse.

Do they seriously believe this? No, not at all, but they make as if to believe it in order to have a pretext for arming themselves and a plausible motive for attack. Yes, for attacking us; for last Tuesday they dared lay hands on some of our comrades who had laid on them not even a finger, but who had responded to all their insults with truths which were no doubt rather disagreeable to ears as delicate as theirs. *They took the liberty of stopping our comrades* and abusing them for several hours, until a committee sent by the International went to the Town Hall to demand them back.[62]

What are the members of the bourgeoisie contemplating? Do they really want to compel us to descend upon the street as well, arms in hand? Yes, they want it. And why do they want it? The reason is very simple: they want to destroy the International.

It is enough to read the bourgeois newspapers, that is, nearly every newspaper in every country, to be persuaded that nothing is now more an object of fear and horror for the European bourgeoisie than the International Working-Men's Association. And as we must, before all else, be fair even to our bitterest foes, we should recognize that the bourgeoisie is a thousand times right to loathe and fear this formidable association.

We know that all bourgeois prosperity, as the exclusive prosperity of an exclusive class, is based on the poverty of the people and their forced labor, labor forced not by law but by hunger. It is true that this slavery of labor is called the freedom of labor in the liberal papers such as the *Journal de Genève*. But this strange freedom is like that of a disarmed and fully naked man who is delivered unto the mercy of another who is armed from head to toe. It is the freedom to be crushed and beaten. Such is bourgeois freedom. We understand that the members of the bourgeoisie love it dearly and that the workers cannot stand it at all; because for the former this freedom means wealth, whereas for the latter it means poverty.

The workers are tired of being slaves. They do not love freedom any less than the members of the bourgeoisie do, on the contrary they love it more, for they understand very well and know from painful experience that there can be neither dignity nor prosperity without freedom. But they do not conceive of freedom other than together with equality; for freedom with inequality is privilege, that is, the pleasure of some based on the suffering of all. The workers want political and economic equality together, for political equality without economic equality is a fable, a trick, and a lie, and they want no more lies. The workers therefore inevitably lean toward a radical transformation of society, which must result in the abolition of classes from the political as well as the economic standpoint, toward an organization of society where everyone will be born, grow up, be educated, work, and enjoy the benefits of life under universally equal conditions. That is the promise of justice and it is also the final goal of the International Working-Men's Association.

But how to reach this paradise, this realization on earth of justice and humanity, from the abyss of ignorance, poverty, and slavery into which the rural and urban proletarians are now plunged? For this, the workers have but a single means: association. Through association they educate and enlighten one another, and by their own efforts they end this deadly ignorance which is one of the main causes of their slavery. Through association they learn to aid, to know, and to support one another, and in the end their influence will be greater than all the bourgeois interests and all political powers put together.

Association has thus become the password of the workers of all trades and all countries, particularly in the last twenty years, and [in that time] all Europe has been covered, as if by magic, with a multitude of workers' societies of all kinds. This is incontestably the most important and at the same time the most comforting event of our times. It is the infallible sign of the approaching full emancipation of labor and of the workers in Europe.

But the experience of these very twenty years has shown that isolated associations are almost as powerless as isolated workers, and that even the federation of all workers' associations of a single country would not be strong enough to combat the international coalition of all the capital exploiters of labor in Europe. Economic science, on the other hand, has demonstrated that the question of the emancipation of labor is by no means a national question; that no country, however rich, powerful, and large, can attempt any radical transformation of the relations of capital and labor without ruining itself and condemning all its inhabitants to poverty—unless this transformation also occurs, simultaneously, in a large number of the most industrialized countries of Europe; and it has shown that the question of delivering the workers from the yoke of capital and from that of its representatives, the members of the bourgeoisie, is as a result mostly an international question. Wherefrom it follows that this question can be solved only on the grounds of internationality.

The intelligent German, English, Belgian, French, and Swiss workers who founded our fine institution understood this. They also understood that the workers of Europe, exploited by the members of the bourgeoisie and oppressed by the States, must count only on themselves to perform this magnificent act of emancipating labor internationally. Thus was the great International Working-Men's Association created.

Yes, great and truly formidable! It has been in existence barely four and a half years and already its adherents number several hundred thousand, scattered throughout nearly every country in Europe and in America as well, and intimately united throughout them all. In so short a time such fruits can be produced only by healthy thoughts; such an undertaking can only be legitimate.

Is this thought hidden, is it a conspiracy? Not a chance in the world. If the International conspires, it does so in broad daylight and discusses it with anyone who wishes to listen.[63] And what does it say? What does it ask? Justice, nothing but the strictest justice, the right to be human, and the obligation of everyone to work. If this sentiment seems subversive and scandalous to modern bourgeois society, then so much the worse for this society.

Is this a revolutionary undertaking? Yes and no. It is revolutionary in the sense that it intends to take a society founded on an oppressive minority's exploitation of the vast majority, on idleness, on iniquity and privilege, and on an authority which protects all these pretty things, and to replace it with a society founded on equal justice for all and freedom for everyone. In a word, it seeks an economic, political, and social organization in which every human being, regardless of natural and individual particularities, would be able to develop and get education, to think and work, to act and enjoy life as a human being. Yes, this is what it seeks, and once more, if what it seeks is incompatible with the present organization of society, then so much the worse for this society.

Is the International [Working-Men's] Association revolutionary in the sense of barricades and a violent overthrow of the political order now existing in Europe? No. It is concerned very little with such politics, to the point of ignoring them. So bourgeois revolutionaries are also very angry at it for its indifference to their desires and all their schemes. Even if the International had not long ago realized that all bourgeois politics, however red and revolutionary in appearance, endeavors not to emancipate the workers but to consolidate their slavery, its eyes would be opened wide enough by the pitiful game that the republicans and even the bourgeois socialists are currently playing in Spain.

The International Working-Men's Association therefore casts completely aside all the political intrigues of the day and now recognizes only one policy: its [own] propaganda, growth, and organization. By the time the great majority of workers in America and Europe have joined it and become truly organized in its midst, the revolution will no longer be necessary; justice will have been done without violence. And if at that time some heads are broken, it will be because the members of the bourgeoisie so desired.

In just a few years of peaceful growth the International will hold such sway that trying to fight against it will be absurd. The bourgeoisie understands this only too well, and that is why its members are trying to provoke us to fight now. They hope that they can crush us today, but they know that tomorrow will be too late. They therefore want to force us to fight them today.

Will we fall into this scurrilous trap, workers? No. We would too much delight the members of the bourgeoisie and for too long a time ruin our cause. We have justice and right on our side but we are not yet strong enough to fight. Therefore let us keep our indignation to ourselves, remaining firm and resolute yet calm, regardless of the provocations of insolent bourgeois whippersnappers. Let us keep on suffering. Are we not used to suffering? Let us suffer, but let us forget nothing.

And while we wait, let us continue, redouble, and expand ever more widely our propaganda work. The workers of all lands—the peasants in the countryside as well as the urban factory workers—must come to understand what the International seeks, to realize that only its triumph can assure their true emancipation and that the International is the homeland of all oppressed workers, their only refuge against exploitation by the Bourgeois, and the only force capable of overthrowing the arrogant power of the members of the bourgeoisie.

Let us organize ourselves and enlarge our Association, but at the same time let us not forget to consolidate it so that our solidarity, which is our whole power, may become daily more real. Let us build our solidarity in study, in labor, in public action, and in life. Let us become partners in common ventures to make our life together more bearable and less difficult. Let us form as many cooperatives for consumption, mutual credit, and production as we can, everywhere, for though they may be unable to emancipate us in earnest under present economic conditions, they prepare the precious seeds for the organization of the future, and through them the workers become accustomed to handling their own affairs.

This future is near. Let the unity of slavery and poverty, which today engulfs the workers of the entire world, be transformed for us all into a unity of thought and will, of goal and action—and the hour of deliverance and justice for all, the hour of reclamation and full reparation, will then strike.

Organization and General Strike

Workers, keep your greatest composure. If your sufferings are great, be heroic and bear them a bit longer. Read attentively what the newspaper *L'Internationale*[64] tells the workers of the Charleroi basin, which we too should learn.

Listen, then, to the wise counsel of our Belgian brothers:

"May our Swiss brothers be patient a little longer! Like us they must await the signal of the social collapse of a large country, either England, France, or Germany. While we wait, let us continue to gather all the forces of the proletariat, forming alliances. Let us help ourselves so well as we can amid the ills that present conditions compel us to suffer. Above all let us study how to solve the great economic problems which will greet us on the day after victory, and let us seek how best to proceed with the liquidation of the old society and the establishment of the new."

Be patient, be patient, "the day of justice will come." While you wait, close your ranks and strengthen your organization.

The news of the European workers' movement can be summed up in one word: strikes. In Belgium the typographers' strike in several cities, the spinners' strike in Ghent, the upholsterers' strike in Brussels; in England the imminent strike in the manufacturing districts, in Prussia the strike of the zinc miners, in Paris the plasterers' and painters' strike; in Switzerland the strikes in Basle and Geneva.

As we advance, the strikes multiply. What does this mean? That the struggle between labor and capital is ever more urgent, that economic anarchy becomes deeper every day, and that we are advancing with huge steps toward the inevitable result of this anarchy: Social Revolution. Sure, the proletariat's emancipation could be peacefully accomplished if the bourgeoisie desired capital to lose its tithe on labor, if it wanted to renounce its privileges and hold its own Night of August 4.[65] But bourgeois egoism and blindness are so ingrained that you have to be an optimist to hope that the social problem may be solved by a common understanding between the privileged and the disinherited. It is much more likely that the new social order will emerge from the very tumult of the present anarchy.

When strikes spread out from one place to another, they come very close to turning into a general strike. And with the ideas of emancipation that now hold sway over the proletariat, a general strike can result only in a great cataclysm which forces society to shed its old skin. To be sure, we are not yet there, but everything is leading us there. Only the people must be ready, and must not let themselves be manipulated by talkers and dreamers like in 1848. For this they must be vigorously and earnestly organized.

But since the strikes follow each other so rapidly, could the cataclysm arrive before the proletariat is sufficiently organized? We do not think so, in the first place because the strikes indicate a certain collective strength already, a certain understanding among the workers; and in the second place because each strike becomes the point of departure for the formation of new groups.

The necessities of the struggle impel the workers to support one another across political boundaries and professions. The more active the struggle becomes, therefore, the stronger and more extensive this federation of proletarians must become. And some narrow-minded economists accuse this federation of workers, represented by the International, of instigating strikes and creating anarchy! This, very simply, is to mistake the effect for the cause: the International has not created the war between the exploiter and the exploited; rather, the requirements of that war have created the International.

10

On Cooperation[66]

What should be the nature of the economic agitation and development of the workers of the International, and what will be the means of these, before the social revolution, which alone can emancipate them fully and definitively, does so? The experience of recent years recommends two paths to us, one negative, the other positive: *resistance funds and cooperation.*

By the broad term "cooperation," we mean all known systems of *consumption,* of *mutual credit* or *labor credit,* and of *production.* In the application of all these systems, and even in the theory on which they are based, we should distinguish two opposing currents: the bourgeois current and the purely socialist current.

Thus in the associations for consumption, credit, and production that the bourgeois socialists establish or suggest, we may find every element of bourgeois political economy: interest on capital, dividends, and premiums.

Which of these two systems is the good one, the real one?

The first, that of the bourgeois socialists, is accepted most often by those members of the International's sections who like to call themselves practical men. They are in fact very practical in appearance, but only in appearance, for all their ideas amount to is continuing, in the middle of the workers' world, the old bourgeois practice of *exploiting labor through capital.*

What could possibly be the result when a few score workers, or even a few hundred, try to establish an association on bourgeois bases? Either it does not succeed and goes bankrupt, plunging these workers into a poverty greater still than that from which they tried to escape by founding it; or it succeeds, thus creating a few score or a few hundred Bourgeois, without improving the general condition of the working class. The Lausanne Congress expressed this very well in the following resolution: "The Congress thinks that the present efforts of workers' associations (if they become more inclusive and maintain their present form) tend to constitute a fourth estate which has beneath it a still poorer fifth estate."[67]

This fourth estate would comprise a limited number of workers who establish among themselves a sort of bourgeois joint-stock company, necessarily excluding the fifth estate, the great mass of workers not partners in this cooperative venture but on the contrary exploited by it. That is the cooperative system which bourgeois socialists not only preach but even try to establish in the midst of the International, some of them knowing better and others unaware that such a system negates the basis and purpose of our Association.

What is the purpose of the International? To emancipate the working class through the solidaristic action of the workers of all countries. And what is the purpose of bourgeois cooperation? To lift a limited number of workers out of the common poverty and bourgeoisify them, disadvantaging the greater number. Is it not right to say that this practice, which the *practical men* of the International recommend, is a wholly bourgeois practice and that, as such, it should be kept out of the International?*

Let us imagine a thousand persons oppressed and exploited by ten. What if twenty or thirty of them, or more, said to themselves: "We are tired of being victims; but on the other hand, since it is ridiculous to hope for everyone's well-being, since the prosperity of the few absolutely requires the sacrifices of the many, let us abandon our comrades to their fate and think only of ourselves, let us in turn become wealthy bourgeois exploiters."

Would this not be an act of treason? And yet that is exactly what our "practical men" advise us! In theory as well as in practice, in cooperation as well as in administration, they are thus the exploiters and enemies of the working class. They wish to suit their own purposes, not those of the International; but they wish to use the International, the better to suit their own purposes.

We must further remark that they deserve the name *practical men,* which they give themselves, more because of their personal bourgeois intentions than because of their success. Many of them act in good faith and fool only themselves. Never having known, seen, or imagined any kind of association other than a bourgeois one, many of them think it quite fair to resort to this sort of association to fight the bourgeoisie. They are simple enough to believe that what destroys the workers can emancipate them, that they can use against the bourgeoisie the weapon with which the bourgeoisie itself crushes them.

This is a big mistake. These naïve persons do not take into account the vast advantage that the bourgeoisie enjoys against the proletariat through its monopoly on wealth, science, and secular custom, as well as through the approval—overt or covert but always active—of States and through the whole organization of modern society. This fight is too unequal for success reasonably to be expected. Under these conditions, bourgeois weapons—which are only frenetic competition, the war of all against all, and the victory of individual prosperity through the ruination of others—can serve only the bourgeoisie, and they would inevitably destroy the proletariat's only strength, its solidarity.

*[A footnote in *L'Égalité* at this point cites, in support of the argument presented, the resolutions of the Brussels Congress of the International (1866) on cooperative credit unions and on consumption and production cooperatives; see note 33.—Ed.]

The bourgeoisie knows this well. So what do we see? While the bourgeoisie rashly continues to fight resistance funds and trade unions, which are the only really efficacious weapons the workers now can use against it, it is entirely reconciled—after a certain hesitation, it is true, but not a long one—to the system of bourgeois cooperation.

All the bourgeois economists and publicists, even the most conservative, sing of the praises of this system in every key, and the bourgeoisie's still all too numerous partisans in the International[68] try to add every workers' cooperative to the chorus. Mr. Coullery and the *Journal de Genève,* Mr. Henri Dupasquier, the Protestant conservative of Neuchâtel, and Prof. Dameth, that apostate of socialism converted by the Protestants in Geneva, all agree in this regard.

They all shout themselves hoarse: "Build cooperatives, workers!"

Yes! Build these fine bourgeois cooperatives, so that you may be demoralized and ruined for the benefit of some wealthy entrepreneurs to whom you would be stepping-stones, so that they in their turn may become members of the bourgeoisie. Build bourgeois cooperation, it will hypnotize you, and after it exhausts all your energies it will leave you unable to organize your international strength, without which your right would never prevail against the bourgeoisie and triumph over them.

We want cooperation too. We are even convinced that the cooperative will be the preponderant form of social organization in the future, in every branch of labor and science. But at the same time, we know that it will prosper, developing itself fully and freely, embracing all human industry, only when it is based on equality, when all capital and every instrument of labor, including the soil, belong to the people by right of collective property. Therefore before all else, we consider this demand, the organization of the international strength of the workers of all countries, to be the principal goal of our great International [Working-Men's] Association.

Once this is acknowledged, we hardly oppose the creation of cooperative associations; we find them necessary in many respects. First, and this appears to us even to be their principal benefit at present, they accustom the workers to organize, pursue, and manage their interests themselves, without any interference either by bourgeois capital or by bourgeois control.

It is desirable that when the hour of social liquidation is tolled, it should find many cooperative associations in every country and locality; if they are well organized, and above all founded on the principles of solidarity and collectivity rather than on bourgeois exclusivism, then society will pass from its present situation to one of equality and justice without too many great upheavals.

But for cooperative associations to fulfill their purpose, the International must sanction only those that are based on its own principles.

In subsequent articles, we shall discuss cooperation according to the principles of the International,* and already today we are publishing a rough draft which seems to us to take an important step toward realizing these principles.[69]

*[These articles did not appear.—Ed.]

11

The International Working-Men's Movement

If anything now shocks the most stubborn conservatives, it is the increasingly universal and imposing movement of the working masses not only in Europe but in America as well. Every address delivered by aristocratic or bourgeois Statesmen and politicians of every country testifies to their uneasiness. They no longer let a single opportunity escape to express their so profound and above all so sincere sympathies for this so numerous and so *interesting* mass of workers, a mass which has for ages served as a passive, mute pedestal to every ambition and to all the world's politics, a mass which has finally grown tired of playing so unprofitable and undignified a role, a mass which is now giving notice of its resolute will to live and work no longer for any but itself.

Indeed, one must be gifted with a great deal of stupidity, one must be blind and deaf not to recognize the importance of this movement. And whoever has preserved in himself a spark of vitality and rightmindedness uncorrupted by self-interest or by doctrine, will recognize with us that only one movement today is no ridiculous and fruitless disturbance, only one movement carries an entire future within itself, and that is the international working-men's movement.

What is there, aside from this movement? First of all at the very top, there is something that is without a doubt very respectable but quite unproductive and very ruinous in the bargain: the organized brutality of the States. Next, under the protection of this brutality, come the large financial, commercial, and industrial works and great international plunder; a few thousand internationally solidaristic individuals who rule over the whole of society thanks to their mighty interests.

Underneath them are the moyenne and petite bourgeoisie, a clever and comfortable class in times past, but one now stifled and overwhelmed and driven down into the proletariat by the progressive intrusions of financial feudalism. This class is now so much poorer [than before] that it combines all the conceits of a privileged world with all the real poverties of an exploited world. It is a class condemned by its own history and physiologically exhausted. It had influence in earlier times, when it advanced; now it draws back, afraid, condemning itself to nothingness. If it had retained a bit of this vigorous vitality, a bit of this sacred fire which in the past inspired it to conquer a world, it would have found the courage to acknowledge to itself that it is now in an impossible predicament, ruined in every way unless it makes a heroic effort, dishonored, destroyed, and threatened with death from complications. There are only two influences today and they are preparing for a fatal meeting: that of the past, represented by the States, and that of the future, represented by the proletariat.

What effort can save this class, not as a separate class of course, but as an aggregation of individuals? The answer is very simple: *thrust into the proletariat by the force of circumstances, the moyenne and especially the petite bourgeoisie should enter it without restraint and with all its will.*

We shall return to this question shortly. Meanwhile, we shall end this article with the following reflections, borrowed from our Viennese colleague and organ of social democracy, the *Volksstimme.*[70]

"Only the blindest egoism can fail to recognize that only the triumph and the realization of the socialist principle can now put an end to the appalling putrefaction that has invaded all strata of society, founding in place of the present anarchy a social order consonant with justice and the general well-being. Really, we don't need scientific treatises to show that vast social reforms are needed. Socialism today is inevitably taking hold of all spirits. The future belongs to it. There can no longer be any doubt in the matter, for the winds of the workers' movement grow ever higher and more threatening in every country. The principal strength of the working masses is concentrated, above all, in the capitals and other large cities of Europe—our organized battalions are everywhere pushing forward. Already, in Spain, the red flag has been baptized with blood.

"The electoral activities in France[71] and the recent crimes of the privileged class in Belgium in particular show that it has everywhere been decided to answer the legitimate complaints of the workers with the arguments of brute force and the eloquence of bayonets. In Vienna as well, a certain newspaper uttered this sinister cry: 'It is time to get it over with!' We are threatened, and yet, without letting ourselves be the least bit intimidated by these threats, we are not afraid to say that if we feel a single burning desire, then that desire is to see all these social reforms, which have now become absolutely necessary, peacefully achieved by universal fraternal agreement.

"*For us,* the red flag is the symbol of universal human love. Let not our enemies think, then, of turning it into a flag of terror *against themselves.*"

12

On Russia[72]

What is now happening in Russia deserves the attention of every socialist-democrat in Europe.

We must affirm that there have been up to now some wholly mistaken ideas about the character, the tendencies, and the economic situation of the peoples inhabiting those vast regions. Thus was it not a rather general opinion in Europe—and is it not still—that the present Tsar [Alexander II], the benefactor and liberator of these peoples, is the object of their every reverence? That he has really emancipated the Russian peasants and established on solid foundations the well-being of the rural communities that are all the strength and richness of the Empire of All the Russias? Has it not been said and believed that the Tsar owes his power to all the happiness he has created and all the gratitude he has deserved, that he need only make a sign for millions of fanatic barbarians to launch themselves against Europe?

It has been said and repeated in a thousand different ways; some doubt the fact, but others know full well, that by doing so they render an immense service to the Tsars' much detested power, which is based less on its actual deeds than on imagination and on the panic terror which it knowingly propagates and which its diplomats can always explain.

Was thus it not believed in 1861, on the basis of Prince Gorchakov's dispatches, of the Russian press, and of the non-Russian press funded by the government of St. Petersburg, that the entire Russian people, including every class—the nobility, the priests, the shopkeepers, and above all the young people in the universities and the peasants—unanimously supported the suppression and annihilation of Poland; that the government, which may perhaps have wished to act more moderately, was forced to become the hangman of this unfortunate nation, which it drowned in blood merely to obey the unanimous will and vast passion of the people?

The whole European world believed it with hardly an exception, and if this general belief did not restrain European public opinion, it did quite a bit to neutralize the effects thereof. Aided by the cowardice and the divisions in European diplomacy, everyone stopped short in the face of this impressive manifestation of the supposed power of a whole people. They did not dare confront it or provoke it to fight and, with no resistance save a few ridiculous protests, they calmly allowed a great new crime to be committed in Poland.

Then came the sophists, Russian and non-Russian, some hired and others foolishly blind—in whose ranks Proudhon, the great Proudhon, unfortunately stood—explaining to us that the Polish revolutionaries were Catholics and aristocrats, representatives of a world condemned to perish, that the Russian government with all its hangmen represented the cause of democracy, the cause of the oppressed peasants, and the cause of the new principle of economic justice.[73]

These are the lies which they dared to spread and which were believed in Europe; and in Europe all this helped to increase considerably the prestige and power of the idea (and the power of ideas must never be disregarded) of the Empire of All the Russias.

To have believed all these fictions, spread by Russian diplomacy either directly or indirectly, the European public must have been totally ignorant of everything in that vast land and of everything happening there. And what is more peculiar, the Polish *émigré* press of every country lent a hand to Muscovite diplomacy by unanimously identifying the Russian people with the government of St. Petersburg. Would the Poles' legitimate hatred for their oppressors so blind them, that they would not realize the service they thus render to the very government they detest? Or might they actually desire to preserve the present economic order so much, that they would prefer even the Tsars' savage regime to a social revolution of the Russian peasants?

Whichever the case, it is time that this disgraceful and dangerous ignorance cease. As representatives of the cause of the international emancipation of labor and of the working-men of all countries, we cannot and must not have national preferences. The oppressed workers of all countries are our brothers; and as we pay no attention to the interests, ambitions, and vanities of the political homelands, the only foreigners or enemies we know are the exploiters of the people's labor.

It is very important for us to know, as representatives of the great international struggle of labor against exploitation by the nobility or bourgeoisie, whether the seventy million who are now imprisoned and enslaved within our close neighbor the Empire of All the Russias, and the hundred million Slavs who live in Europe, will be for us or against us on the great day of the battle. It would be more than a mistake for us to be unaware of them, for us not to try to understand their nature and their customs, their position and their current inclinations: it would be criminal lunacy.

The most obvious event, which now fills the columns of every official or semiofficial newspaper in St. Petersburg and Moscow, is the unforeseen closing of universities, academies, and other State schools, the arrest of a large number of young students in St. Petersburg and Moscow, in Kazan and other Russian provinces. After that, police orders enjoined all innkeepers and headwaiters from serving meals to more than two students at a time, enjoined house owners from letting one student spend the night at another's, enjoined even a gathering of more than two students in one room during the day. The prisons, the police stations, the dungeons of the secret chancellory, and the fortresses are full of young people seized in the two capitals or brought from the heart of Russia.

So what is happening? Isn't everything in Russia calm and satisfactory? What do these young people want? Are they asking for a constitution like in Belgium or Italy, or like the one that lucky Spain, for instance, will receive? No, not at all. Have you read the program of Russian social democracy which, translated into French, caused such scandal among the good bourgeois socialists at the Berne Congress?[74] Well, it's their program, it's what they want. They want nothing more nor less than the dissolution of this monstrous Empire of All the Russias, whose oppression has stifled the people's vitality for centuries but which has not succeeded in killing it, regardless of how things look. They want a social revolution such as the West, which has been moderated by civilization, scarcely dares to picture in its imagination.

And are these lunatics small in number? No, they are a legion, forming an army of several tens of thousands: *déclassé* young people, a few nobles, many children of common employees and priests, and the youth of the people both urban and rural. But are they isolated from the people? Not at all. On the countrary, this is a movement of the enlightened youth who come from the lowest dregs of Russian society and seek the light with a vigor and a passion we no longer know, a movement which is growing and expanding despite all the terrible measures of repression familiar to this country's government, a movement which every day seeks to blend in further with the movement of a people reduced to despair, to the most unimaginable poverty, by the famous emancipation and other reforms of the "Liberator-Tsar."

A little longer—two years, a year, perhaps several months—and these two movements will be one, and then: then we shall see a revolution which will without doubt be greater than every revolution heretofore.

13

A Few Words to My Young Brothers in Russia

You rise anew. So they have not succeeded in burying you. Then this spirit that arouses you to destroy the State is not the ephemeral product of some juvenile excitement but the expression of a vital need and of a real passion. It rises from the very depths of the life of the people.

If your revolutionary tendencies were only an outward sickness, the simple longing of youth's vanity, then the heroic attempts of our paternal government to cure you would have long ago been successful. You would long ago have renounced the dangerous mania of thinking, renounced all in man which is human, and become—among this throng of officially titled and unreasoning beasts who ravage the people and devour the country—new beasts. You would have merited the name of patriots of *the Empire of All the Russias.*

The outcast lettered youth of Russia, as young as it is, has already weathered quite a few storms. In our days, under the naïvely despotic regime of the Emperor Nicholas, twenty years and more were needed to go through half the proofs which you have undergone in the last eight or nine.

After the fires of 1861, during and after the Polish insurrection [of 1863], and above all since Karakozov's act, this good Emperor Alexander has not spared his efforts to complete your political education.[75] Encouraged, excited by our entire *patriotic* learning, by the Slavophiles and Panslavists as well as by the partisans of the bourgeois civilization of the West, at the same time by our planters and by our liberals, he has liberally used against you all the methods bequeathed him by the Tatars which were later so well perfected by the bureaucratic science of the Germans: truncheon, whip, torture, death by gallows and death by hunger, imprisonment for life, exile *en masse* and forced labor—he used them all to take the measure of your strength, your obstinate will, your faith in the people's cause.

Nothing shook you, you sustained yourselves, and so you are strong. Many of your comrades perished. But for each victim buried, ten new fighters rise from the earth: it is thus near at hand, the end of this infamous Empire of All the Russias.

Where do you find your strength and your faith? A faith without God, a strength without personal goal or expectation! Where do you find this strength consciously to condemn to nothing your entire existence, to confront torture and death without vanity and without phrases? What is the source of this merciless thought of destruction and coldly passionate resolve in the face of which our adversaries' spirit takes fright and their blood runs cold in their veins? Our official and semi official literature, which claims to express the thought of the Russian people, halts before you altogether disconcerted. It no longer understands anything.

If you were the faithful servitors to the Emperor and the State, spies, executioners, private or public thieves, burglars or otherwise, well-thinking riffraff, servile liberals, butchers of peasants or of Poles, if you had caused the deaths of thousands or tens of thousands of human beings, this precious literature would have understood you and amnestied you, and if you had in the least the means and the will to show your gratitude to the editors of the newspapers, they would have declared you the saviors of the Empire, as they did Muravyov the Hangman. All of that is customary in the Byzantino-Tatar and Germano-bureaucratic civilization of our State; none of it is opposed to the official and semi official patriotism of the Empire of All the Russias.

If you young people were visionary, doctrinaire, or sentimental, if you trifled with dreams of science and art, of freedom and humanity in theory, in your conversations, or in books, they would still amnesty you; for the worthy veterans of this disgraceful literature had their youth as well. They too dreamt when they were still only students. Enthusiasts of pretty theories, they too swore to devote their lives to the cult of the ideal, to noble exploits, to the service of freedom and humanity. Then came experience, acquired in the most abject world imaginable, and under the influence of this world they became what they are—scoundrels. But, recalling with compassion the dreams of their youth, they would pardon you yours so willingly that they would be convinced that, with the same experience and under the influence of the same reality, you would certainly become still more villainous than they.

What they will never pardon is that you wish to be neither thieves nor dreamers. You have as much scorn for this hateful world whose reality oppresses you as for that ideal world which has served until now as a refuge for *pure souls,* against reality's ignominy. That is what frightens our patriotic literature. It knows neither what you want nor where you go.

The editors of the St. Petersburg and Moscow newspapers have, in their consternation, found a subterfuge. They have unanimously decided that the present movement among the Russian youth results from Polish intrigues! One could not imagine anything more cowardly, nor more stupid!

Is it not infamy and cruel cowardice to inflame the executioner against the victim he tortures! And on the other hand, it is truly stupid not to see the abyss that separates the program of the largest majority of Polish patriots from that of our youth, which represents the socialist and revolutionary idea of the Russian people.

Between the Polish patriots and us there is only one sentiment and one goal in common: *Hate for the Empire of All the Russias, and the firm will to destroy it at all cost as quickly as possible.* That is the only point on which we agree. One step more, and the abyss opens between us. We wish the definitive abolition of everything that constitutes the State, in Russia as well as outside it; and the Poles work only for the reconstitution of their historical State.

The dream of the Poles is, we think, not good, since every State, however liberal and democratic its forms, ruins the popular masses who work to profit a small minority that does not work. The Poles dream the impossible, for States in the future will not reconstitute themselves but fall, annihilated by the emancipation of these masses. The Poles, without knowing it and certainly without wishing it, dream a new slavery for their people. And if they succeed in realizing this dream—not with the strength of the people, who will certainly not lend themselves to it, but with the aid of foreign bayonets—then they will become our enemies as well as their people's oppressors.

We will fight them then in the name of social revolution and universal freedom. But until then we are their friends and we should help them, for their cause—the destruction of the Empire of All the Russias—is also ours.

For Russian and non-Russian peoples emprisoned today in the Empire of All the Russias, no enemy is more dangerous, more mortal, than this Empire itself.

The Polish patriots have never understood this, and that is why their influence on Russia's revolutionary movement has always been nil. This is unfortunate, for if they as well as we really merited the calumny of the Russian press, we would better understand one another, if only for the first act of the Slav tragedy that is being heralded: which would not prevent us from separating or even from fighting during the three following acts, if we have to, only to be reconciled in the fifth.

No, it is not the influence of Polish intrigues, it is a wholly other gigantic strength that agitates the Russian youth and urges them on: *it is the awakening of the life of the people.*

The current reign bears a remarkable resemblance to that of Tsar Alexis, the father of Peter the Great, who despite his historical good nature pillaged and unmercifully oppressed the people for the greater glory of the State and for the benefit of the tribe of nobles and bureaucrats, just as the so-called emancipator of the peasants, this excellent Emperor Alexander II, does today.

Then as now the unfortunate people, crushed, tortured, reduced to most dire poverty and decimated by hunger, abandoned their villages and took refuge in the forests. Now as then this entire, vast population, finally understanding this imperial swindling, is becoming restless, counting no longer on any emancipation but that from below, in the way shown only two centuries ago by the hero *Stenka Razin.**

*To explain the immense figure of Stenka Razin and the secret of his vast popularity, we would first have to outline the Russian people's position in seventeenth-century society. To understand this position it is necessary to know that they were a free people up to the end of

One senses the approach of a new bloody encounter, a last struggle to the death between the Russia of the people and the State.

Who will triumph this time? The people, without doubt. Stenka Razin was a hero, but among them all he was alone and above them. His truly gigantic personal influence was nevertheless insufficient to resist the already largely organized power of the State. He perished, and everything perished with him. It will be otherwise today. There will probably not be a hero as influential or as popular as Stenka Razin, who concentrated the whole strength of the rebellious masses in his single person. But he will be replaced by this legion of nameless, socially outcast young people who already thrive on the life of the people and who stay united by the same thought and passion and by a common goal.

The union of these youths with the people assures the triumph of the people.

These youths are strong and resolute only because they draw their thought and their implacable will from the passion of the people. They seek not their own triumph but the triumph of the people. Stenka Razin is felt behind them. Not the personal hero but the collective hero, invincible for that very reason: the entire, spendid, assembled young people over whom his spirit already hovers.

---

the sixteenth century, and that it was only in the last decade of that century that the peasants, who had kept their freedom of movement up to then, attached themselves to the land.

The traditional idea in Russia, which still today is one of the two pillars of the people's consciousness there, is that the land belongs to the people. The other idea, just as old, is that the people should administer their own affairs according to the resolutions of their communal assemblies, in which every head of family takes part.

These two ideas are so deeply rooted in the consciousness of the Russian people that despite three centuries of slavery, they are today preserved intact. They will be the very basis of the Russian people's future political organization.

The Russian people are deeply socialist by instinct as well as by tradition, but they lack political education. That is why, as free as they were to begin with, they could have been enslaved.

In the West, the alliance of the crown and the people against the property-owning nobility led to the development of monarchical power, but in Russia that power was based on the alliance of the crown, the nobility, and the clergy against the people. That is why the Russian nobility and clergy always remain the willing slaves of the Tsar, who rewards them by guaranteeing [to them] the peasants' slavery; it is also why the people have always been the only real, the only earnest revolutionaries in Russia.

During the first years of the seventeenth century, the communes rose up *en masse* against the tyranny of the Tsar, the clergy, the nobility, and the Muscovite bureaucracy, and this memorable revolution failed to destroy the Empire, which was reconstituted by the free election of a new Tsar. Then that Tsar's son, Alexis (1645-1676), forgetting all the promises sworn by his father, plunged the Russian people and especially the peasants into a theretofore unimaginable slavery. It was during this reign that the celebrated revolt of Stenka Razin erupted.

Stenka Razin was a man of remarkable intelligence and will. He was a man of iron who knew pity neither for himself nor for others. He was nothing but a simple Don Cossack. His father had been hanged by a Prince Dolgorukii, commander of a Muscovite army against Poland. Stenka Razin fled down the Volga in 1667. There he formed a band with whom he

That is the real meaning of the current movement, which is rather innocent in appearance but which, despite seeming so, throws our whole official and semiofficial, patriotic, literary world into consternation.

Friends! Leave all the more quickly, then, this world condemned to destruction. Leave these universities, these academies, these schools from which you are now being expelled, where they sought only to separate you from the people. Go among the people. There should be your career, your life, your knowledge. Learn amid these masses whose hands are hardened by labor how you should serve the people's cause. And remember well, brothers, that the cultured youth should be neither master nor protector nor benefactor nor dictator to the people, only the midwife of their spontaneous emancipation, the uniter and organizer of their efforts and their strength.

Do not concern yourself at this moment with the knowledge in the name of which you would be tied down and flogged. This *official science* must perish with the world that it expresses and serves; and a new science, rational and alive, will appear in its place after the victory of the people, from the very depths of their unchained life.

Such is the faith of the best men of the West, where, as in Russia, the old world of States founded on religion, on metaphysics, on jurisprudence, in a word on bourgeois civilization, is collapsing, along with its indispensable complement, the rights of hereditary property and of the

---

descended in boats to the Caspian Sea, pillaging the Persian coasts and returning to the Don rich with his spoils.

In 1670 he reappeared on the Volga and declared war to the death on the entire nobility, bureaucracy and clergy; he proclaimed the peasants' freedom to full and integral possession of the land. The whole people from the Oka to the Volga pronounced themselves in his favor, killing every noble, every functionary of the Tsar, and every priest. In a short time, Stenka Razin had taken Astrachan, Tsaritsyn, and Saratov. His procedure was the simplest: he massacred everyone who was not of the people and left it to the latter to seize the land and thrive upon it. Everywhere he plundered, there rose the free commune of peasants who fully possessed the land.

When Razin defeated regular troops, his first concern was to make the soldiers themselves kill all their officers. He told the soldiers that he would not make war on them, that they were free to join him or to go their own way. But if they went their own way, he made the others pursue and massacre them.

Everywhere he went, he burnt all the acts and papers of the Tsar; but as we have seen he didn't spare men either. He was hardly religious; when he was reproached for killing priests, he replied: "Hey, what do you need priests for? If you want to get married, walk around a tree three times and it's settled." On the other hand, he was a poet; he wrote magnificent songs of brigandage which are still sung on the Volga and throughout Russia. Taken prisoner in 1671, he was conveyed to Moscow, where the people had awaited him as a liberator; after being tortured, he was beheaded.

In the midst of the most monstrous tortures, he uttered not a sound. His nature was of iron. He is still today the greatest hero of popular legend.

The Russian people, who are superstitious but not religious, and superstitious only when superstition coincides with their desires, await his return in 1870.[76]

juridical family, collapsing and preparing to give way to the international and freely organized world of the workers.

It is a lie that Europe rests shrouded in a deep sleep. On the contrary, she wakes, and one must truly be deaf and blind not to sense the approach of a final struggle.

Organizing itself for this struggle and extending its hand across the borders of all States, the world of the workers of Europe and America appeals to your fraternal alliance.

Part Five

Patriotism and Human Progress

Detail of a map, drawn in 1869, showing Berne, Neuchâtel, and the St. Imier Valley, which runs from La Chaux-de-Fonds east-northeast to Sonceboz. The heavy dark lines are railroads, overprinted on the map in 1908. Along the line that runs through the St. Imier Valley appear the towns of St. Imier and Sonvil[l]ier. (The latter is where Bakunin gave the "Three Lectures to Swiss Members of the International.") Southwest from La Chaux-de-Fonds is Le Locle, and between these two towns is Crêt[-du-Locle]. To the northeast of Sonceboz is Moutier. Bakunin's grave is in the Bremgarten Cemetery, Berne.

14

Open Letters to Swiss Comrades of the International*

1

Friends and brothers,

Before leaving your mountains I feel the need to express to you once more, in writing, my profound gratitude for the fraternal reception that you have given me. Is it not marvelous that a former Russian noble, of whom you previously knew nothing, may set foot in your land for the first time and, having scarcely arrived, find himself surrounded by hundreds of brothers! This wonder could occur today only through the *International Working-Men's Association,* for one simple reason: only it today embodies the historical vitality and creative force of the political and social future. Those united by a living thought, by a volition and the same great passion and by a common will, are truly brothers, even when they do not realize it themselves.

[The Economic Component of Patriotism]

There was a time when the bourgeoisie, endowed with this life force and constituting by itself the historic class, offered the same spectacle of fraternity and unity in both its thoughts and its actions. That was the finest hour of the bourgeoisie, a class doubtless still worthy of respect but one which has since become impotent, stupid, and sterile: during those days it advanced most strongly. That was the bourgeoisie before the Great Revolution of 1793, as well as before the revolutions of 1830 and 1848 though to a much lesser degree. In those days the bourgeoisie had a world to conquer, a place to take in society, and it organized for combat; intelligent, audacious, and feeling that it stood for universal rights, it was endowed with an irresistible omnipotence; unaided, it accomplished three revolutions against the combined forces of the monarchy, the nobility, and the clergy.

At that time the bourgeoisie also founded a formidable worldwide international association: *Freemasonry.*[77]

It would be a great mistake to judge the Freemasonry of the eighteenth

*[This selection and the next, "Physiological or Natural Patriotism," are of a piece. The inserted, bracketed subheadings correspond to the four components of patriotism that Bakunin enumerates below.—Ed.]

century, or of the beginning of the nineteenth, by what it is today. The erstwhile increasing influence of Freemasonry, a preeminently bourgeois institution, reflected the growth and influence of the bourgeoisie; later, its decadence reflected the moral and intellectual decadence of that class. Today, having sadly become a jabbering old intriguer, it is useless and worthless, sometimes malevolent and always ridiculous, whereas before 1830 and especially before 1793 it was active, powerful, and genuinely beneficent, uniting through its organization the choicest minds and the most ardent hearts, the most fiery wills and the boldest personalities, with but a very few exceptions. It was the vigorous incarnation of the humanitarian idea of the eighteenth century, as well as its practical implementation. All the great principles of liberty, equality, and fraternity, of human reason and human justice—worked out at first in theory by the philosophy of that century and developed within Freemasonry—emerged as practical principles, as the bases of a new morality and politics: the soul of a colossal project of demolition and reconstruction. At that time, Freemasonry was nothing less than the worldwide conspiracy of the revolutionary bourgeoisie against feudal, monarchical, and divine tyranny. It was the International of the bourgeoisie.

We know that nearly all the main actors of the first Revolution were Freemasons and that when this Revolution erupted it found, thanks to Freemasonry, friends and powerful allies in every other country. This certainly contributed to its triumph. But it is just as clear that the triumph of the Revolution was Freemasonry's undoing, for once the Revolution had granted most of the wishes of the bourgeoisie by giving it the nobility's social position, the bourgeoisie, which had for so long been an exploited and oppressed class, became very naturally in its turn the privileged, exploitative, oppressive, conservative, and reactionary class, the friend and firmest supporter of the State. After the *coup d'état* of Napoleon I, Freemasonry became an imperial institution in most European countries.

The Restoration revived it slightly. Seeing itself threatened by the return of the old regime and forced to surrender to the coalition of Church and nobility the position it had won through the first Revolution, the bourgeoisie necessarily became revolutionary again. But what a difference between this reheated revolutionism and the ardent, powerful revolutionism that inspired it at the end of the eighteenth century! In those days, the bourgeoisie was sincere, it earnestly and naïvely believed in human rights, it was driven and inspired by the genius of demolition and reconstruction, it was in full possession of its intelligence and at the height of its strength. It believed itself and felt itself to be the representative of the people, and this it truly was. It did not yet sense the abyss that separates it from the people. The Thermidorean reaction and the conspiracy of Babeuf dispelled this illusion forever. The abyss that separates the working people from the dominating, exploiting, property-owning bourgeoisie has opened, and nothing less than the dead body of the entire bourgeoisie and its whole privileged existence will ever fill it.

Thus, after the Restoration, it was no longer the whole bourgeoisie but only a part of it, which recommenced to conspire against the regime of the Church and the nobility, against the legitimated kings.

In my next letter, if you allow me, I shall develop my ideas on this last phase of constitutional liberalism and of bourgeois Carbonarism.

2

In my last article I said that reactionary, legitimist, feudal, and clerical activities revived the revolutionary spirit of the bourgeoisie, but that there was an enormous difference between this new spirit and the one that animated it before 1793. The eighteenth century's bourgeoisie were giants, compared to whom the most daring members of the nineteenth's appear mere pygmies.

One need only compare their programs to be convinced of this. What was the program of the eighteenth century's philosophy and of its Great Revolution? No more nor less than the full emancipation of all of humanity; the achievement of every individual's right and full, real freedom by means of the political and social equalization of all individuals; the triumph of the human world over the wreckage of the divine world; the reign on earth of justice and fraternity. But this philosophy, this revolution erred in not realizing that human fraternity cannot be achieved so long as States exist, that the real abolition of classes and the political and social equalization of individuals will be possible only when the economic resources for upbringing, education, employment, and subsistence are the same for everyone. We cannot criticize the eighteenth century for not having understood this. Social science is not created and studied with books alone, it needs the great lessons of history; and it was necessary to accomplish the Revolution of 1789 and 1793, and further to undergo the experiences of 1830 and 1848, in order to arrive at this henceforth irrefutable conclusion—that any political revolution that does not have economic equality as its *immediate and direct* goal is, from the standpoint of the interests and the rights of the people, nothing but hypocritical and camouflaged reaction.

This truth, so clear and simple, was still unrecognized at the end of the eighteenth century, and when Babeuf posed the economic and social question, the revolution's strength was already exhausted. But the immortal honor remains his, of having stated the greatest problem ever stated in history—the emancipation of all of humanity.

In comparison with this vast program, what was the goal of the program of revolutionary liberalism under the Restoration and the July Monarchy? Sham constitutional freedom: a very prudent, very modest, very regulated, very limited freedom, created entirely for the tempered disposition of a half-sated bourgeoisie which was weary of combat and impatient to enjoy its spoils, which already felt threatened (though now from below rather than from above), and which was anxiously watching while innumerable millions of exploited proletarians appeared on the horizon like a dark crowd tired of suffering and preparing to demand their rights.

Since the beginning of the present century this nascent spectre, later baptized the red spectre, this dreadful ghost of universal rights which opposes the privileges of the rich and which, as it develops, will reduce to dust the sophisms of bourgeois economy, jurisprudence, politics and metaphysics—this justice and reason of the people has become, amid the modern triumphs of the bourgeoisie, its unremitting killjoy, diminishing its confidence and its spirit.

And still the social question was nearly unrecognized under the Restoration, or rather, nearly forgotten. Certainly, there were a few isolated great dreamers like Saint-Simon, Robert Owen, and Fourier, whose genius and great hearts understood the necessity of radically transforming the economic organization of society. Around each of them, like so many small churches, gathered a small number of devoted and ardent followers who were, however, known only to their masters and who exerted no outside influence. There was only the communist testament of Babeuf, transmitted by his illustrious friend and comrade Buonarroti to the most vigorous proletarians through a secret organization of the people.[78] But this work was underground at the time and its effects were felt only later, during the July Monarchy; it was not noticed at all by the bourgeois class during the Restoration. The people, the mass of workers, remained quiet and did not yet demand anything for themselves.

It is clear that if the spectre of popular justice had any life at this time, it could only have been in the false consciousness of the members of the bourgeoisie. Whence came this false consciousness? Were the members of the bourgeoisie any more wicked during the Restoration than their fathers who made the Revolution of 1789 and 1793? Not in the least. They were virtually the same persons but they were set in different surroundings and in other political conditions. They were enriched by a new experience, and hence they possessed a different consciousness.

The bourgeoisie of the last century sincerely believed that they emancipated the entire people by emancipating themselves from the monarchical, clerical, and feudal yoke. And this sincere but naïve belief was the source of the heroic daring of all their marvelous power. They felt themselves united with everyone, and they marched into battle carrying with them universal strength and universal rights. Thanks to the strength and the rights of the people which the bourgeoisie embodied, its members could, over the last century, scale and capture the fortress of political power after which their ancestors had lusted for so many centuries. But the very moment they planted their banner, a new idea struck them. As soon as they gained power, they began to realize that the interests of the bourgeois class no longer had anything in common with those of the popular masses, that on the contrary these were radically opposed, that the exclusive influence and well-being of the property-owning class could depend only on the poverty and the political and social subordination of the proletariat.

From that moment, the relations between the bourgeoisie and the people were radically transformed, and even before the workers had realized that the members of the bourgeoisie were their natural enemies—this out of necessity rather than out of ill will—those latter had already recognized this inevitable antagonism. This is what I call the bad conscience of the bourgeoisie.

3

I said that the false consciousness of the members of the bourgeoisie has paralyzed the entire intellectual and moral development of the bourgeois class since the beginning of the nineteenth century. Let me correct myself and replace the word *paralyzed* with another: *distorted.* For it would be wrong to say that a spirit has been paralyzed or atrophied, which has passed from the theory of the positive sciences to their application: it has invented all the wonders of modern industry—steamboats, railroads, and the telegraph—and it has pushed to their most extreme conclusions political economy and the historical criticism of the growth of wealth and of the civilization of peoples, giving birth to a new science—statistics—and establishing the bases of a new philosophy—socialism—which is nothing but the very negation of the bourgeois world, sublime suicide from the standpoint of the exclusive interests of the bourgeoisie.

The paralysis came only later, after 1848, when the bourgeoisie, terror-stricken by the effects of its own works, consciously leapt backwards, renounced every thought and volition so as to preserve its wealth, submitted to military protectors, and abandoned itself—body and soul—to the purest form of reaction. Since then it has created nothing and it has lost, along with its courage, the creative force itself. It no longer has even the force or the spirit of self-preservation, for everything it has done and still does to save itself pushes it inevitably toward the abyss.

The bourgeoisie was still full of spirit up to 1848. Undoubtedly, this spirit no longer had the vigorous strength that enabled it to create a new world between the sixteenth and eighteenth centuries. No longer was it the heroic spirit of a class whose daring had allowed it to conquer all. It was the moderate and thoughtful spirit of a new proprietor who, after having gained an ardently coveted piece of property, now had to make it prosper and turn it to his profit. The spirit of the bourgeoisie in the first half of the nineteenth century is characterized above all by an almost exclusively *utilitarian* tendency.

The bourgeoisie has been criticized for this, but wrongly so. On the contrary, I believe that it has rendered one last great service to humanity by preaching, more by example than by its theories, the cult of—or rather, the respect for—material interests. These interests have, at bottom, always prevailed in the world: but until then they had always appeared as some kind of hypocritical or unwholesome idealism, which is precisely what transformed them into malicious and unjust interests.

Whoever pays the slightest attention to history cannot fail to see that the most abstract, sublime, and ideal religious and theological struggles are always underlain by some great material interest. No war between races, nations, States, and classes has ever had any purpose other than *domination,* which is the necessary condition and guarantee of the possession and enjoyment of wealth. From this standpoint human history is only the continuation of the great struggle for life which, according to Darwin, constitutes the basic law of the organic world.

In the animal world this battle is waged without ideas, without words, and also without resolution. So long as the earth exists, the animal world will devour itself: this is the natural condition of its life. Human beings, who are preeminently carnivorous, began their history with cannibalism. Today they aspire toward worldwide association, the collective production and collective consumption of wealth.

But what a bloody and horrible tragedy there is between these endpoints! And we are not yet finished with this tragedy. After cannibalism came slavery, after slavery serfdom, after serfdom wage-labor, after which the terrible day of justice must first come, and much later, the age of fraternity. These are the phases through which the animal struggle for life is gradually transformed, historically, into the human organization of life.

And amid this fratricidal struggle of men against men, during this mutual ruination, this subjugation and exploitation of [the many] by those [few] who have until now held out over the centuries under changing names and forms, what has been the role of religion? Always to sanctify violence and transform it into right. It transported humanity, justice, and fraternity into an imaginary heaven, leaving behind the reign of injustice and brutality on earth. It has blessed these successful thieves and, in order to enrich them further, it has preached resignation and obedience to their innumerable victims, the peoples. And the more sublime the ideal that it adored in heaven appeared, the more horrible the reality on earth became. For it is the very essence of all idealism, religious as well as metaphysical, to scorn the real world and to exploit it while scorning it—from which it follows that all idealism inevitably engenders hypocrisy.

Man is material, and material cannot be scorned with impunity. Man is an animal and cannot suppress his animality. But he can transform, must transform and humanize it through freedom, that is, through the combined action of justice and reason, which in their turn can comprehend freedom only because they are its products and its highest expression. On the contrary, every time that man has tried to abstract his animality, he has become its plaything and slave, and even more often its hypocritical servant: witness the priests of the most idealist and most absurd religion of the world, Christianity.[79]

Compare their well-known lewdness with their vow of chastity, compare their insatiable lust with their doctrine of renouncing the goods of this world, and you will agree that no one is as materialist as these preachers of Christian idealism. At this very moment, which question most disturbs the Church? The preservation of Church properties, which that other Church—the State, the expression of political idealism—is now everywhere threatening to confiscate.

Political idealism is no less absurd, pernicious, and hypocritical than religious idealism, of which it is moreover only a different form: its worldly and terrestrial expression. The State is the younger brother of the Church—and patriotism, that virtue and cult of the State, is but a reflection of the cult of the divine.

According to the precepts of the idealist school, which is simultaneously a religious and a political school, the virtuous must serve God and devote themselves to the State. That is the doctrine that bourgeois *utilitarianism* has begun, since this century began, to treat as it deserves.

4

[The Political Component of Patriotism]

One of the greatest services rendered by bourgeois utilitarianism, I have said, is to have killed patriotism, the religion of the State.

As we know, patriotism is an ancient virtue which arose under the Greek and Roman republics, where no real religion other than that of the State ever existed, nor any object of veneration other than the State.

What is the State? The metaphysicians and doctors of law tell us that it is the public cause: it is collective welfare and universal rights, as opposed to the disintegrating action of the egoistic interests and passions of the individual. It is justice and the realization of morality and virtue on earth. As a result the individual has no duty greater, nor can he perform any act more sublime, than devotion and self-sacrifice to—and, if necessary, self-immolation for the sake of—the State's triumph and its influence.

There, in a few words, is the whole theology of the State. Let us now see whether this political theology does not, like religious theology, conceal beneath its very attractive and poetic appearance some very vulgar and sordid realities.

Let us analyze first the very idea of the State, as it is portrayed by its enthusiasts. It is the sacrifice of the natural freedom and interests not only of each individual but also of every relatively small collectivity—associations, communes, and provinces—to the interests and the freedom of everyone, to the well-being of the great whole. But what, in reality, is this everyone, this great whole? It is the agglomeration of all these individuals and of all those more limited human collectivities which they compose. But what does that whole, which is supposed to represent them, actually represent as soon as all individual and local interests are sacrificed in order to create it and coordinate themselves into it? Not the living whole wherein each person can breathe freely, becoming more productive, stronger, and freer as the full freedom and well-being of individuals develops in its midst; nor natural human society, in which every individual's life is reinforced and broadened through the life of every other: on the contrary, it is the ritual sacrifice of each individual and of every local association, an abstraction which destroys living society. It is the limitation, or rather the complete negation, of the so-called good of everyone, of the life and the rights of every individual who is party to this "everyone." It is the State, the altar of political religion on which natural society has always been immolated: a universality which subsists on and devours human sacrifices, just like the Church. The State, I repeat again, is the younger brother of the Church.

To demonstrate the identity of the Church and the State, I ask the reader to note that both are based essentially on the idea of the sacrifice of life and of natural rights, and that they proceed similarly from this principle. According to the Church, natural human wickedness can be overcome only through divine grace and the death, for God's sake, of man as he is found in nature; according to the State, it can be overcome only through law and the immolation of the individual on the altar of the State. Both strive to transform man: the one into a saint, the other into a citizen. But man as found in nature must die, for sentence is passed on him unanimously by the religion of the Church and that of the State.

That is the self-same theory of the Church and the State in its ideal purity. It is a pure abstraction. But every historical abstraction presupposes historical events. These events, as I said in my last article, are of an entirely real and brutal character: violence, spoliation, conquest, and enslavement. It is human nature that man is not satisfied just to act; he must also justify and legitimate what he has done, in his own eyes and in those of the world. Thus religion appeared in the nick of time to consecrate the accomplished facts and, as a result of this benediction, the unjust and brutal action was transformed into a right. As we know, juridical science and political rights sprang first from theology and then from metaphysics, which is nothing but disguised theology, a theology which ridiculously claims not to be absurd and vainly strives to give political rights a scientific aspect.

Let us see now what role this abstraction called the State, which parallels that historical abstraction called the Church, has played and still plays in real life, in human society.

The State, as I have said, is basically a vast cemetery wherein every manifestation of individual and local life, every interest of those parties who together constitute society, is sacrificed, dies, and is buried. It is the altar on which the real freedom and welfare of peoples are immolated for the sake of political grandeur; and the more complete this immolation, the more perfect the State. From this I conclude, and it is my conviction, that the Russian Empire is the State *par excellence,* the State without rhetoric or phrase-mongering, the most perfect State in Europe. On the contrary, all States in which the peoples still have some room to breathe are incomplete States from the standpoint of the ideal, just as all other Churches, in comparison with the Roman Catholic Church, are deficient.

As I have said, the State is an abstraction which consumes the life of the people. But for an abstraction to be born, develop, and continue to exist in the real world, there must be a real collective body interested in its existence. This collective cannot be the great masses of the people, for they are precisely its victims: it must be a privileged body, the sacerdotal body of the State, the governing and property-owning class, which is to the State what the sacerdotal class of religion, the priests, is to the Church.

And indeed, what do we see throughout all history? The State has always been the patrimony of some privileged class: the priesthood, the nobility, the bourgeoisie, and finally, after every other class has been exhausted, the bureaucratic class, when the State falls or rises—whichever you wish—into the condition of a machine. But for the State to be preserved, there absolutely must exist some privileged class interested in its existence. It is exactly the solidaristic interest of this privileged class that is called *patriotism.*

5

[The Physiological or Natural Component of Patriotism]

Has patriotism, in the complex sense in which the word is normally used, ever been a passion or a virtue of the people? Basing myself upon the lessons of history, I do not hesitate to answer this question with a decisive *no.* To prove to the reader that this reply is correct, I should like to analyze the basic elements which, combined in various ways, constitute this thing called patriotism.

These elements are four in number: (1) the natural or physiological element, (2) the economic element, (3) the political element, and (4) the religious or fanatical element.

The physiological element is the essential basis of all naïve, instinctive, and brutish patriotism. It is a natural passion which is in flagrant contradiction with all politics precisely because it is excessively natural—that is, altogether animal—and, what is worse, it greatly obstructs the economic, scientific, and human development of society.

Natural patriotism is a purely animalistic reality, to be found at all levels of animal life and even, one might say, to a certain degree in plant life. Patriotism taken in this sense is a war of destruction, the first human expression of this great inevitable battle for life which is the essence of all evolution and existence in the natural or material world: an incessant battle, a universal and mutual carnivorism in which each individual, each species, is nourished by the flesh and blood of members of other species, a battle which thus inevitably renews itself every hour, every instant, resulting in the prosperity and development of the fullest, most intelligent, and strongest species, at the expense of all others.

Those who are in agriculture or gardening know the costs of preserving their plants from the invasion of the parasitic species that join battle with them over the light and the chemical elements of the earth, without which they cannot survive. The strongest plant, which is best adapted to the particular conditions of climate and soil and which still develops with relative vigor naturally tends to stifle all others. It is a silent struggle, but one without truce. And the whole force of human intervention is required to protect the preferred plants against this deadly invasion.

In the animal world the same struggle recurs, only with more dramatic commotion and noise. The extinction is no longer silent and insensitive. Blood flows; the devoured, tortured animal fills the air with its cries of distress. Man, the animal that can speak, finally utters the first word in this struggle, and that word is *patriotism*.

The struggle for life in the animal and plant world is by no means only an individual struggle; it is a struggle of species, groups, and families, some pitted against others. In each living being there are two instincts, two great basic concerns: food and reproduction. From the standpoint of nourishment, every individual is the natural enemy of every other, regardless of the bonds of family, groups, and species. The proverb that wolves do not eat other wolves is correct only so long as the wolves find animals of other species for sustenance, but we know very well that as soon as wolves begin to miss these latter, they devour each other without qualms. Cats, pigs, and many other animals ofter devour their own offspring, and there is no animal that will not do so if forced by hunger. Didn't human beings begin with cannibalism? And who has not heard those distressing stories of sailors on some frail craft, shipwrecked, lost in the ocean, deprived of nourishment, deciding by lot which of them is to be sacrificed and eaten by the others? Finally, during this terrible famine which has just decimated Algeria, did we not see mothers devouring their own children?

Hunger is a harsh and invincible despot, and the need to eat, an entirely individual need, is the first law, the ultimate condition of life. It is the basis of all human and social life, and of animal and plant life too. To rebel against it is to destroy what remains, condemning oneself to nothingness.

But along with this fundamental law of material life, there is another just an essential: reproduction. The first leads to the preservation of individuals, the second to the establishment of families, groups, and species. Individuals, impelled by an innate need, in order to reproduce themselves, seek to mate with those individuals who are organically closest to them, who are their fellow-creatures. Differences among organisms can render mating sterile or even altogether impossible. This impossibility is clear between the plant world and the animal world; but even in the latter, the mating of quadrupeds, for example, with birds, fish, reptiles, or insects is equally impossible. If we limit ourselves to quadrupeds alone, we again find the same impossibility between various groups, and we come to the conclusion that the ability to mate and the power to reproduce exist for each individual only among a very limited sphere of individuals whose organisms are identical or similar to his own, and who belong to the same group or family.

Since the instinct of reproduction establishes the sole link of solidarity that exists among individuals in the animal world, animal solidarity ceases to exist where this ability to mate is not found. All those with whom an individual finds it impossible to reproduce, form a different species, an absolutely foreign and hostile world, condemned to be destroyed; and all that lies within composes the great homeland of the species—for example, the human race for human beings.

But this destruction and mutual carnivorism of living beings are found not only at the boundaries of this limited world that we call the great homeland, but also in the very midst of this world, which is just as ferocious and sometimes more ferocious, because of the very resistance and competition that are found there, and because there the equally cruel battles of love are added to those of hunger.

Moreover, every animal species is subdivided into various groups and families, under the influence of the geographic and climatological conditions of the various countries it inhabits. The various differences in conditions of life leads to corresponding differences in the very organisms of these individuals who are members of the same species. We know further that every individual animal seeks naturally to mate with the individual most like it, from which follows naturally the development of a great number of variations within the same species. Since the differences that distinguish all these variations from one another are based primarily upon reproduction, and since reproduction is the sole basis of all animal solidarity, it is clear that the great solidarity of the species must be subdivided into many more limited solidarities, that the great homeland must parcel itself out among a multitude of small animal homelands that are mutually hostile and mutually destructive.

15

Physiological or Natural Patriotism

[continued*] 1

In my last letter I showed how patriotism, as a natural passion or disposition, derives from the physiological law that separates living beings into species, families, and groups.

The patriotic passion is clearly a solidaristic passion. To be observed in its most explicit and clearly resolved form in the animal world, it must be sought among those animal species which, like man, are endowed with a highly sociable nature: for example, among ants, bees, beavers, and many others which have stable common habitats, as well as among species which wander in herds. The animals that live in established, collective habitats exhibit, from the standpoint of nature, the patriotism of agricultural peoples, whereas those that wander in herds exhibit that of nomadic peoples.

It stands to reason that the latter patriotism, which involves only the bond among individuals within the herd, is less complete than the former, which adds to it the bond of individuals with the soil or locality they inhabit. Habit is second nature for animals as well as for man, and the particular ways of life of which habit is composed are much better resolved and more established among collectively sedentary animals than among wandering herds; and these different habits, these particular ways of life, constitute an essential element of patriotism.

Natural patriotism may be defined as follows: an automatic and wholly uncritical, instinctive attachment for hereditary or traditional ways of life which are collectively accepted, and an equally automatic and instinctive hostility toward any other way of living. It is love for one's own and hatred for everything foreign. Patriotism is thus collective egoism on one hand, and war on the other.

It is by no means so strong a solidarity that the individual members of an animal collectivity will not devour one another if they must; it is, however, strong enough for all these individuals to unite, forgetting their civil discords, against every intruder who comes from a foreign collectivity.

Take the dogs of a town, for example. Certainly, dogs do not by nature form a collective republic; left to their own instincts, they live in errant packs, like wolves, and only under man's influence do they become settled

*[See the note at the bottom of p. 169, above.—Ed.]

animals. But once they have established this way of life, they constitute in each village a sort of republic, not a communitarian one, but one based on individual freedom, pursuant to the formula of which bourgeois economists are so enamored: every man for himself, and the Devil take the hindmost. It is *laissez-faire* and *laissez-aller* without limit, a competition, a civil war with no quarter and no truce, in which the stronger always bites the weaker—exactly as in bourgeois republics. But just let a dog from a nearby village trot down their street, and you see all these contentious citizens immediately throw themselves *en masse* on the unfortunate stranger.

I ask, is this not the faithful imitation, or rather the original that is copied every day in human society? Is it not a perfect demonstration of that natural patriotism which I have called, and which I dare to call again, nothing but an altogether animal passion? It is without doubt animal, both because dogs are incontestably animals and also because man—an animal like the dog and all other animals on earth, but an animal endowed with the physiological ability to think and talk—begins his history with animality in order to attain, many centuries later, the conquest and the perfect foundation of his humanity.

Once we understand this origin of man, we need no longer be astonished at his animality, which is one natural fact among so many other natural facts, nor need we even be indignant about it, for, whereas the whole of man's human life is only an incessant fight on behalf of his humanity, against his natural animality, it follows that we must struggle most vigorously against man's animality.

I wish merely to establish that the patriotism extolled to us as an ideal and sublime virtue by the poets, by politicians of every school, by governments, and by every privileged class, is rooted not in man's humanity but in his animality.

And indeed at the beginning of history, and today in the least advanced parts of human society, we see natural patriotism reign supreme. To be sure, patriotism is a much more complex feeling in human communities than in other animal communities, for the very reason that human life, the life of the animal that thinks and speaks, comprehends infinitely more than does that of the other animal species. To purely material customs and traditions there are added, in man, traditions that are more or less abstractive, intellectual, and moral, plus a horde of ideas and representations, true or false, along with different religious, economic, political, and social customs. All these compose, as elements of man's natural patriotism, in one combination or another, a particular manner of being for a collectivity, a traditional way of life, thought, and action, which is distinct from all others.

But whatever difference there be between the natural patriotism of human collectivities and that of animal collectivities, they have this in common: they both are instinctive, traditional, habitual, and collective passions, and their intensity in no way depends upon the nature of their content. On the contrary, we may say that the simpler and less complex the content is, the more intense and strongly intolerant is the patriotic feeling that manifests and expresses that content.

Animals are clearly much more attached to the traditional customs of the collectivity to which they belong than are men. This patriotic attachment is unavoidable for them, and they can shake it off only under man's influence. Likewise in human collectivities: the less advanced the civilization, the simpler and less complex is the very foundation of social life, and the more intense is natural patriotism, i.e., the instinctive attachment of individuals to all the material, intellectual, and moral habits that represent the traditional and customary life of a particular collectivity, as well as their hatred for everything different and foreign. From this it follows that natural patriotism is inversely proportional to [the degree of] civilization, which latter is the very triumph of human nature among human societies.

No one will dispute that the instinctive or natural patriotism of the wretched tribes inhabiting the arctic zones, which have hardly been touched by civilization and whose material life is stricken by poverty, is infinitely stronger and more exclusive than the patriotism of, for example, a Frenchman, an Englishman, or a German. The Frenchman, the Englishman, and the German can live and acclimatize themselves anywhere, while the native of the polar regions would very soon perish of homesickness, were he far removed from there. And yet, how much poorer and less human his existence is! This shows again that, far from being a mark of humanity, the intensity of natural patriotism is a mark of animality.

Aside from this positive component of patriotism, which consists of the instinctive attachment of individuals to the particular way of life of the collectivity to which they belong, there is, further, the negative component, just as essential as the first and inseparable from it. This is the equally instinctive abhorrence of everything foreign—instinctive and, as a result, altogether animal. Yes, truly animal, for this abhorrence is so much stronger and harder to conquer that the less the one experiencing it thinks about and understands it, the less human he is.

Today this patriotic repulsion against everything foreign is found only among savage peoples. In Europe it can still be found among those half-savage natives whom bourgeois civilization has not deigned to enlighten, but whom it has not forgotten to exploit. In the greatest European capitals, even in Paris and above all in London, rays of enlightenment have never brightened some streets, which have been abandoned to a wretched populace. A stranger need only appear there, and he will be surrounded by a mob of wretched human beings—men, women, and children, scarcely dressed, whose countenance and appearance show signs of the most ghastly poverty and abject degradation—who will insult and sometimes maltreat him, just because he is a stranger. By all means, then, is not this brutal and savage patriotism the most glaring negation of everything we call humanity?

And still, some very enlightened bourgeois newspapers—the *Journal de Genève,* for example—are not ashamed to exploit this barely human prejudice, this thoroughly animal passion. However, wishing to do them justice, I freely acknowledge that they exploit these people without dividing them in any way, doing so only because they find that exploitation useful—just as nearly every priest of every religion today preaches religious nonsense without believing it, only because it is clearly in the interest of the privileged classes for the popular masses to continue believing it.

When the *Journal de Genève* has exhausted its arguments and proofs, it says: this is a *foreign* thing, or idea, or man. And it has so low an opinion of its compatriots that it hopes the advance of this fearful word *foreign* will suffice for them to forget everything—common sense, humanity, justice—and go over to its side.

I am scarcely a Genevan, but I respect the residents of Geneva too much not to think the *Journal* mistaken about them. Surely they would not wish to renounce humanity for guilefully exploited animality.

2

I have said that, insofar as patriotism is instinctive or natural, having all its roots in animal life, it presents nothing more than a particular combination of collective habits—material, intellectual and moral, economic, political and social—developed by tradition or by history within a limited human society. These habits, I added, may be good or bad, since the content or object of this instinctive feeling does not influence its intensity; and even if one conceded some kind of difference in this respect, it would tend more often toward the good habits than toward the bad. This is because the force of inertia exerts in the intellectual and moral world a force just as powerful as in the material world. As a result of the animal origin of every human society, in every society which is not yet declining but which is progressing and marching onward, the bad habits are more deeply entrenched than the good, because they are older. This explains why, of the sum total of present collective habits in the most advanced countries of the civilized world, at least nine-tenths are worthless.

It should not be imagined that I wish to declare war on the habit that society and men have generally allowed themselves to be governed by *habit.* In this, as in many other things, they are only inevitably obeying a natural law, and it would be absurd to rebel against natural laws. The action of habit in the intellectual and moral life of individuals, as well as in that of societies, is identical to that of vegetative forces in animal life. Both are conditions of existence and of reality. To become something real, the good as well as the bad must become habit, either with the members of mankind each taken individually, or with society. Every practice and study to which men apply themselves has no goal other than this, and the better things take root in man and become second nature only by force of habit. The question, therefore, is not to rebel foolishly against habit, for it is an inevitable influence which neither human intelligence nor human will can reverse. But if we earnestly wish to be enlightened by the reason of the age and by the idea of true justice which we have formed, we need do but a single thing: constantly engage our willpower—that is, the habit of willing which circumstances independent of us have developed in us—for the elimination of our bad habits and for their replacement by good ones. To humanize society completely, it is necessary to destroy ruthlessly all causes and conditions—economic, political, and social—which produce the tradition of the bad in individuals, and to replace them with conditions that will engender necessarily, among those same individuals, the rise of the habit and the practice of the good.

From the standpoint of modern consciousness, humanity, and justice, such as we have come finally to understand them thanks to the past developments of history, patriotism is a bad, narrow, and disastrous habit, for it is the negation of human equality and solidarity. The social question, which the working people of Europe and America are now posing in their practice and which can be resolved only by abolishing State boundaries, tends inevitably to destoy this traditional habit in the consciousness of the workers of all countries. I will show later how, since the beginning of the nineteenth century, this habit has already been greatly undermined in the consciousness of the high-financial, commercial, and industrial bourgeoisie by the prodigious and wholly international development of its wealth and economic interests. But I must first show how natural and instinctive patriotism, which by its very nature can only be a very narrow and very limited feeling, an altogether local collective habit, has been greatly modified, weakened, and impaired since the beginning of history by the successive formation of political States, well before this bourgeois revolution.

To be sure, patriotism as an altogether natural sentiment—i.e., as produced through the truly solidaristic life of a collectivity, and until now weakened only a little, if at all, by reflection or by the effect of economic and political interests, or by that of religious abstractions—is animal patriotism in very great part if not altogether, and it can only encompass a very restricted world: a tribe, a commune, a village. At the beginning of history, as now among savage peoples, neither nations nor national languages nor national cults existed; thus, there was no fatherland in the political sense of this word. Every little locality, every village had its particular language, its god, its priest or sorcerer, and was only a diverse, extended family which, at war with every other tribe, negated all the rest of humanity by its own existence and grew stronger by enduring. Such is natural patriotism in its vigorous and simple crudity.

Vestiges of this patriotism are still found, even in some of the most civilized countries of Europe. In Italy, for example, especially in the southern provinces of the Italian peninsula, the lay of the land, the mountains, and the sea produce barriers among the valleys, communes, and towns, separating and isolating them, rendering them almost alien to one another. Proudhon, in his pamphlet on Italian unity,[80] correctly observed that this [national] unity was still only a wholly bourgeois idea and by no means a popular passion, that the rural population has remained largely foreign (and I would even add hostile) to it because this unity, which is in contradiction on the one hand with their local patriotism, has brought them on the other hand nothing but oppression, ruin, and unmerciful exploitation.

Even in Switzerland, especially in the backward cantons, do we not very often see local patriotism vying with cantonal patriotism, and this latter with the political, national patriotism of the whole republican confederation?

To sum up, I conclude that patriotism, as a natural feeling, being in essence and in reality an altogether basically local feeling, is a serious obstacle to the formation of States, and that as a result these latter, and civilization along with them, have been able to establish themselves only by destroying—if not altogether, then at least to a considerable degree—this animal passion.

3

[The Religious or Fanatical Component of Patriotism]

Having examined patriotism from the standpoint of nature and shown that *from this point of view* it is, on the one hand properly an animal sentiment, since it is common to all animal species, and, on the other hand essentially local, because it can never extend beyond the very limited space or world in which the man deprived of civilization spends his life, I shall now proceed to the analysis of exclusively human patriotism, of *economic, political,* and *religious* patriotism.

Naturalists have proven, and it is henceforth axiomatic, that the number of animals in a pack always corresponds to the amount of the means of subsistence in the region it inhabits. The pack grows as these means are found in greater quantity; it is reduced as this quantity decreases. When a pack of animals has consumed all the provisions of a region, it migrates. But this migration shatters all its old habits and its daily routine ways of life, and causes it to hunt for the means of subsistence in wholly unknown regions, with no idea and no clue at all, by instinct and altogether at random. It is always accompanied by privations and vast sufferings. The greater part of the migrant animal pack perishes from hunger, often serving as food for the survivors; and only the smaller part succeeds in acclimatizing itself and in finding new ways of life in a new region.

Then comes war: war among the species that feed on the same foods, war among those who must devour one another to survive. Considered from this point of view, the natural world is nothing but a bloody slaughterhouse, an appalling and dismal tragedy writ by hunger.

Those who admit the existence of a God-the-Creator do not suspect the handsome compliment they pay him by portraying him as the creator *of this world.* Indeed! A God-the-Omnipotent, God-the-Omniscient, God-the-Omnificent could not have created so hideous a world.

It is true that the theologians have an excellent argument to explain this revolting contradiction. They say that the world was created perfect, and that an absolute harmony did reign at first, until God, furious at man who had sinned, condemned man and the world.

The fuller this explanation is of absurdities, the more edifying it is; and we know that all the theologians' strength rests with the absurd. For them, the more absurd and impossible a thing is, the truer it is. All religions are only deifications of the absurd.

So a perfect God created a perfect world, and that is how this perfection goes to the dogs and draws its creator's malediction, becoming an absolute imperfection after having been an absolute perfection. How could perfection become imperfection? To this they reply that, however perfect the world was at the moment of creation, it was nevertheless not an absolute perfection, since God alone is absolute and More-than-Perfect.[81] The world was perfect only in a relative way, in comparison to what it is now. But why use this word "perfection," which admits of nothing relative? Is not perfection necessarily absolute? Then say that God created an imperfect world, but one which was better than that which we now behold. But if it was only better, if it was already imperfect upon emerging from its creator's hands, then it did not exhibit this harmony and absolute peace of which the theologians continually remind us. And then we will ask them: According to your own words, should not every creator be judged from his creation, and a worker from his works? The creator of an imperfect thing is inevitably an imperfect creator; since the world was imperfect, God, its creator, is imperfect, because his creation of an imperfect world can be explained only by his lack of intelligence, lack of power, or lack of goodwill.

But, they will say, the world was perfect, only less perfect than God. To this I shall reply that one cannot speak of more or less where perfection is involved. Either perfection is complete, whole, and absolute, or it does not exist; therefore, if the world was less perfect than God, the world was imperfect. From this it follows that God, the creator of an imperfect world, was himself imperfect, that he remains imperfect, that he never was God, and that God does not exist.

To preserve God's existence, the theologians will then be forced to concede that the world he created was perfect in the beginning. But then I will ask them two little questions. First, if the world was perfect, how could two perfections exist one outside the other? Perfection can only be unique. It does not admit of duality, for in duality the one limits the other, rendering it imperfect. Accordingly, if the world was perfect, there was no God above or even outside it; the world itself was God. One other question. If the world was perfect, how did it fall? It is a pretty perfection that can degenerate and be spoilt! And if they admit that a perfection can fall, then God can fall too! Which means that God existed in men's credulous imagination, but that human reason, which is increasingly triumphant in history, destroyed him.

Finally, how unique he is, this God of the Christians! He created man in such a way that man could, that man *must* sin and fall. Since omniscience is one of his infinite attributes, God, in creating man, could not have been unaware that the latter would fall. And since God knew it, man had to fall; otherwise, it would have given an impudent lie to divine omniscience. And they speak to us of human freedom? It was fate! Even the simplest family head would have been able to foresee in the place of God Almighty that man falls in yielding to this fatal inclination. And then see how Divine Perfection gets terribly angry, ridiculously and hatefully angry: God curses not only the transgressors of his law, but all of human descent, even though it does not yet exist and is accordingly absolutely innocent of the sin of our first parents; and, not content with this revolting injustice, he curses further this harmonious world, which happened to be there, and transforms it into a repository of crimes and horrors, a perpetual slaughterhouse. Then, slave of his own anger and of the curse he himself declared on men and on the world, his own creation, remembering a bit late that he was a God of love, what does he do? It is not enough to have bloodied the world with his anger: he further spills the blood of his only Son, this bloody God; he sacrifices him under the pretext of reconciling the world with his Divine Majesty! If only he had succeeded! But no, the natural, human world remains as torn asunder and stained with blood as before this vicious expiation: from which it follows clearly that the God of the Christians, like all other Gods who had preceded him, is a God as impotent as he is cruel, and as absurd as he is wicked.

And these are the kinds of absurdities that they wish to force on our freedom and reason! It is with monstrosities just like these that they claim to moralize and humanize men! If only theologians had the courage frankly to renounce all claims to humanity as well as to reason. It is not enough to say with Tertullian, "*Credo quia absurdum,* I believe what is absurd."[82] Let them try, if they can, to force their Christianity on us by the knout like the Tsar of All the Russias, by the stake like Calvin, by the Holy Inquisition like good Catholics, and by violence, torture, and death, as the priests of every religion possible would still like to be able to do—let them try all these fine ways, but let them never expect to triumph any other way.

As for us, let us once and for all leave these absurdities and divine abominations to those who foolishly believe that in their name they can still exploit the common people, the toiling masses, for a long time to come. Returning to our fully human reason, let us always remember that human wisdom, the only thing that can enlighten and liberate us and make us worthy and inspire us, is to be found, in relation to the present day, not at the beginning of history but at its end; and that man, in his historical development, proceeds from animality progressively to attain humanity. Let us, therefore, never look back but always look ahead, for ahead is our light and our well-being. If it is also useful to look back sometimes, and if we are so permitted, it is only to ascertain what we have been and what we must no longer be, what we have done and what we must no longer do.

The natural world is the constant theater of an interminable struggle, the struggle for life. It is not for us to ask why this is so. We have not made it so, we have found it so upon birth. It is our natural point of departure, and we are not at all responsible for it. Let it suffice for us to know that it is so, that it has been so, and that it will probably always be so. Harmony in the natural world is established through combat, through the victory of some and the defeat, more often the death, of others. The growth and development of species in the natural world are limited by their own hunger and by the appetite of other species, that is, by suffering and death. We do not say with the Christians that this earth is a vale of sorrows, but we ought to acknowledge that it is not at all as tender a mother as it is said to be, and that living beings need much strength to survive here. In the natural world, the strong live and the weak succumb, and the former live only because the latter do succumb.

Is it possible that this inevitable law of natural life is also a law of the human and social world?

4

Are men by their nature condemned to devour each other in order to live, as do animals of other species?

Alas! We find cannibalism in the cradle of human civilization, during and after wars of genocide among races and peoples: wars of conquest, wars to maintain the balance of power, political wars and religious wars, wars on behalf of great ideas such as those waged by France under her present emperor [Napoleon III], and patriotic wars for great national unity like those contemplated on the one hand by the Pangermanic minister [Bismarck] of Berlin and on the other hand by the Panslavist Tsar [Alexander II] of St. Petersburg.

And what do we find at the bottom of all this, common to all these hypocritical phrases they use to give themselves an appearance of humanity and right? Always the same economic issue: *the tendency of some to live and prosper at the expense of others.* All the rest is mere humbug. The ignorant, the naive, and the fools let themselves be taken in, but the strong men who control the destinies of the States know full well that at the bottom of every war lies but a single concern: plunder, the acquisition of others' wealth, and the subjugation of others' labor!

That is the simultaneously cruel and brutal reality that the Gods Almighty of every religion, the Gods of battles, have never failed to bless—beginning with Jehovah, God of the Jews, the eternal Father of our Savior Jesus Christ, who commanded his chosen people to massacre every native of the Promised Land, and ending with the Catholic God, symbolized by the Popes, who, as a reward for the massacre of heathens, Mohammedans, and heretics, gave the land of these hapless peoples to their happy butchers, each one of whom was dripping with their blood. To the victims, Hell; to their executioners, their spoils, the goods of the earth. Such is the purpose of the holiest wars, religious wars.

It is clear that, at least until now, humanity has hardly been exempt from the general law of animality that dooms all living beings to devour one another in order to live. Only socialism, which puts human justice in the place of political, juridical, and divine justice, which replaces patriotism with the worldwide solidarity of mankind and economic competition with the international organization of a society founded entirely on labor, will be able to put an end to these brutal manifestations of human animality and to war.

But until it triumphs on earth, all the bourgeois Congresses of Peace and Freedom will protest in vain and all the Victor Hugos of the world will preside over them in vain, and men will continue to tear one another to pieces like wild beasts.

It has been well established that human history, like the history of all other animal species, began with war. This war, never having any goal other than obtaining the means of existence, has gone through various phases of development that run parallel to the various phases of civilization, that is, to the various phases of the development of man's needs and of the means of satisfying them.

Thus at first, man the omnivorous animal, like all other animals, subsisted on fruits and plants and by hunting and fishing. No doubt man hunted and fished over many centuries as do animals still today, without the aid of tools other than those that nature endows. The first time that he used the crudest weapon, a simple stick or a stone, he performed an act of thinking and asserted himself, no doubt without suspecting it, as a thinking animal, as a human being. Even the most primitive weapon, which must inevitably be adapted to the proposed goal, implies a certain amount of mental calculation, which essentially distinguishes the human animal from all other animals on earth. Owing to this faculty of reflection, thought, and invention, man perfected his arms—very slowly, it is true, over many centuries—and thereby transformed himself into a hunter or a ferocious armed beast.

Having reached this first stage of civilization, small human groups naturally found it easier to feed themselves by killing living beings (including other human beings) which were to be used as food, than did beasts deprived of these instruments of hunt or war. And *since the multiplication of an animal species is always in direct proportion to the means of subsistence,* it is clear that the number of men was bound to increase at a faster rate than that of other animal species, and that eventually the time would come when uncultivated nature could no longer feed everyone.

5

If human reason were not progressive—if it relied, on the one hand, on the tradition that preserves for the benefit of future generations the knowledge acquired by past generations, spreading, on the other hand, thanks to the gift of speech, which is inseparable from that of thought—then it would never develop any further. If it were not endowed with the unlimited ability to invent new ways to defend human life against all natural forces unfavorable to it, then this insufficiency of nature would inevitably have limited the mulitplication of the human race.

But thanks to the precious faculty that allows him to apprehend, to reflect, and to understand, man can surmount this natural limit which halts the development of all other animal species. When natural sources were exhausted, he created artificial ones. Profiting not by physical force but by superior intelligence, he ceased simply killing for immediate consumption and turned to subduing, taming, and somehow raising wild beasts, in order to make them serve his ends. In this way, over the centuries, groups of hunters were transformed into groups of herdsmen.

With this new source of subsistence, the human race naturally multiplied still further, creating the necessity of producing new means of subsistence. The exploitation of animals no longer sufficing, groups of people set about exploiting the earth. Nomadic peoples and herdsmen were in this way transformed, over still more centuries, into agricultural peoples.

It is at this stage of history that slavery, properly so called, began. Men, wild animals that they were, first began by devouring the enemies they had killed or taken prisoner. But when they began to realize the advantage of exploiting dumb animals instead of killing them immediately, they very soon came to realize what they could gain from the services of man, the most intelligent animal on earth. The vanquished enemy no longer was devoured, but instead became a slave, forced to work in order to maintain his master.

The labor of pastoral peoples is so light and simple that it hardly requires the labor of slaves. Consequently we see that for nomadic and pastoral peoples the number of slaves is very limited, if not zero. Things are otherwise with agricultural and settled peoples. Agriculture' requires assiduous, painful, daily labor. The free man of the forests and plains, the hunter as well as the herdsman, takes to agriculture only with great repugnance. So we see still today among the savage peoples of America, for example, that it is onto the comparatively weaker creature, the woman, that the hardest and most distasteful domestic labors fall. Men know no occupations other than hunting and warring, which our own civilization still considers the most noble callings; and, disdaining all other occupations, they remain slothfully recumbent, smoking their pipes, while their unhappy wives, these natural slaves of the barbarian, succumb to the burden of their daily toil.

One step later in civilization, and the slave takes the part of the women. An intelligent beast of burden, forced to bear the whole load of physical labor, he produces the leisure and the intellectual and moral development of his master.

16

The Agitation of the Socialist-Democratic Party in Austria

The workers' movement in Austria is assuming remarkable proportions. The reader can assess them from the events that we have already pointed out in part and that we shall continue to point out as they occur. In our last issues we published a rather detailed account of the Popular Assembly which occurred in Vienna on 4 May [1869] and which could be held only behind closed doors, but which nevertheless assembled more than 6,000 followers.[83] Now *La Voix du Peuple (Volksstimme),* the newly established organ of this party, which we warmly recommend to every honest socialist-democrat in Europe, brings us news of another popular assembly in Vienna, this time in the open air, which assembled more than 20,000 workers.

But the workers' movement does not stop in Vienna. Despite all the obstacles placed in its path by Herr von Beust's liberal government, which is propped up by the various tendencies in the party of the bourgeoisie, and despite all the enticements of the clerical and feudal party, which is vainly trying to divert it from its goal, the movement is spreading with prodigious speed in nearly every province of Austria, and it is uniting under the same socialist flag and in the name of the same program, the workers of all the different nations whose strained political union has up to now constituted that bulwark of the old Catholic and reactionary Holy Alliance in Europe, the monstrous Habsburg Empire.

This worm-eaten empire is now sinking under the weight of its lies and age-old crimes. Napoleon and Bismarck gave it the *coup de grâce.* It will not rise again despite all the tonics that liberalism—nay, even bourgeois democratism—now tries to administer it. The bourgeoisie is itself too ill to cure an illness which is by now incurable; the dead do not revive the dead, and the living have many more things with which to be concerned than accommodating this dying entity, which will leave no memory in history other than its infamous hypocrisies and its violent, bloody, merciless deeds.

The bourgeoisie, which no longer thinks of effecting its own escape, clings to the unity of Bismarck's Germany or to the imperial institutions of Napoleon III, just as it clings to a kingless throne in Spain and, in general, to all presently existing political States. It is aware that every one of its political and social privileges, as well as its very existence as a class economically distinct from the large number of workers who now work for it [rather than for themselves], will be shattered and destroyed by the very popular storm that will do away with all those States.

However, the disappearance of this empire from the political map of Europe, an event near at hand, will leave a vast void, the filling of which the very interest of civilization will require. The urgency of this task is now becoming so obvious that the dark forces of reaction—encouraged by the fruitlessness of the efforts of the liberal and democratic bourgeoisie in Austria (efforts which seem to hasten the collapse of this empire rather than to avoid it), represented externally by the Panslavist empire of St. Petersburg plus the Pangermanic empire of Berlin and domestically by the ultramontane clergy and the old Austrian oligarchy—are all openly preparing to assume the legacy. Russian diplomacy and Bismarckian diplomacy, imperial princes and counts, former bureaucrats, old soldiers and bishops are all now plotting together in Austria, and they seem to have free rein to excite the most fanatical passions there, religious as well as national, in every possible way. By whipping up these foolish and blind passions, they hope to kill the moribund Austrian Empire.

Bourgeois liberalism strives to obstruct this reactionary coalition with the artificial centralization of the States, an obstacle which is no less reactionary from the standpoint of socialist democracy and which is, moreover, too feeble and inadequate to the task. Terror-stricken by the imminence of the cataclysm that threatens to engulf all privileged positions and fortunes, the bourgeois members of the Reichsrat[84] have made a superhuman effort to conceal an enormous deficit and have given the emperor an army of 800,000 men besides. This is the final effort of the empire. Once these last resources are exhausted, it will have nothing left to live for. But history teaches us that once a State has reached this point, it can not survive much longer.

The Austrian Empire is therefore condemned to die. Who will assume its legacy? Will it be foreign reaction, allied with domestic reaction? This would be a very great calamity, but it will not come to pass. The heir that awaits its legitimate legacy, and is alone powerful enough to collect it, is neither imperial Russia nor royal Prussia. It is *the party of socialist democracy,* which is not Austrian, although it is of good Austrian birth, for it represents the cause of the workers of the entire world.

It is above all in Austria that we feel, see, and touch, so to speak, this indisputable truth: life has now deserted the bourgeois class, as before it deserted the nobility; the body of the bourgeoisie is intellectually and physiologically dead or close to dying, and the entire future—I almost said the present—belongs to the workers alone. While the liberal and democratic members of the bourgeoisie exhaust themselves in ineffectual attempts to establish something resembling a party, the party of socialist democracy, which is composed principally of workers if not entirely so, which reaches into every Austrian province and as a result of natural attraction unites members of the most different nationalities in its midst, already counts well over 100,000 followers. And it was formed hardly a year ago. Isn't this a tremendous result?

The fact is that Austrian workers are perhaps the best situated in Europe to usher in unselfishly the social policy of the future. The workers of other lands must still somewhat fight the demoralizing grip and stifling prejudices of national feeling or patriotism. Austrian patriotism was invented only to mask the imperial bureaucracy and army. By no means is it a natural national sentiment; it is an official virtue worth as much as every other official virtue.

If the Austrian worker wished to be patriotic, in the very limited way of one of the numerous nationalities which compose the Austrian Empire, he would have to surrender all claims to unity with the workers of every nation in the same empire. That is to say, he would have to surrender all claims to the only instrument with which he can humanize his life and obtain well-being, freedom, and—the supreme goal of the workers of all countries today—equality. Accordingly, he can become a real force only by trampling underfoot the principle of nationality.[85]

The Austrian workers understand this necessity so well that the first act of the party of socialist democracy was to eliminate the national question from its program. The heads of national Slav parties—urged on the one hand by feudal and clerical politics and on the other by bourgeois-liberal, bourgeois-socialist, and bourgeois-democrat German politicians—are vainly trying to win the workers of Vienna over to their opposing camps. These courageous workers, deaf to all the Sirens' voices,[86] and inspired by the principle that brought them together, have declared in a memorable manifesto that they wish to belong neither to the Confederation of Northern Germany, over which Bismarck presides, nor to the political combination of the bourgeois socialists of Vienna, Munich, and Stuttgart;[87] that they recognize no homeland other than the international camp of the workers of all countries who fight against bourgeois capital; and that for them there are neither Germans, nor Slavs, nor Magyars, nor Italians, nor French, nor English, but only human beings: their friends if they are workers, their enemies if they are bourgeois exploiters and dominators.

The program of the proletariat of all countries can be expressed no more clearly.

What follows? That the Austrian workers, in every effort they make to emancipate themselves, serve not a national cause but that of the workers of the whole world. Do they not in this respect surpass the working populations of all other countries, even the workers of France, who, their heroic virtues aside, greatly err in never forgetting that they have the honor of being French and that Paris is the capital of France, nay, of the world?

The Viennese workers are attached no more to Vienna than to any other city. They do not consider themselves the center of the world. They have no heroic and revolutionary tradition in their past, and are thereby fortunate in having no reason for conceit; but they are also free of all the memories of 1789 and 1793, a splendid but ponderous burden that too often renders the creative force of French socialism powerless. For it must certainly be admitted that revolutionary classicism still weighs heavily on the political and social thought of the French today, as the classicism of Corneille and Racine has long weighed on their poetry.

The Austrian workers have none of these glories and none of these burdens. They enter both politics and socialism wholly virgin and fresh, and hence full of life. They will be able to create everything; a great future awaits them, and they will quite probably be called upon to lay the first foundations of the international State of the future: *the worldwide economic republic,* the inevitable coming of which was announced to his bewildered bourgeois electors by Mr. Thiers himself—this most vile bourgeois celebrity, this skeptical septuagenarian moneybags who has conducted a lifelong fight against socialism but whose long and unhappy experience has turned him into a prophet.

The Viennese workers, who in general follow the vagaries of Lassalle and who educate themselves by reading his writings, auspiciously discuss a State of the Austrian people in their program. But they must first make allowances for their present political position: they are still Austrian *subjects* and, as such, are subjected to very severe and restrictive laws as well as to the arbitrariness of a police that was formed under the old despotism and has not been much reformed by the new liberalism. Moreover, *did not the Viennese liberals—what am I saying, did not the Viennese democrats and bourgeois socialists—nearly a year ago denounce,* in their newspapers and speeches, *the earnest socialism of the Viennese workers to this very police?* The workers of Austria must therefore by prudent, since they are surrounded on all sides by informers and enemies. A trustworthy source tells us that they would before long be incorporated as sections of our great International[Working-Men's] Association, were they not formally prevented by Austrian laws.

And in spite of all this, in spite of all these restrictive laws and under the very pressure of such a police, we must say that they display more revolutionary audacity, a much greater initiative, and international sympathies far more magnanimous in other respects, than we do, who are also members of the International and who enjoy in Switzerland every liberty of the bourgeois republic. To prove this, we need only cite the text of the telegram that the last popular assembly, held in Vienna on 30 May [1869] by 20,000 workers, sent to the workers of Paris and Lyons after the last elections: "Greetings and congratulations to the workers of Paris and Lyons. We have received happily the news of your victory, which is ours as well. Long live the French people, long live the vanguard of the proletariat!"

We believe that Lassalle errs when he forgets that history has shown the worldwide political State to be impossible, since every political State inevitably must be a limited national or territorial State, and says, in the middle of so many wonderful things, a bit too much about the State, for the existence of the State is, as just indicated, incompatible with the solution of the economic question, which is essentially an international and worldwide question. But let us suppose that the Austrian workers, too blindly drawing their inspiration from Lassalle's writings, seriously believe it possible to transform the present Austrian Empire into a genuinely democratic State of the people. Where can their efforts lead if they succeed? Only to the destruction of this empire and to the liquidation of every political State on the land it occupies.

What do the Austrian workers want? What all bold, thoughtful workers want now: not just the political abolition of classes but their economic abolition as well; the social and economic equalization of individuals in their upbringing, their labor, and their enjoyment of the fruits of labor—so that all human individuals on earth may have but a single way of life regardless of nation or sex, so that this new life may be expressed by each individual's fullest freedoms and founded on the strictest solidarity of them all. Well, we defy them to realize this goal in any political State!

Whoever talks about a political State—whether it is an absolute monarchy, a constitutional monarchy, or even a republic—is talking about domination and exploitation. It is the domination of either one [dynasty] or one nation or one class over every other one, it is the very [negation] of socialism.

What does socialism want? To establish a just human society, free of all tutelage, free of all authority, free of political domination and economic exploitation, founded only on collective labor that is guaranteed by collective property.

What is to be done to reach this goal? The States must be abolished, for their only mission is to protect individual property, that is, to protect the exploitation by some privileged minority, of the collective labor of the masses of the people; for in that very way they prevent the development of the *worldwide economic republic*.

Once the political States are abolished, and the old system of organizing society by means of authority from the top down is accordingly rendered forever impossible, how will the new society reorganize itself? Through the free federation of local associations into a vast international association: local associations no longer political as they now are, but economically productive as they will inevitably become as soon as they are delivered from all political tutelage.

Well, the Austrian workers are now in such a position that they must inevitably take this path, unless they renounce all hope of improving their lot. Indeed, to unite all nations of the Austrian Empire under the same banner, don't the Austrian workers have to recognize that all these nations have the same rights? To do that, they have to put an end to the monarchy in Austria. They have to destroy the empire.

And once this empire is destroyed, nothing will prevent the workers' associations of every other country in Europe, once they are emancipated, from joining the association of Austrian workers—which already includes so many different nationalities, forming the nucleus of a vast international organization—and establishing the worldwide association together with it.

These are the reasons we greet the splendid progress of the socialist-democratic party in Austria with deep joy.

17

Panslavism

Panslavism is the order of the day in our official and semiofficial world. It is the dominant idea of the present reign. Having emancipated our peasants, as we know, having given us freedom and happiness, our generous benefactor Tsar Alexander II now thinks only of the deliverance of the Slav peoples, our brothers, who groan under the yoke of the Germans and the Turks.

No one speaks anymore of anything else at the court of St. Petersburg, or in the lofty spheres of the army and the bureaucracy. The salons of St. Petersburg and Moscow offer, at this moment, a spectacle as amusing as it is instructive. Great ladies who ordinarily speak only French and who disdain Russian because it is the language of our peasants, thoroughbred Germans who serve the emperor, men of State, generals, officers and civil functionaries who have only two ideas in their head and two feelings in their heart—first to please the emperor and second to make their fortune and career—all of them are now dying out of their love for our unhappy brothers, the Slav peoples. A well-organized empire has marvelous discipline! The master orders, and immediately everyone is animated by suitable ideas and intentions.

We had a memorable example of this magical production of feelings on command during and after the Slav Congress held in Moscow in 1867,[88] when with the permission of their master—or, more truthfully still, following an order which they had received from their master—the Emperor of Russia's valets, whom he has given titles of one sort or another, offered their generous hospitality to the Slav subjects of the Emperor of Austria and of the Sultan of Turkey. The program of feelings, conforming to the political situation and officially imposed, was worked out at the Ministry of Foreign Affairs, as we know, with great care. Once the roles were distributed, each one learned his own by heart, reciting it so naturally and so seemingly freely that our Slav guests, who asked no better than to let themselves be fooled, were carried away by it all.

This was high comedy, where every spectator was simultaneously an author. Naturally, a good number of simpletons took their roles seriously, believing in good faith that Slav emancipation was what it was all about. They wasted their congratulations and their tears of sincere joy, while liars gave them the Judas kiss.

This congress was a true saturnalia of slaves, an orgy of mutual hypocrisy and official lies. On the part of all its Russian members it was an act of cynicism, and on the part of the Slav members it was one of cowardice. For the introduction to and the basis of this congress was: the massacre of a great Slav nation, Poland; the subjugation of another Slav nation, Little Russia [i.e., Ukraine]; and finally the *de facto* slavery which—under the name of emancipation—still oppresses a third great Slav people, the people of Great Russia.

And it was in the name of the Tsar who organized all these massacres—the cause of this slavery as well as its ultimate aim—that the Slavophile Russians promised resurrection and deliverance, and that the Slav delegates announced such to their fellow-citizens! Our Russian Slavophiles, mostly functionaries or semiofficial agents of the empire and fools only in some small part, clearly acted in the interest of the empire. But the Slav delegates, the Riegers, the Palackýs, the Brauners: in whose interest did they seek to defraud their peoples?[89]

We do not hesitate to speak of fraud, for the eminent men whom we have just named are too intelligent, too aware, too practical, and too clever to be fooled themselves. They know better than anyone what the Empire of Russia is and what the Slav peoples can expect from it.

They see very clearly how this boa constrictor strives to crush in its vast entrails the last vestiges of nationality among the Slav and non-Slav peoples it has devoured. Consummate experts in the history of the Slav peoples, they know that nothing until now has been as disastrous for those peoples as the protection of the government of St. Petersburg, which, having ceased fomenting unrest among them, has never failed to betray them, defenseless, to their vengeful Turk and German oppressors. Finally, they are political men too perspicacious and too well-informed not to know that at this very hour, when an innumerable throng of this government's agents is running around all the Slav countries of Austria and Turkey, preaching holy war in the name of the Liberator-Tsar and announcing to everyone that the hour of common deliverance is near at hand, that at this very hour, Russian diplomacy—too wise to dream of conquering all the Slav countries at the same time, which would be impossible—is already preparing the elements of a new partition, in which it will ask only the concession to Austria, at least temporarily, of Turkish Serbia, Montenegro, and perhaps even Bosnia, so long as it is itself allowed to grab all of Romania and to create the quasi-independent viceroyalty of the Bulgarians, under the high and very liberal protection of the Emperor of Russia, with a prince of the house of Romanovs.

Moreover, Messrs. Palacký, Rieger, Brauner & Co. can also not be unaware that there has long existed an entente between the courts of St. Petersburg and Berlin, according to which—in the event that the united arms of Prussia and Russia triumph over the Austro-French coalition—Russia will seize Galicia while the kingdom of Prussia, transformed into the Empire of Germany, will lay its hands on Bohemia, Moravia, and a large part of Silesia.

They know all this and they have always known it. Why then did they go to Moscow? Why are they defrauding their peoples by portraying Emperor Alexander II as the future liberator of the Slav world?

This is a question that the Slav patriots must resolve themselves. We are content to pose it. Permit us, however, to give them counsel: that all Slav peoples—sorely tried by experience and acquainted above all with the example of unhappy Poland—who today feel oppressed might follow the example of the Bulgarians today, who seek their emancipation and well-being in revolution, in the revolutionary solidarity of all peoples, Slav and non-Slav, and never in reaction, nor ever in schemes of diplomacy, and never above all in the dissolving, corrupting, and fraudulent protection of the Emperors of All the Russias.

Notes

Introduction

1. Bakunin's connection with Nechaev is therefore not directly addressed here, although it is contemporaneous with this period; but Bakunin himself kept that connection separate from his other activities. The Bibliographies in this volume may guide the interested reader to English-language and other materials on this matter and on other matters.

2. Of the items not appearing in these two newspapers, one was published in a workers' almanac in French Switzerland, one is from another newspaper, and one was given as a series of lectures in a public hall. Full information on sources may be found in the Comment on Texts and Translation.

3. Isaiah Berlin, "Herzen and Bakunin on Individual Liberty," in Joint Committee on Slavic Studies [of the ACLS and SSRC], *Continuity and Change in Russian and Soviet Thought,* ed. with introd. by Ernest J. Simmons (Cambridge: Harvard University Press, 1955), p. 473; Amédée Dunois, "Michel Bakounine," *Portraits d'hier,* no. 6 (1 June 1909): 146.

4. Cited by Carlo Cafiero and Elisée Reclus, "Editor's Preface" [sic], in Bakunin, *God and the State* (Boston, Mass.: B. R. Tucker, 1883), p. 4. An acquaintance of Bakunin's from this period has left a description of his "bizarre method of writing, which was itself a function of his complete lack of order":

> [Bakunin] usually began with a letter to one of his neophytes; little by little the letter became as long as an article for a review, which article then took on the dimensions of a pamphlet. Sometimes, even in this context, his vagabond thought was unable to find a home, and a rather thick tome emerged. The first pages would have been long ago set in type and corrected when, upon finishing the manuscript, he would say that there was no money to publish it; the printers' proofs were arranged on shelves, awaiting more favorable circumstances. Another time, a subsidiary question came to his mind while he was in the middle of writing; Bakunin then abandoned what he had begun and concerned himself to develop the issue. What was left unfinished or unpublished was certainly not lost; Bakunin drew liberally on his archives and used old writings for new literary enterprises. Moreover, this was facilitated by the fact that all his cogitations, whatever he wrote, came back to a single thought: the worldwide revolution had to be set off and collectivist anarchism installed. His phraseology, a direct heir to Hegel, easily adapted itself to the most diverse subjects.
>
> . . . He announced to me in one of his letters that he proposed to write a pamphlet polemicizing against me; but to publish it he needed 300 francs, which he asked me to lend him. This insolent manner of borrowing money from an adversary in order to assail him seemed so original to me that I sent it to him. But this brochure too failed to see the light of day; the money, apparently, was necessary for other "needs" of the propaganda.

G. N. Vyrubov, "Revoliutsionnyia vospominaniia" [Revolutionary Reminiscences], *Viestnik Evropy,* 48 (February 1913): 56–57.

5. A chronological table of Bakunin's life may be found in the list of Milestones, based on

and expanded from N. M. Pirumova, *Bakunin* (Moscow: Molodaia gvardiia, 1970), pp. 394-96.

6. E. H. Carr, *Michael Bakunin* (New York: Random House, Vintage Books, 1961), p. 20.

7. M. A. Bakunin, *Sobranie sochinenii i pisem* [Collection of Works and Letters], ed. by Iu. M. Steklov, 4 vols. (Moscow: Izdatel'stvo vsesoiuznogo obshchestva politkatorzhan i ssyl'no-poselentsev, 1934-36), I, 328-29; translated in Arthur Lehning (ed.), *Michael Bakunin: Selected Writings* (London: Jonathan Cape, 1973), pp. 34-35.

8. Bakunin, *Sobranie sochinenii i pisem*, II, 70.

9. The two articles are reprinted together in ibid., II, 317-85.

10. "Reaction in Germany," in Lehning (ed.), *Michael Bakunin: Selected Writings*, p. 49.

11. Ibid., p. 48.

12. Ibid., p. 36.

13. Ibid., pp. 49-50.

14. Hence Bakunin's opposition, at the Basle Congress (1869) of the International, to the notion of "direct legislation," which is now a commonplace known as the referendum.

15. Frederick Engels, "Origin of the Family, Private Property and the State," in Karl Marx and Frederick Engels, *Selected Works in One Volume* (New York: International Publishers, 1968), p. 514.

16. Engels, "Apropos of Working-Class Political Action," in ibid., p. 314.

17. Bakunin, "Vsesvetnyi Revoliutsionnyi Soiuz Sotsial'noi Demokratii" [World Revolutionary Union of Social Democracy], in *Archives Bakounine*, 8 vols. in 9 by 1984 (Leiden: E. J. Brill, 1961-), V, 100. This translation is based on the one found in G. P. Maximoff (comp. and ed.), *The Political Philosophy of Bakunin* (Glencoe, Ill.: The Free Press of Glencoe, 1953), p. 384, but is greatly modified from this.

18. Bakunin, "Aux Frères de l'A[lliance] en Espagne," cited in Max Nettlau, *Michael Bakunin: Eine Biographie* (London: By the Author, 1896-1900), p. 288.

19. Bakunin, "Programma obshchestva mezhdunarodnoi revoliutsii (okonchanie)" [Program of the World Revolutionary Alliance (Conclusion)], *Anarkhicheskii vestnik*, no. 7 (May 1924): 40. The first part of this document is in nos. 5-6 (November-December 1923): 37-41.

20. Marx, "On the Jewish Question," in Loyd D. Easton and Kurt H. Guddat (trans. and eds.), *Writings of the Young Marx on Philosophy and Society* (Garden City, N.Y.: Doubleday, Anchor Books, 1967), p. 231.

21. Marx and Engels, *The German Ideology* (London: Lawrence & Wishart, 1965), pp. 45, 78.

22. Marx, "Private Property and Communism," in Easton and Guddat (eds.), *Writings of the Young Marx*, p. 304.

23. Marx, "Critique of Hegel's Philosophy of the State," in ibid., pp. 173-75.

24. Bakunin, "Reaction in Germany," in Lehning (ed.), *Michael Bakunin: Selected Writings*, p. 39.

25. *La Réforme* (Paris), 27 January 1845.

26. Ibid.

27. M. Bakounine, *17e anniversaire de la révolution polonaise* (Paris: Bureau des Affaires polonaises, 1847), p. 1.

28. Ibid., pp. 13-14; this translation is taken from Carr, *Michael Bakunin*, p. 150, and checked against the original. Samuel Dolgoff (ed.), *Bakunin on Anarchy* (New York: Random House, 1972), p. 60, for some reason renders the last word as "Russia."

29. Bakunin, *Sobranie sochinenii i pisem*, IV, 140; this translation is slightly revised from Lawrence D. Orton (ed.), *The "Confession" of Mikhail Bakunin*, trans. by Robert C. Howes (Ithaca, N.Y.: Cornell University Press, 1977), p. 76.

30. Engels, "Democratic Panslavism," in Marx and Engels, *Collected Works*, 13 vols. by 1984 (London: Lawrence & Wishart, 1975-), VIII, 366-67.

31. Ibid., p. 369.

32. Marx and Engels, "The Communist Manifesto," in *Selected Works in One Volume*, pp. 35-36.

33. Marx and Engels, "The Eighteenth Brumaire of Louis Bonaparte," in ibid., p. 175.

34. Marx, "Critique of the Gotha Program," in ibid., p. 330.

35. Bakunin, "Lettre à *La Liberté*," in *Archives Bakounine*, II, 161; translation slightly revised from Lehning (ed.), *Michael Bakunin: Selected Writings*, pp. 253-54.

36. Bakunin, "Lettre à Celso Ceretti," in *Archives Bakounine*, I, pt. 2, 245.

37. Marx, "Le Conseil général au Comité central de l'Alliance internationale de la Démocratie socialiste," in *Archives Bakounine*, II, 275. An English translation of the full text may be found in Institute of Marxism-Leninism, *The General Council of the First International: 1868-1870* (Moscow: Progress Publishers, n.d.), pp. 379-83.

38. Bakunin, "Lettre à *La Liberté*," in *Archives Bakounine*, II, 161.

39. Marx and Engels, "The Communist Manifesto," in *Selected Works in One Volume*, p. 53.

40. Bakunin, "L'Empire knouto-germanique et la Révolution sociale," in *Œuvres*, 6 vols. (Paris: P. V. Stock, 1895-1913), II, 327.

41. M. Bakunin, *Narodnoe dielo: Romanov, Pugachev, ili Pestel?* [The People's Cause: Romanov, Pugachov, or Pestel?] (London: Trübner & Co., 1862), reprinted in M. P. Dragomanov [Drahomaniv] (ed.), *Pis'ma M. A. Bakunina k A. I. Gertsenu i N. P. Ogarevu* [Letters of M. A. Bakunin to A. I. Herzen and N. P. Ogaryov] (Geneva: Ukrainskaia tipografiia, 1896), pp. 396-418.

42. M. A. Bakounine, *A mes amis russes et polonais* (Leipzig: Wolfgang Gerhard, 1862).

43. Not to be confused with the "Catechism of the Revolutionary" that was found in Nechaev's possession. An English translation of the "Revolutionary Catechism," abridged, may be found in Dolgoff (ed.), *Bakunin on Anarchy*, pp. 76-97.

44. This brochure was set in type in 1867, and printers' proofs were corrected; however, it was not published until after Bakunin's death. It may be found in *Œuvres*, I, 1-206. The principal passages are translated into English in Lehning (ed.), *Michael Bakunin: Selected Writings*, pp. 94-110.

45. Translation taken from Carr, *Michael Bakunin*, p. 356. This passage does not correspond exactly with the minutes of the Congress in *Bulletin sténographique du deuxième Congrès de la Paix et de la Liberté* (Berne), no. 2 (23 September 1868): 119, probably because Carr's source uses a Russian translation of a separately published French edition of the speech, which Bakunin would have had the opportunity to emend. The changes do not affect the substance of Bakunin's speech, constituting mainly clarification and elaboration of the ideas expressed.

46. See Bakunin, "Kuda idti i chto delat'?" [Where Are We to Go and What Is to be Done?], in *Archives Bakounine*, III, 187-200.

47. Bakunin, "[Lettre] à Pablo," cited in Nettlau, *Michael Bakunin: Eine Biographie*, p. 284. Emphasis in the original.

48. Bakunin, "Reaction in Germany," in Lehning (ed.), in *Michael Bakunin: Selected Writings*, p. 43.

49. Ibid., p. 40.

50. Bakunin, *Sobranie sochinenii i pisem*, IV, 153. This translation is based on Orton (ed.), *The "Confession" of Mikhail Bakunin*, p. 91, but is revised against the original text. The most significant change is to render *vlast'* as "power" rather than "government." In the paragraph preceding the one cited, Bakunin did use the word *napravlenie*, which does mean "government," and the context of that usage led the original Russian editor to infer that Bakunin was repeating a question which the Tsar had given him on a list to answer (*Sobranie sochinenii i pisem*, IV, 152, 475, n. 142). Orton duly notes that inference in his own edition (p. 172, n. 79), and that is the only possible basis for retaining the English word "government" when Bakunin switches from *napravlenie* to *vlast'*; the very fact of the switch, however,

strongly suggests that Bakunin intended another meaning. The whole of his revolutionary activity and political philosophy argues against the use of the word "government" in this context.

51. Bakunin, "Pis'mo k Sergeiu Nechaevu" [Letter to Sergei Nechaev], in *Archives Bakounine*, IV, 118-19; translation taken from Lehning (ed.), *Michael Bakunin: Selected Writings,* pp. 191-92. Emphasis in the original.

52. The epithet is Max Nomad's.

53. Bakunin, "Appendice [à 'L'Empire knouto-germanique et la Révolution sociale']: Considérations philosophiques sur le Fantôme divin, sur le Monde réel et sur L'Homme," in *Œuvres,* III, 219, 234.

54. Ibid., p. 235.

Comment on Texts and Translation

1. Alexander Fraser Tytler, Lord Woodhouselee, *Essay on the Principles of Translation* (London: Dent, 1791).

2. B. Nikolajewsky, "M. A. Bakunin in der 'Dresdner Zeitung'," *International Review for Social History*, 1 (1936): 185-92.

3. Dysgloss: a neologism that I may propose for general adoption, as no word in English now has the requisite sense—the prefix meaning "abnormal" and the root meaning "language," from the Greek.

4. Jean Dubois, *Le vocabulaire politique et social en France de 1869 à 1872* (Paris: Larousse, [1962]).

The Basic Bakunin

1. In late October 1870, Bakunin wrote: "However much I try to convince myself to the contrary, I believe that France is lost, betrayed to the Prussians by the incapacity, the cowardice, and the cupidity of the bourgeoisie. The militarism and the bureaucracy, the aristocratic arrogance and the Protestant Jesuitry of the Prussians, in affectionate alliance with the knout of my dear sovereign lord and master the Emperor of All the Russias, will triumph over the Continent of Europe for I know not how many decades. Goodbye to all our dreams of approaching liberation." Thus the Knouto-Germanic Empire. (Cited in James Guillaume, *L'Internationale: documents et souvenirs*, 4 vols. [Paris: Société nouvelle de librairie et d'édition, 1905-10], II, 112; translation taken from E.H. Carr, *Michael Bakunin* [New York: Random House, Vintage Books, 1961], p. 424.) Between November 1870 and February 1871 Bakunin composed, and in April 1871 he published, the pamphlet *L'Empire knouto-germanique et la Révolution sociale* (Geneva: Imprimerie coopérative, 1871), in which he expanded on this theme; only fragments have appeared in English, in G. P. Maximoff (comp. and ed.), *The Political Philosophy of Bakunin* (Glencoe, Ill.: The Free Press of Glencoe, 1953), pp. 220-22, 259-60, 281-82, 368, 388-89, 392-93, 404-8.

Other parts of the manuscript gained greater notoriety after Bakunin's death. The title page of the 1871 publication had added: "Part I"; from Part II, written in February-March 1871, was drawn the famous "God and the State," not to be confused with another fragment of this same manuscript, composed in April-May 1871, published by Nettlau under the title "Dieu et l'Etat" in *Œuvres*, 6 vols. (Paris: P.V. Stock, 1895-1913), I, 261-335, and translated in part in Arthur Lehning (ed.), *Michael Bakunin: Selected Writings* (London: Jonathan Cape, 1973), pp. 139-52. The "Preface to Part II," which Bakunin wrote in June 1871, is none other than "The Paris Commune and the Idea of the State," which is translated integrally in ibid., pp. 195-213.

More information on this history of the manuscript, and on its still more numerous fragments may be found in Paul Avrich, "Introduction to the Dover Edition," in Bakunin, *God and the State* (New York: Dover, 1970), pp. viii-xii. Since Avrich wrote, the fragment called "An Essay against Marx" has been partially translated in Lehning (ed.), *Michael Bakunin: Selected Writings*, pp. 263-66. The entire manuscript, with many variants appearing for the first time, has been published as vol. VII of the *Archives Bakounine*. Arthur Lehning's "Introduction" to this volume is the definitive history of the work's composition.

2. More literally but less alliteratively: "War on the castles and peace to the hovels!" (In the German: Friede den Hütten, Krieg den Palasten!) In *The Peasant War in Germany*, Engels opined that this popular movement was not progressive because it opposed the historically necessary centralization of Germany; to Bakunin, however, so widespread a popular revolt could not be in the wrong.

3. The phrase is the title of a folksong with the refrain: "Do not speak of liberty, poverty is slavery." Pierre Lachambeaudie, *Fables*, 10th ed. (Paris: Pagnerre, 1852), pp. 188-89.

4. Cf. *Œuvres*, I, 41: "... whereas socialism seeks to found a *republic of men*, [pure republicanism, "the darling of the Robespierres and Saint-Justs"] seeks only a *republic of citizens*, even if—as in the constitutions which came as a necessary sequel to that of 1793, from the moment when, after a brief hesitation, [pure republicanism] came to the point of deliberately ignoring the social question—even if the *active citizens*, to use an expression of the Constituent Assembly, must base their civic privilege on exploiting the labor of the *passive citizens*." (Translation taken from Lehning [ed.], *Michael Bakunin: Selected Writings*, pp. 100-101; emphases in the original.) Those who characterize Bakunin as a Jacobin tend erroneously to discount such sentiments as these, which are found throughout his writings.

5. The book Bakunin refers to is: Ph. Buonarroti, *Conspiration pour l'égalité dite de Babeuf, suivie du procès auquel elle donna lieu, des pièces justificatives, etc., etc.*, 2 vols. (Brussels: Librairie romantique, 1828). The only English translation of this work appeared in 1836, but Babeuf's speech to the court that condemned him is more widely available: *The Defense of Gracchus Babeuf before the High Court of Vendôme*, ed. and trans. by John Anthony Scott (New York: Schocken Books, 1972).

6. Bakunin refers to his fourth speech at the Berne Congess (1868) of the League of Peace and Freedom, which is a rare item and has not been translated into English: *Bulletin sténographique du deuxième Congrès de la Paix et de la Liberté*, no. 4 (25 September 1868): **214–39. See, however, "On Russia" and "A Few Words to My Young Brothers in Russia" in this volume.**

7. "... les gros capitaux doivent nécessairement écraser les petits capitaux, les gros bourgeois doivent ruiner les petits bourgeois." The grande, moyenne, and petite bourgeoisies were capitalists of varying wealth; Bakunin "invented" the *gros capitaux* and *gros bourgeois* (on the construction of *gros capitalistes*, which locution was current in Lyons near the end of 1870 when he was there) in order to play on the double meaning of *petits bourgeois*. See the lexicographical study by Jean Dubois, *Le vocabulaire politique et social en France de 1869 à 1872* (Paris: Larousse, [1962]), esp. pp. 48-49, 110-11, 229-31, 236-39.

The haute (also vieille or ancienne) bourgeoisie were aristocrats, probably descended from the noblesse de robe. Because all these terms have specific and interdependent connotations, they are as a rule kept in the translations here, rather than replaced with others less definite (such as "upper middle-class," which would not only confound the haute and grande bourgeoisies but also be anachronistic).

8. In 1911 Guillaume commented: "Things have greatly changed in the St.-Imier Valley since 1871. The watchmaking industry has entered large-scale production; most workers who make watches now labor in factories, and their salaries have greatly diminished." *Œuvres*, V, 325, n. 1.

9. The anonymously printed *Lettres à un Français sur la crise actuelle, septembre 1870* [Neuchâtel: Imprimerie G. Guillaume fils, 1870], reprinted in *Archives Bakounine*, VI, 106-

31, were the result of Guillaume's extensive editing of a Bakunin manuscript composed in Lyons under the title "Lettre à un Français" (see ibid., VI, 3-103). The original manuscript has been fairly widely but only fragmentarily translated into English: see Lehning (ed.), *Michael Bakunin: Selected Writings*, pp. 232-35; Maximoff (ed.), *Political Philosophy of Bakunin*, pp. 174-75, 203-4, 370-72, 373, 389-92, 393-97, 397-403, 405, 406-7, 408, 410-11; and Sam Dolgoff (ed.), *Bakunin on Anarchy* (New York: Random House, 1971), pp. 183-217, despite the plural title "Letters."

10. Bakunin participated in the aborted Lyons insurrection.

11. Following the transcription in *Archives Bakounine*, VI, 245 ("Ceignons nos reins..."); Michel Bakounine, *De la guerre à la Commune*, ed. F. Rude (Paris: Editions anthropos, 1972), p. 404, gives "serrons nos reins," which it rectifies to "serrons nos rangs" (respectively: let us close our loins, let us close our ranks), but the manuscript is ambiguous. Paris, Bibliothèque nationale, Salle des manuscrits, Nouvelles acquisitions françaises, folio 23690, p. 446.

12. Held in Berne in 1868. After this vote by the Congress Bakunin, who had been a member of the League's Central Committee, withdrew from the League with his associates and founded the International Alliance of Socialist Democracy.

The "Program of the Alliance," which Bakunin wrote upon his withdrawal from the League, is so concise a statement of his anarchist principles and objectives, that it is worth reproducing here. This translation is taken from Lehning (ed.), *Michael Bakunin: Selected Writings*, pp. 174-75:

> 1. The *Alliance* stands for atheism, the abolition of cults and the replacement of faith by science and divine by human justice.
>
> 2. Above all, it stands for the final and total abolition of classes and the political, economic and social equalization of individuals of either sex, and, to this end, it demands above all the abolition of the right of inheritance, so that every man's possessions may in future be commensurate to his output, and so that in pursuance of the decision reached by the last working men's Congress in Brussels, the land, the instruments of work and all other capital may become the collective property of the whole of society and be utilized only by the workers, in other words by the agricultural and industrial associations. [See note 33 below.]
>
> 3. It stands for equality of the means of development for all children of both sexes from the cradle onward—maintenance, upbringing and education to all levels of science, industry and the arts—being convinced that while at first the effect of equality will be only economic and social it will increasingly lead to greater natural equality among individuals by eliminating all artificial inequalities, the historic products of a false, iniquitous social system.
>
> 4. Hostile to all despotism, acknowledging no political form other than the republican form, and totally rejecting any alliance with reaction, it also repudiates all political action whose target is anything except the triumph of the workers' cause over Capital.
>
> 5. It recognizes that all the political and authoritarian States of today must scale down their functions to the simple administration of the public services in their respective lands and merge into the universal union of free Associations, both agricultural and industrial.
>
> 6. The concrete, final solution to the social question can only be realized on the basis of international workers' solidarity, and the *Alliance* repudiates any policy based on so-called patriotism and national rivalry.
>
> 7. It stands for the universal Association of all local associations, through Liberty.

13. From the League's untitled circular of 14 May 1869. Bakunin does not mention that the contributions being solicited were to have been redeemable for shares in a company

"which we are organizing to assure the appearance of the newspaper *Les Etats-Unis d'Europe*."

14. A Berlin newspaper, founded by Johann Jacoby in 1867 and closely allied to the Volkspartei, which Bakunin once called the "principal organ of Prussian democracy." See Guillaume, *L'Internationale*, I, 51, n. 1, and 212.

15. "Après nous, le déluge!"—a remark attributed to Jeanne, Marquise de Pompadour (1721-1764), mistress of Louis XV, toward the end of her life.

16. Bakunin elsewhere expresses the principle of authority thus: "With God . . . humanity is divided into men greatly inspired, less inspired, and uninspired. . . . The greatly inspired *must* be listened to by the less inspired, and the less inspired by the uninspired. Thus we have the principle of authority well established and with it the two fundamental institutions of slavery: Church and State." *God and the State*, p. 53, translation modified slightly according to the original text in *Œuvres*, III, 86; emphasis in the original. Cf. P.-J. Proudhon, *General Idea of the Revolution in the Nineteenth Century* [Idée générale de la révolution au XIXe siècle, 1851], trans. by John Beverley Robinson (London: Freedom Press, 1923), Fourth Study.

17. The International Students' Congress, held from 29 October through 1 November 1865, and attended by over a thousand persons. Bakunin met a number of them later in the decade, in Geneva and through the League of Peace and Freedom. For more, see *Archives Bakounine*, IV, 454, nn. 55-57.

18. Bakunin heard of this while in the United States (perhaps from Charles Sumner), or while he was travelling to or from the United States, after his escape from Siberia and on his way to London.

19. Cf. P.-J. Proudhon, *What Is Property? An Inquiry into the Principle of Right and of Government* [Qu'est-ce que la propriété? ou Recherches sur le principe du droit et du gouvernement, 1840], trans. by Benj. R. Tucker (New York: Humboldt, [ca. 1890]; reprint ed. [with a new Introduction by George Woodcock], New York: Dover, 1970), First Memoir, chap. III, sec. 7, esp. p. 146: ". . . an artist's talent may be infinite, but its mercenary claims are necessarily limited . . ."

20. This is an idea with which Mao, in a different social and political context, had the opportunity to experiment. A brief description in English is provided by Rennselaer W. Lee, "The *Hsia Fang* System: Marxism and Modernization," *China Quarterly*, no. 28 (October-December 1966): 40-62.

21. "L'hypocrisie est un hommage que le vice rend à la vertu"—aphorism no. 218 in the *Réflexions ou sentences maximes* of François, duc de la Rouchefoucauld.

22. Syrian god of riches, whose name was often used to refer to great unearned wealth.

23. The brief first installment of this series may have been written jointly by Bakunin and Charles Perron (1837-1909), the principal editor of *L'Égalité* whom Bakunin replaced for several months in the summer of 1869.

24. The agendum was, "How should the International's goal be realized?" Resolutions repudiating *La Montagne* and endorsing *L'Égalité* and *Le Progrès* were passed; the assembly was unanimous but for three votes. Coullery had used *La Montagne* to attack the resolutions of the IWMA's Brussels Congress (1868) on collective property. (See note 33.) He did not appear at the meeting on 30 May 1869 but declared the following day that, had he been there, he could easily have refuted his opponents' arguments; given this opportunity that very evening by his followers, who also invited Bakunin, Coullery stayed home. After his earlier bravado, this was taken as his acknowledgment of defeat. The series of articles on Coullery was catalyzed by his own attacks a month later, again printed in *La Montagne*, against the "aberrations" of the socialist-revolutionaries who had turned their backs on him. See also note 30.

25. On the front page.

26. The President of the League had, at Bakunin's behest, sent a letter to his counterpart in the International, inviting representatives of the latter to the League's Congress in Berne;

the International adopted a resolution declining the invitation. (See Guillaume, *L'Internationale*, I, 72, n. 1, and 67 for these documents and more information; see also the interesting commentary in the League's organ, *Les Etats-Unis d'Europe*, no. 38 [20 September 1868].)

27. After 1815 Neuchâtel was governed by aristocratic families loyal to the King of Prussia, even though it had become a Swiss canton. A workers' revolt, centered in Le Locle and La Chaux-de-Fonds, failed in 1831, but 1848 saw the proclamation of a republic, ending Prussian sovereignty and installing an elected Grand Conseil. A royalist attempt at counterrevolution was defeated in 1856.

28. Guillaume explains: "What is involved here is not, as one might think, those *privileges* which, to the detriment of the proletariat, make the aristocracy and bourgeoisie into privileged classes, but a simple detail of the Neuchâtel legislation on bankruptcy. Concerning this Coullery had written (*Voix de l'Avenir*, 26 May 1867), 'We ask the destruction of every privilege. We wish that, in case of bankruptcy, no creditor be privileged save the mortgagee, for this type of credit is a covenanted contract between the two parties.'" *Œuvres*, V, 93, n. 1.

29. Dupasquier had launched an attack on various European and American republics, culminating in the assertion that the Civil War in the United States had been waged for purposes of oppression. This statement drew remarks from the hall, including: "Let him go to the French Senate if he wants to insult a Republic!" Hector Varela, a Venezuelan minister, demanded the floor to refute "this calumny." See *Annales du Congrès de Genève, 9-12 septembre 1867* (Geneva: Vérésoff & Garrigues, 1868), pp. 259-63.

30. Guillaume explains: "This title alludes to one of Coullery's maneuvers. Having carefully avoided both being present at the 30 May [1869] meeting in Crêt-du-Locle and running into Bakunin the following day, Coullery, after a month's delay, had the idea of asking to be judged by the Chaux-de-Fonds section. In *La Montagne* he invited his 'accusers,' whom he did not name, to attend a meeting of that section on 5 July, so that the case might be decided between them and him. Naturally only the Coullery faithful attended the meeting, where they applauded their chief." In its 10 July 1869 issue, *Le Progrès* labelled the entire proceeding a ridiculous farce. *Œuvres*, V, 96-97, n. 2.

31. The Preamble is retranslated from the French. It had previously appeared in *L'Egalité* on 8 May 1869, reproduced from *Congrès ouvrier de l'Association internationale des Travailleurs tenu à Genève du 3 au 8 septembre 1866* (Geneva: Imprimerie J.-C. Ducommun et G. Œttinger, 1866), pp. 12-14, which text had been adopted by the IWMA at its 1866 Congress in Geneva. Here is the original English text as published in *Address and Provisional Rules of the Working Men's International Association, established September 28, 1864, at a public meeting held at St. Martin's Hall, Long Acre, London* ([London]: Printed at the "Bee-Hive" Newspaper office, 1864), which served as the basis for that French translation:

> That the emancipation of the working classes must be conquered by the working classes themselves; that the struggle for the emancipation of the working classes means not a struggle for class privilege and monopolies, but for equal rights and duties, and the abolition of all class rule;
>
> That the economical subjection of the man of labour to the monopolizer of the means of labour, that is the sources of life, lies at the bottom of servitude in all its forms, of all social misery, slavery, mental degradation, and political dependence;
>
> That the economic emancipation of the working classes is therefore the great end to which every political movement ought to be subordinated as a means;
>
> That all efforts aiming at that great end have hitherto failed from the want of solidarity between the manifold divisions of labour in each country, and from the absence of a fraternal bond of union between the working classes of different countries;
>
> That the emancipation of labour is neither a local, nor a national, but a social problem, embracing all countries in which modern society exists, and depending for its solution on the concurrence, practical and theoretical, of the most advanced countries;

That the present revival of the working classes in the most industrious countries of Europe, while it raises a new hope, gives solemn warning against a relapse into the old errors and calls for the immediate combination of the still disconnected movements.

32. A comparison of this sentence with the original in note 31 yields the observation of a discrepancy between the English and its French translation, in the omission in the latter of the words "as a means." This requires a comment, for the difference—which was not believed to be a serious one by those who noticed it at the time—became the subject of controversy after the London Conference (1871) of the International, where a resolution was passed suggesting that "unfaithful translations" of the IWMA's General Rules had given rise to "false interpretations."

The French translation published by the IWMA, *Association internationale des Travailleurs: Statuts et Règlements* (London: Imprimerie coopérative internationale, 1866), did translate "as a means" by *comme moyen*, following Longuet's version in *Manifeste de l'Association internationale des Travailleurs suivi du Règlement provisoire* (Brussels: Alliance typographique, M.-J. Poot et Cie., 1866), pp. 15-18. But the latter publication was hardly distributed outside Belgium, while the former was completely unknown in the French-speaking countries.

In February 1870, the French sections of the IWMA decided to reissue the General Rules, using the 1866 Geneva text as a basis. This new translation can be found in *Procès de l'Association de Travailleurs* (Paris: Par la Commission de propagande du Conseil fédéral de l'A.I.T., 1870), pp. 201-9. In it, "as a means" is rendered by *comme simple moyen*, passing into French and Swiss currency.

That the 1871 London resolution was actually part of Marx's campaign against Bakunin, and that no falsification or distortion was involved, is suggested by the fact that after the 1870 translation with *comme simple moyen* appeared, Bakunin cited it many times in his published explanations of the General Rules. One such instance, in fact, is found in this volume on pp.142-43, in a selection written in mid-1871.

The information on historical sources included in this note is drawn from *Archives Bakounine*, I, pt. 1, 313-16, n. 5, and pt. 2, 485, n. 369, which contain much more information and can be considered definitive on the issue.

33. The Brussels Congress (1868) of the International adopted a resolution on "Property in Land, Mines, Railroads, &c.," expressing the belief that "the economical development of modern society will create the social necessity of converting arable land into the common property of society," although it continued, "and of letting the soil on behalf of the State to agricultural companies" composed of "working men bound by contract to guarantee to society the rational and scientific [exploitation of the land] at a price as nearly as possible approximate to the working expense."

The resolution on "Credit Institutions for the Working Classes" began with the consideration that "interest and profit of every kind accruing to capital, whatever form it may assume, is a black mail levied upon the labour of to-day for the benefit of him whom the labour of yesterday has already enriched, and that if he has the right to accumulate, he has no right to do so at the expense of others," and concluded that "the foundation of banks of exchange, based upon cost price, [is] the means of rendering credit democratic and equal . . . "

The resolution on "Property in Land, Mines, Railroads, &c.," defined terms for the collective ownership of fixed capital, and that on "The Effects of Machinery in the Hands of the Capitalist Class" based such ownership on the "organization of mutual credit." International Working Men's Association, *Resolutions of the Congress of Geneva, 1866, and the Congress of Brussels, 1868* (London: Printed by the Westminster Printing Co., [1870]), pp. 10-13.

34. See *Archives Bakounine*, V, 510, n. 105.

35. Bakunin refers to Proudhon's participation in the debate over a motion in the Constituent Assembly. The motion called for opening a State credit of two million francs to

permit the definitive closure of the *ateliers nationaux*, which had provided employment for the jobless after the February 1848 revolution. The principle at issue was the right to work, for a key section of the motion read, "It is important that the intervention of the State conserve the character of benevolent assistance and that no payment be made as either salary or remuneration." Proudhon had introduced a counterproposal which guaranteed employment and which an official report severely criticized. The debate may be found in *Compte rendu des séances de l'Assemblée nationale* [*constituante de 1848-1849*] (Paris: H. & C. Noblet, 1849), II, 757-87; Proudhon's interventions are at 770-82, esp. 780-82; excerpts from his speeches were also published separately at the time, as a folio broadside.

The 17 May 1869 issue of *Le Progrès* published excerpts from this session (31 July 1848) of the Consituent Assembly, very possibly at Bakunin's suggestion, as he had been strongly impressed by Proudhon's position at the time itself; Bakunin without doubt had this issue in mind when, in a letter to Georg Herwegh written during the first half of August 1848, he called Proudhon "the only man in Paris, the only one in the politico-literary world, who still has any sense." It is also in this letter to Herwegh that Bakunin for the first time expresses his disillusionment with parliamentarism (repeated in his *Confession*; n.b., this letter antedates his experiences during the wave of insurrections across Central Europe in which he participated in 1849), and he concludes: "I believe neither in constitutions nor in laws; the best constitution possible would not satisfy me. We need nothing less than the bursting-out-into-life of a new world, lawless and therefore free." (But see Bakunin's distinction between man-made and natural law, p. 121 above.) M. A. Bakunin, *Sobranie sochinenii i pisem* [Collection of Works and Letters], ed. by Iu. M. Steklov, 4 vols. (Moscow: Izdatel'stvo vsesoiuznogo obshchestva politkatorzhan i ssyl'no-poselentsev, 1934–36), III, 317–18.

Bakunin erred in saying that Proudhon was alone in the Constituent Assembly; the motion to open the credit was passed by a vote of 691 to 2.

36. See notes 31-32.

37. See note 3.

38. The June Days comprised nearly a week of bitter street fighting in 1848 by the working poor and the unemployed of Paris, including probably some members of the *ateliers nationaux*. After General Cavaignac moved in with infantry and artillery, the defeat of the insurrection was only a matter of time, although the rebel quarters were conquered with difficulty, street by street and barricade by barricade. In simplest terms, the June Days were a revolt by the propertyless against the propertied. The sentiments of the latter, whether they were large or small property-owners, were uniform.

The December Days, in 1851, followed the *coup d'état* that abolished the republic and made Louis Napoleon, who had been its president, the Emperor Napoleon III. These Days were not as hard-fought and were over sooner than those in June 1848, for the Parisian masses did not participate as widely. It is said that deputies to the no longer existing Parliament, rather than workers, manned the barricades.

39. This letter was printed, in French translation, in *L'Égalité*, no. 27 (24 July 1869), pp. 1-2, having been borrowed from the Brussels newspaper *L'Internationale*, no. 27 (18 July 1869), pp. 1-2. It made the rounds of a number of newspapers adhering to the IWMA's cause after some bourgeois newspapers (including the *Journal de Genève*) reported the interesting case of a worker who killed himself and his family, without however mentioning his motivation. The key passage in the letter reads: "It is better to die this way that to wait for death to come to us with the slow tortures of poverty and hunger; however, we should perhaps succumb quickly, for we are hardly strong, Emma, the children and I. My wife and I love each other much; separation would be worse than death, and we adore our children. We adore them too much to give them over to poverty and to abandon them. My wife and I suffer now an indescribable agony."

40. An allusion to the then well-known observation of General de Failly concerning the Battle of Mentana (3 November 1867): "The chassepots worked wonders," chassepots being a new kind of rifle named for its inventor, Albert-Antoine Chassepot (1835-1903).

41. Briareus, a sea monster with fifty heads and a hundred hands, son of Uranus and Gaea in Roman mythology, revolted with his brothers against Jupiter. Although Jupiter defeated and enchained the rebels, consigning them to an abyss in the earth, he later called on them for help in his struggle with the Titans.

42. See *Herr Bastiat-Schulze von Delitzsch, der ökonomische Julian, oder Capital und Arbeit* (Berlin: C. Ihring Nachf., 1874).

43. See note 20.

44. Those whose supreme value is precious metal.

45. *The Essence of Christianity* [Das Wesen des Christenthums, 1841], trans. by George Eliot (New York: Harper and Row, 1957), p. 23.

46. It was Talleyrand (1754-1838) who said, in a speech to the Chambre des Pairs on 24 July 1821: "There is someone who has greater sense than Voltaire, Bonaparte, or any cabinet minister past, present, or yet to come—and that is everyman." This phrase does not appear in the *Procès-verbal des séances de la Chambre des Pairs*, however, but only in Talleyrand's speech separately printed: Chambre des Pairs de France, *Opinion de M. le Prince de Talleyrand sur le projet de loi relatif aux journaux et écrits périodiques* [Impression no. 96 de la] Session de 1820, Séance du mardi 24 juillet 1821 (Paris: P. Didot, 1821), pp. 11-12. At issue was an extension and intensification of press censorship; Talleyrand, avowing his desire for a "repressive law," opposed the proposed law as too harsh. It was nevertheless adopted.

47. Not the positivism of Auguste Comte (1798-1857), which Bakunin abhorred as a new religion legitimizing the hegemony of the licensed intellect, but rather scientific philosophy in general, based on observation and experiment. Bakunin read Comte's *Cours de philosophie positive* in December 1869-January 1870, and discussed it extensively in his "Considérations philosphiques sur le Fantôme divin, sur le Monde réel et sur l'Homme," which was planned as an appendix to *L'Empire knouto-germanique et la Révolution sociale* (see note 1) but was not published until 1908 (in *Œuvres*, III, 216-405).

48. See note 16.

49. See Lambert A. J. Quetelet, *A Treatise on Man and the Development of His Faculties* [Sur l'homme, et le développement de ses facultés, 1835] (Edinburgh: William and Robert Chambers, 1842; reprint ed. [with an Introduction by Solomon Diamond], Gainesville, Fla.: Scholars' Facsimiles & Reprints, 1969), p. 108, col. 2.

50. Bakunin uses the word *hierarchy* in its etymological sense, meaning "ecclesiastic government."

51. Bakunin misunderstands Tertullian, who, referring to the Resurrection, wrote, "Certum est quia impossibile est" (It is certain because it is impossible), often quoted as "Credo quia absurdum" (I believe [it] because [it is] absurd). See his *De carne Christi*, chap. 5.

52. The resolution is retranslated from Bakunin's French; all italics are his. The English text of the original resolution follows, according to International Working Men's Association, *Resolutions of the Congress of Geneva, 1866, and the Congress of Brussels, 1868,* p. 12: "Cognisant that it is impossible at present to organise a rational system of education, the Congress invites the different sections to establish courses of public lectures on scientific and economical subjects, and thus to remedy as much as possible the short comings of the education actually received by the working men. It is understood that the reduction of the hours of labour is an indispensable preliminary condition of any true system of education."

It should be noted, in order to avoid misunderstanding, that in this volume *éducation* has been translated as "upbringing," *enseignement* as "instruction," and *instruction* as "education."

53. In Greek mythology the Sirens were women whose voices lured sailors to their death as the latter's boats crashed against the rocky shores of the island inhabited by the former.

54. This report was adopted at the General Assembly of the Geneva Sections of the International, probably held 21 August 1869, and it was presented in their name a few weeks later at the Basle Congress of the IWMA.

55. No such committee was formed; but see "All-Round Education" in this volume.

56. Bakunin begins by refuting the previous speaker, Tolain, who had stated, "I do not think we have the right to take a decision on the collectivity of land in the absence of representatives of agriculture."

There are some differences between the record of Bakunin's speeches as published in the minutes of the Congress by the International and in *L'Égalité*. Although the differences for the most part are not major, involving phraseology and emphasis, it is the latter transcript which is used as the basis of this translation, for that transcript was provided by Bakunin himself. Cf. Jacques Freymond (ed.), *La Première Internationale: Recueil des documents*, 4 vols. (Geneva: Droz, 1962-71), II, 67, 94-95.

57. See note 46.

58. The minority report, based in part on a report presented by the Brussels section of the IWMA, called for a new State to liquidate and reorganize existing society.

59. Bakunin based this summary on the French version printed in Paris in 1870; here it is retranslated from his own French. (See notes 31-32.) The concluding slogan, "No obligations without rights, no rights without obligations," appeared on the masthead of *L'Égalité*.

60. Bakunin refers to a proclamation which Gambetta had issued in early September 1870. Having entered Marseilles, Gambetta declared himself the bearer of "*the instructions and the orders* of those who have accepted the mission of delivering France from foreign [domination]" (emphasis in the original). Calling on the people to follow him in his crusade against the Prussians, Gambetta described the "great duties" which "the situation in Paris" imposed on the people in the provinces: "The first, for everyone, is not to let yourself be diverted by any preoccupation which is not war, the fight to the death; the second is, until peace comes, *to accept fraternally the command* of the republican power which has issued from necessity and from law." Cited in *Gambetta, 1869-1879* (Paris: Librairie Sandoz et Fischbacher, 1879), pp. 68-71; emphasis added.

61. The significance of the strikes lies in the fact of solidarity, previously undemonstrated, among the different trades, and in the support they received from the IWMA. The two strikes to which Bakunin refers, by stonecutters and bricklayers, broke out in mid-March 1869, over the failure of some employers to honor the pay scale agreed upon to resolve a previous strike. All the workers in the building trades sided with the strikers. Then on 20 March 1869, the typographers struck over their employers' refusal to accept new wage demands. Guillaume continues the story: "At this the Genevan bourgeoisie assumed a clearly provocative attitude. The 'golden youths' took up arms and looked for run-ins with the workers, stopping strikers [in the street]; a large bourgeois assembly (31 March [1869]) addressed an appeal to the government, inviting it to make the 'freedom to work' respected, and denouncing the International, which 'throws the canton of Geneva into ruins with decrees sent from London and Paris.' " Bakunin, believing that streetfighting would destroy the strikers' organization and possibly hurt the International, then collaborated with Charles Perron (the erstwhile editor of *L'Egalité*) to write this article. *Œuvres*, V, 37, n. 1.

62. It was actually the police who made the arrest after the "golden youths" had induced them to break up meetings in which strikers were explaining their situation to unwitting strikebreakers from out of town. *L'Égalité*, no. 11 (1 April 1869).

63. The members of the Parisian sections of the International made a similar declaration a year later, when the arrest of "all individuals who direct the International" was ordered in the French capital. On 2 May 1870, the International's Federal Council of Paris published a protest which read in part: "It is untrue that the International was involved in this new conspiracy, which is doubtless no more real than any similar invention we have heard before.... So long as all exploters, capitalists, priests, and political adventurers have not disappeared, the International Working-Men's Association, a permanent conspiracy of all the oppressed and exploited, will [continue to] exist, despite the powerless persecution against its supposed chiefs." Cited in *Œuvres* V, 44, n. 1.

64. A Brussels newspaper, from the 27 March 1869 issue of which *L'Egalité* reprinted an article commemorating the bloody repression of strikes and then of riots resulting therefrom.

The principal passages of the *L'Internationale* article are reprinted in *Œuvres*, V, 48-49, n. 2. Here are the most significant excerpts:

> Be patient, workers, be patient. A day will come, if you desire it, when today's slaves will be the masters; but for that you must know how to contain your legitimate anger until all workers act in concert for their common deliverance.
>
> Don't let those who tell you such a day will never come, discourage you; if you desire it, it will come; it will come, and you will be astonished at ever having doubted it.
>
> It will come, the day of justice, and at its coming everyone will salute, saying, "How could we have been so long in the darkness?"
>
> Dawn is already breaking; its first rays are already beginning to pierce the darkness; have courage, friends, the great day is near.

65. During a session of the National Assembly held late into the night of 4 August 1789, the French nobility approved a decree in which they renounced their remaining feudal rights.

66. It is possible that this article was written jointly by Bakunin and Charles Perron.

67. There is no authoritative English version of this resolution. It is interesting, however, to note the addendum proposed by Eccarius, which also carried: "The supposed danger of an inferior rank of working men within the working class, resulting from the efforts of working men's associations, will vanish in the same degree as the development of modern industry renders production on a small scale more and more impossible." See *The Times* (London), 10 September 1867, p. 8. The unnamed correspondent of the newspaper is in fact Eccarius. He was clearly somewhat dissatisfied with the outcome of the proceedings: "I wonder whether those voluble Frenchmen have any idea of making themselves ridiculous in the eyes of the practical people. . . . " The original French resolutions, a series of which those cited here are only a part, may be found in the minutes of the Congress, reproduced in Freymond (ed.), *La Première Internationale*, I, 126-30, 201-9.

68. In using this phrase, Bakunin probably had in mind the Volkspartei and Arbeitervereine, which met respectively in Stuttgart and Nuremberg in September 1868 to endorse the program of the International. (Marx thereupon took these two organizations to be the exclusive representatives of the German proletariat.) The Stuttgart and Nuremberg Congresses both sent delegates to the Berne Congress (1868) of the League of Peace and Freedom, where they voted *with the majority* against the proposals motivated by Bakunin and the collectivist minority. Guillaume, *L'Internationale*, I, 75, n. 1.

69. Guillaume summarizes this project: "The project in question, signed by 'A Group of Internationalists,' proposed the creation in Geneva of a cooperative society, which would have been attached to the central resistance fund that the Geneva sections of the International intended to establish. Each member of the Geneva sections would have been assessed thirty centimes each month, but only one-third of the total would have been turned over to the resistance fund. The other two-thirds would have been put at the disposal of the cooperative. This cooperative would have started with about 650,000 francs and made a net profit of four percent, or 26,000 francs, of which half would have been turned over to the resistance fund . . . . In the case of a strike, aid would have been distributed partly in money, through the resistance fund itself, and partly in kind, through the account which the resistance fund would have at the cooperative . . . . In this way, the resistance and the cooperative became indissolubly linked, to the great advantage of both." *Œuvres*, V, 218, n. 1.

70. This passage is taken from the *Volksstimme*, no. 3 (3 May 1869), which later carried a summary of the assembly on 4 May, including the major speeches, which Bakunin translated in *L'Égalitié*, nos. 19, 21 (29 May, 12 June 1869). Also see note 83.

71. In particular, the legislative elections of 23-24 May 1869, in France, where many so-called "unreconciled" candidates were chosen.

72. The young revolutionary S. G. Nechaev (1847-1882) arrived in Belgium from Russia in March 1869; before the end of March he landed in Geneva and immediately entered into

relations with Bakunin. Guillaume writes of having received a letter from Bakunin, in which the latter expresses his excitement at Nechaev's arrival: "At this moment I am excessively preoccupied with what is happening in Russia. Our young people, perhaps the most revolutionary in the world, both in theory and in practice, are so restless that the government has been forced to close the universities, academies, and several schools in St. Petersburg, Moscow, and Kazan. I now have a specimen of these young fanatics who neither doubt nor fear anything, who have adopted the principle that, although many of them must perish under the hand of the government, they will not rest an instant until the people revolt. They are admirable, these young fanatics—believers without God and heroes without phrases." Cited in *Œuvres*, V, 53, n. 1.

73. For Proudhon, see his *Si les Traités de 1815 ont cessé d'exister? Actes du futur Congrès* (Paris: E. Dentu, 1863).

74. The program in question was written by Bakunin and first appeared in Geneva in the first issue (1 September 1868) of the Russian-language newspaper *Narodnoe delo*; it has not been translated into English. That newspaper was founded by Bakunin and an associate, but from the second issue on, it was controlled by N. I. Utin (1845-1883), a Russian member of the International who was extremely active in Marx's campaigns against Bakunin.

75. In St. Petersburg. They were the pretext for a series of judicial pursuits against various groups of students, on whom blame for the fires was, probably unjustly, placed.

76. In early 1870 came the end of the nine-year period following the abolition of serfdom, during which the Russian peasants were forbidden to oppose the repurchase, by their former masters, of the land they received through the 1861 decree that "emancipated" them.

77. According to Carr (*Michael Bakunin*, p. 128), Bakunin became a Freemason in 1845, though his activity in the lodge was negligible. In the mid-1860s, however, his interest revived (ibid., p. 303), and it is possible that this influenced the atheism—or "anti-theologism"—in Bakunin's anarchist thought. Probably he also regarded the Freemasons as a potential network for revolutionary activity, due to the group's clandestinity.

78. See note 5.

79. F. Rude, in *Le Socialisme libertaire* (Paris: Denoël, 1973), p. 50, n. 1, accuses Guillaume and Nettlau of falsification for having printed "Catholicism" for "Christianity" in the 1895 edition (*Œuvres*, I, 221); this is somewhat peculiar. It is no secret that Nettlau alone produced the first volume, whereas Guillaume did the rest over a decade later. More important, passages a few pages on—particularly one in which Bakunin calls the Roman Catholic Church the most perfect religion—give this accusation of false ring; Rude's suggestion that Bakunin's earlier editors were trying to play up to the Protestants makes little sense in view of the uncensored anti-Protestantism in "*La Montagne* and Mr. Coullery" (published in *Œuvres*, V), or in view of the Catholic preponderance among French-speakers.

80. P.-J. Proudhon, *La Fédération et l'unité en Italie* (Paris: E. Dentu, 1862), pp. 23-27, 37-39, 44-51, and esp. p. 33: "In Italy, unity is like Robespierre's indivisible republic, the cornerstone of despotism and bourgeois exploitation."

81. *Plus-que-parfait,* also the French name of verbal tense known as English as the past perfect or pluperfect; a play on the double meaning of "imperfect," a tense in French with no precise English equivalent, though the past progressive is closest.

82. See note 51.

83. This assembly had been convoked in order to address two questions, the right to coalition and the nationality question. On the first point, after hearing speakers who inveighed against the exploitation of workers in Austria, the assembly adopted a resolution inviting the Reichsrat (see note 84) to vote the full right to coalition, including international coalition, without delay. As for the nationality question, the following resolution was unanimously adopted: "Considering that the struggle of the nationalities in Austria inhibits the development of the Socialist-Democratic Party, the assembly declares that it is the workers' obligation to turn their back on the so-called nationalist parties; that it is everywhere their duty to shake off the yoke of the privileged classes, and to concentrate all their efforts on

the conquest of their rights, their liberty, and their equality, in both political and economic respects." See also note 70.

84. The Reichsrat was the name given to the bicameral Austrian parliament: membership of the first chamber, the Herrenhaus, was either hereditary or granted by the emperor; the members of the second, the Abgeordnetenhaus, were elected by provincial assemblies.

85. According to *Archives Bakounine*, I, pt. 1, 343-44, n. 142, this passage is the first instance where the solution to the national question that Bakunin proposes, is not to detach the Slav populations from Prussia and Austria but to accept that their economic history may serve as a context for the solution of national and social problems. It is also observed there that this view would conform with Proudhon's federalist ideas, which envisaged a fusion of races and languages, rejecting nationality as the political basis of an independent unitary entity.

86. See note 53.

87. The "manifesto" was probably simply a broadside containing the text of the two resolutions adopted by the public assembly of 4 May 1869. See note 83.

88. Bakunin refers to the Panslav Congress organized in Moscow by the Society for the Natural History of Anthropology and Ethnology, which complemented an exhibition on Slav ethnology.

89. In early 1872 Bakunin wrote that the Palacký-Rieger-Brauner triumvirate "are enemies more dangerous to [the Slav proletariat] than even the Germans themselves, precisely because they are indigenous oppressors and exploiters." "Aux compagnons de la Fédération des sections internationales du Jura," in *Archives Bakounine*, II, 17.

Biographical Glossary

ALEXANDER II (1818-1881). Emperor of All the Russias from 1855 to 1881. Known as the Liberator-Tsar for his emancipation of the serfs in 1861, he was assassinated on the very day when he had signed a decree approving a plan for a representative assembly in Russia.
ALEXIS (1629-1676). Tsar of Muscovy from 1645 until his death, father of Peter the Great. Captured and executed Stepan Razin.
ARAGO. Family name of three prominent French republicans. François (1786-1853) was Minister in the 1848 Provisional Government, in which his brother Étienne (1802-1892) also served; his son, Emmanuel (1812-1896), was a lawyer who defended in court the radical opponents of the July Monarchy. François was also a physicist and astronomer whose accomplishments include discovery that magnetism is induced by rotation, and creation of an experiment to prove the wave theory of light. Bakunin was certainly acquainted with Étienne, and probably with all three, during his stay in Paris in the 1840s.
BABEUF, François-Noël (1760-1797), called Gracchus. French revolutionary, egalitarian communist who attacked Robespierre from the left and attempted to overthrow the Directory with friends and associates in the famous "Conspiracy of Equals"; having been denounced before he could act, he was arrested and executed.
BALZAC, Honoré de (1799-1850). Prolific French author best known for his series of novels collectively titled *The Human Comedy,* in which individual characters reappear from book to book in sequel and are "studied" in relation to their changing and diverse social environments.
BARNI, Jules-Romain (1818-1878). Professor of History at the Academy, now the University, of Geneva. Founded the League of Peace and Freedom and presided at its Berne Congress (1868).
BECK, Theodore. Founding member of the League of Peace and Freedom and Secretary at its Berne Congress (1868). A lawyer who practiced in Berne but was not born there, he was otherwise of little note.
BEUST, Count Friedrich Ferdinand von (1809-1886). Saxon and Austrian politician. President of the Saxon Council from 1858 on, he tried to combine the small German States into a third force between Austria and Prussia. After Prussia defeated Austria at the battle of Sadowa (also called the battle of Königgrätz) in 1866, he resigned and became Minister of Foreign Affairs under Franz-Joseph. He negotiated the Austro-Hungarian compromise in 1867 with Deák, then resigned himself, after 1871, to the rapprochement between Austria and the German Empire.
BISMARCK-Schönhausen, Otto Eduard Leopold (1815-1898). German Statesman. During the March 1848 revolution in Prussia, he was instrumental in Friedrich-Wilhelm IV's decision in favor of repression. Prussian plenipotentiary in Frankfurt during the 1850s, he was ambassador to St. Petersburg and Paris in the early 1860s; in 1862, Wilhelm I named him Prime Minister. By 1866 Bismarck had incited Austria to war against Germany and defeated her. After the King of Prussia, in 1870, refused French requests for guarantees against the candidacy of a Hohenzollern prince to the Spanish throne, Napoleon III declared war on Prussia and was quickly defeated. As a result the southern German States rallied to Bismarck's Northern Confederation, enabling the establishment of the German Empire (18 January 1871). Thereafter, until 1890, Bismarck governed Germany at the head of a succession of parliamentary coalitions and was the fulcrum of the balance of European diplomacy. Having decided in the mid-1880s that Germany should become a colonial power, he resigned in 1890, partly over disagreement with Wilhelm II about that decision. In

retirement he wrote his memoirs, bitterly criticizing his successors and the emperor.
BRAUNER, František (1810-1880). Czech politician, liberal lawyer, one of the chiefs of the Austrian Slav movement.
CALVIN, Jean (1509-1564). French religious reformer who lived in Geneva after 1541. He coauthored the fundamental document of the Reformed Church in Geneva, reorganized the Academy of Geneva, and, continually writing and preaching on religious instruction, inevitably played a large political role in the city as well.
CASTELAR y Ripoll, Emilio (1832-1899). Spanish writer and politician, head of republican opposition leading to the fall of King Amedeo Ferdinando Maria de Savoia (the third son of Victor-Emmanuel II) in 1873. As President of the Spanish Republic, September 1873 to January 1874, he was unable to withstand the onslaught of extremist and Carlist demagogy and exiled himself after the return of Alphonso XII, returning, however, a few years later to serve in the Cortes.
CHAUDEY, Ange-Gustave (1817-1871). French lawyer and journalist, federalist republican, a member of the International. One of Proudhon's favorite followers, he was assistant to Ferry during the Paris Commune and was executed by its ex-Prefect of Police Rigault as troops from Versailles entered the city in May 1871.
CLÉMENT, Sylvain. Photographer in St.-Imier in the Swiss Jura.
CORNEILLE, Pierre (1606-1684). French dramatist and poet, one of the greatest names in literature who, unlike some such writers, found his talents rewarded in his own lifetime.
COULLERY, Pierre (1819-1903). Founder of the newspaper *La Voix de l'Avenir* in La Chaux-de-Fonds, where he was a deputy in the Council of Neuchâtel. Breaking with radicalism, he became involved in a polemic with Bakunin. Later he was a precursor of the Socialist Party in La Chaux-de-Fonds.
DAMETH, Claude-Marie-Henri (1812-1884). Professor of Political Economy and Statistics at the University of Geneva, delegate to the Geneva Congress (1867) of the League of Peace and Freedom.
DANTON, Georges Jacques (1759-1794). French politician, object of diverse historical judgments; considered a sincere patriot by some, a venal opportunist by others. Sympathetic to the Revoution, he nevertheless did not declare against the monarchy until June 1792. A brilliant orator, he was elected to the Convention and sat with Robespierre, and was attacked with him by the Girondins. An instigator of the Terror, he nevertheless opposed it after being eliminated from the Committee of Public Safety, having fallen under Robespierre's suspicion. After being implicated in a financial scandal, he was executed with most of his followers.
DARWIN, Charles (1809-1882). English naturalist, geologist, biologist, and psychologist, best known for his theory of evolution by natural selection, epigrammatically called "the survival of the fittest."
DOLGORUKII, Iurii Alexeevich (d. 1682). Commander of the armies of Tsar Alexis against Poland.
DOUGLAS, Stephen Arnold (1813-1861). American political leader, skillful debater, opponent of slavery. In 1858 he and Abraham Lincoln met in a series of debates during their contest for senator from Illinois; Douglas won the seat but lost the presidency two years later to Lincoln, after the secession of the southern states had split the national Democratic Party in half. He was one of the strongest advocates of maintaining the integrity of the union at all hazards, and he denounced secession as criminal at the outbreak of the Civil War.
DUGAN, Walter (d. 1869). London goldsmith who, with his wife and children, took poison to escape the hardships of hunger and poverty, thereby acquiring different sorts of notoriety in the various European circles of the time concerned, in different ways, with the condition of the working class.
DUMAS. Family name of Alexandre Davy de la Pailleterie (1802–1870), called Dumas *père,* and of Alexandre Dumas (1824–1895), called Dumas *fils,* both French novelists, who were father and son. The former wrote *The Three Musketeers, The Count of Monte Cristo,* and other historical novels. Although not exiled, he left France after the *coup d'état* of Napoleon III in 1851 and wrote his *Memoirs.* During the 1850s he travelled widely, returning

to France to spend the last decade of his life. In 1859 he met Garibaldi and become one of his partisans. The younger Dumas was primarily a playwright who concerned himself with the moral problems of love; his works address the values and behavior in the bourgeois society of his time.

DUPASQUIER, Henri (1815-1875). Industrialist and politician in the Swiss Jura, editor of *La Montagne*.

FAVRE, Gabriel-Claude-Jules (1809-1880). French lawyer and political figure. He was deputy to the Constituent Assembly (April 1848), then to the Legislative Assembly (May 1849). Opponent of the *coup* of 2 December 1851 by Napoleon III, he was nevertheless again a deputy after 1857, and he opposed the declaration of war on Prussia in 1870. Minister of Foreign Affairs in the Government of National Defense after the fall of the Second Empire, he signed the armistice (28 January 1871) capitulating to the Prussians after the siege and bombardment of Paris. Remaining Minister of Foreign Affairs in the government of Thiers, he negotiated the peace of Frankfurt (May 1871) but resigned soon therafter.

FERRY, Jules-François-Camille (1832-1893). French lawyer and political figure who became known in the late 1860s for exposing in the press the financial abuses of the Second Empire. He was named Mayor of Paris after the fall of Napoleon III (4 September 1870) and, charged with assuring supplies to the population and maintaining order during the ensuing siege, he acquired the ingracious sobriquet Ferry-la-Famine. During his later career, he introduced measures to reform public education and greatly increased French colonial holdings.

FOURIER, Charles (1772-1837). French philosopher and economist, critic of industrial society who, although he also opposed the ideas of Owen and of Saint-Simon, was classified with them by Engels as a "utopian socialist." According to Fourier's project, which was not realized despite his attempts but which nevertheless gained numerous adherents, the unit of social organization would be the "phalanstery," a group of about 1200 workers cooperatively associated.

GALILEO Galilei (1563-1642). Italian mathematician, physicist, and astronomer, one of the last geniuses to be remembered by posterity under his first name. Condemned by the Inquisition for having propagated Copernican ideas about the solar system, he helped to destroy the credibility of the Biblical cosmology and the myth of anthropocentrism, insisting also on a unified theory of terrestrial and celestial mechanics.

GAMBETTA, Léon Michel (1838-1882). French politician, opponent of Napoleon III's declaration of war on Prussia in 1870. Minister of the Interior in the Government of National Defense, he resigned in protest against France's capitulation in January 1871 and refused to sign the peace treaty. Reelected to the Chamber of Deputies in July 1871, he sat on the extreme left and was able, after the 1873 victory in the elections, to push through legislation proclaiming a Republic in 1875. He was excluded from power until his party's victory in 1881, but the government he then tried to form was quickly overturned. He was injured in an accident soon thereafter and died of its complications.

GARIBALDI, Giuseppe (1807-1882). Italian politician, member of Mazzini's organization "Young Italy" in his youth. He rallied to Victor-Emmanuel in the 1850s and was amnestied by him after involvement in an 1862 uprising. In 1866 and 1867 he successfully directed military forces against Austria but was defeated at Mentana during his campaign against the Papal States. A native of Nice, he was elected to the National Assembly of France in February 1871 but did not serve, and did not respond to appeals from the Paris Commune. Although he did not cease to express republican convictions during his political career in Italy, he remained loyal to the Italian king.

GOEGG, Armand (1820-1897). Journalist, publicist, member of the Baden government of 1849. One of the most influential members of the League of Peace and Freedom, he was also delegate to the Basle Congress (1869) of the International.

GORCHAKOV, Prince Alexander Mikhailovich (1798-1883). Russian politician and diplomat, Minister of Foreign Affairs from 1856 to 1862. A partisan of Russian rapprochement with Prussia, he was under Bismarck's influence after 1863.

GUIZOT, François-Pierre-Guillaume (1787-1874). French politician and historian who held a succession of posts in the cabinet and foreign service of Louis-Philippe. He opposed the parliamentary and electoral reforms demanded by the French public during the 1830s and 1840s. He was President of the Council of State in 1847 when Bakunin was expelled from Paris at the demand of the Russian ambassador to France. Bakunin had given a fiery speech at a banquet, several times forbidden by the authorities but always postponed and rescheduled, which commemorated the Polish insurrection of 1830; Guizot fell as a result of his policy of forbidding such banquets, which were at the time a principal forum for political activity. Soon afterward, Louis-Philippe fell, and both went into exile. After returning to France in 1849, Guizot devoted himself to historical studies.

HAUSMANN, Julius (1816-1889). Württemberg democrat and republican, participant in the revolutionary movement of 1848-49. Later one of the leaders of the Volkspartei, he was also coeditor of the Stuttgart newspaper *Beobachter*. Delegate to the Berne Congress (1868) of the League of Peace and Freedom, he strongly opposed Bakunin there.

HUGO, Victor-Marie (1802-1885). French poet and novelist. A poor politician, taken seriously as a writer but not as an orator, he exiled himself under the Second Empire and published satires on Napoleon III. After the establishment of the Third Republic, he returned to Paris and was elected to the Senate but did not participate in debates there, preferring to continue writing prolifically and bask in the universal adulation and acclaim.

JACOBY, Johann (1805-1877). German doctor, writer, and politician. Member of the Frankfurt Parliament in 1848-49 and of the Prussian Parliament from 1862 on, he eventually forsook bourgeois democracy in favor of socialism. By the end of his life he no longer believed in parliamentary socialism; reelected in 1874 despite his refusal to renew his candidacy, he resigned. Bakunin and he first met in Frankfurt in April 1848 through the radical German poet Georg Herwegh.

JANIN, Jules-Gabriel (1804-1874). French writer and literary critic.

JEANRENAUD, Louis. An engraver in La Chaux-de-Fonds who, having poetic intrerests, became a journalist and was later given the editorship of *La Montagne* by Coullery.

KARAKOZOV, Dmitrii Valdimirovich (1840–1866). Student at Kazan and Moscow, of aristocratic origins, who failed in his attempt to assassinate Tsar Alexander II in April 1866.

LASSALLE, Ferdinand (1825-1864). German socialist, founder of the General Association of German Workers, the embryo of the German Social-Democratic Party. He believed that universal suffrage and the national idea were the bases of German socialism, and so supported Bismarck's fight for national unity even while combating his government. He proposed the creation of production associations in industry and agriculture, for which the capital would be created by taxes and furnished by a State bank. Bakunin respected Lassalle, although disagreeing with a number of ideas; when the atheist Bakunin entered a synagogue for the first and only time in his life, it was to pay respect to Lassalle's memory.

LEMONNIER, Charles (1806-1891). Editor of the works of Saint-Simon and one of the organizers of the League of Peace and Freedom.

LINCOLN, Abraham (1809-1865). Sixteenth president of the United States. He presided during the Civil War and was assassinated after its conclusion.

LOUIS NAPOLEON. See Napoleon III.

LOUIS-PHILIPPE (1773-1850). Jacobin during the French Revolution and lieutenant general of its army who became King of the French from 1830-1848. Following Dumouriez in 1792, he passed over to the Austrians, but refused to take up arms against France. After some years of travelling, he returned under the Restoration and, though prudently not involving himself in politics, gained favor with the liberals and the commercial bourgeoisie. The influence of Thiers led to his eventual designation as king after the revolution of 1830. His policies thereafter became more conservative and he presided over a cabinet which in the 1830s repressed riots demanding a republic and which passed restrictive press laws. The triumph of conservatism was signalled by his appointment of Guizot as prime minister in 1840. The revolution of 1848 ended his reign.

LUTHER, Martin (1483-1546). German religious reformer. During the 1520s he changed his attitude toward political power by differentiating it from the spiritual sphere. Thus when the

German peasants revolted in the middle of that decade, he preached the duty of the subject to submit to civil power and to suffer, rather than to repel injustice. At the same time he denounced the misgovernment of the German princes.

MELANCHTHON (1497-1560). Hellenized name of Philipp Schwarzerd, Professor of Greek at the University of Wittenberg, who became the chief disciple of Luther and the head of the Reformed Church after the latter's death.

MÜNZER, Thomas. (1489?-1525). German religious reformer, member of the Augustinian order who met Luther in 1519 and adhered to the Reformation though disagreeing with the doctrine religiously and politically. He preached an evangelical communism as the Anabaptist leader of a peasant revolt in Mülhausen, where he and his followers took power but were executed after being defeated, and was portrayed by Engels as one of the first modern revolutionaries in *The Peasant Wars in Germany*.

MURAVYOV, Mikhail Nikolaevich (1796-1866). Governor General in Vilna during 1863-65 who crushed with great cruelty the Polish uprising of 1863; maternal relative of Bakunin. Implicated with his brother and cousin in the Decembrist plot in 1825, he was able to avoid punishment.

NAPOLEON I (1769-1821). Title assumed by Napoleon Bonaparte, Emperor of the French from 1804 to 1814.

NAPOLEON III (1808-1873). Name assumed by Charles Louis Napoleon Bonaparte, also called Louis Napoleon. Nephew of Napoleon I, he became president of the Second Republic after the revolution of 1848, then emperor after the *coup d'état* of 2 December 1851. He wasted France's strength through colonial wars on foreign continents while Bismarck was founding German unity, and was unable to compensate for the weakness of France through European diplomacy. His empire fell on 4 September 1870, when he surrendered with eighty thousand troops to Bismarck's army during the Franco-Prussian War.

OWEN, Robert (1771-1858). English social reformer, magnate of the textile industry, philanthropist, for whom the three tyrannies of the Western world were private property, marriage, and religion. Convinced that a healthy social environment was the basis for improving the workers' condition, he created cooperative associations founded on the absence of profit.

PALACKÝ, František (1798-1876). Leading politician in Bohemia and founder of modern Czech historiography who saw the nature of Czech history as "constant contact and conflict between the Slavs on the one hand and Rome and the Germans on the other." President of the Slav Congress of 1848 in Prague, where Bakunin spoke in favor of revolutionary Panslav federalism, he supported the Austro-Slavonic conception of a federal Austria, composed of nationalities with equal rights, such that Bohemia would have autonomy; later he based his federalism instead on the historic provinces of the Hapsburg Empire. He was appointed a member of the Herrenhaus in 1861.

PELLETAN, Eugène (1813-1884). French journalist and politician. Parliamentary deputy after 1863, founder of *La Tribune* in 1868, he opposed Napoleon III but entered the government after the Second Empire had fallen, as Minister without Portfolio in the Government of National Defense.

PÉRIER, Casimir (1777-1832). Regent of the Bank of France, deputy after 1817. Under the Restoration he was a member of the liberal opposition, eventually supporting, after long hesitation, the 1830 revolution. In 1831, as head of government and Minister of the Interior, he suppressed the silk-weavers' revolt in Lyons.

PERROCHET, Edouard. An editor of *La Montagne*.

PETER I, the Great (1672-1725). First Russian emperor. He abolished the Moscow Patriarchy, replacing it with a synod subordinated to the Tsar; reformed central and provincial administration; and introduced a well-organized meritocratic civil service.

PICARD, Louis-Joseph-Ernest (1821-1877). French politician, lawyer, and journalist. Minister of Finance in the Government of National Defense, which was formed after the fall of Napoleon III, he then became Minister of the Interior under Thiers in February-March 1871.

PLATO (c. 428 B.C.-c. 348 B.C.?). Eminent Greek philosopher. In his *Republic*, he justified the tripartition of society into statesmen, the general civilian population, and the army and police.
PROUDHON, Pierre-Joseph (1809-1865). French socialist and political writer who used the word "anarchy" to express the highest perfection of social organization. To the title question of his famous treatise *What Is Property?*, he answered: "Property is theft!" A great friend of Bakunin's in the Paris of the 1840s, he believed that the just measure of an object's value was the amount of time spent in labor to produce it. He aimed more at economic than political innovation but died too soon to influence personally the course of the International, where his continuators adhered, though not uniformly, to a principle of "mutualism" not always consonant with Bakunin's notion of collectivist socialism.
QUETELET, Lambert-Adolphe-Jacques (1796-1874). Belgian astronomer, meteorologist, and statistician.
QUINET, Edgar (1803-1875). French writer and historian, elected deputy in 1848 and exiled in 1852 for his protests against the seizure of power by Napoleon III in 1851. Living in exile, he participated in the Geneva Congress (1867) of the League of Peace and Freedom. After the Franco-Prussian War he returned to France and was elected deputy.
RACINE, Jean (1639-1699). French tragic dramatist. His perfection of versification sacrificed the warmth of his characters' passions.
RAZIN, Stepan (d. 1671), called Stenka. Don Cossack who led a peasant revolt in 1670, seizing large territories in southeast European Russia, including every town on the Volga from Astrakhan to Samara. He was finally defeated and broken on the wheel in Moscow, becoming a popular hero of Russian folklore.
RIEGER, František Ladislaus von (1818-1903). Leader of the Czech nationalist movement who, with Palacký, fought in vain to establish an autonomous Bohemia within a federalist Austrian empire.
ROBESPIERRE, Maximilien de (1758-1794). French revolutionary, Jacobin *par excellence.* A monarchist still in 1789, he found support among the extreme left in the Constituent Assembly due to his uncompromising democratism. In the Legislative Assembly (1791), he sat with the Jacobins and fought the policies of the Girondins. Later, in August 1792, he associated himself with the insurrection of the Commune and was elected to the Convention. There he demanded the condemnation of Louis XVI and frequently accused the Girondins of treason. After the latter were excluded from the Convention he became a member of the Committee of Public Safety, where he concerned himself more with general policy than with the specialized tasks. He supervised the Terror, using the divisions within the Convention to eliminate his rivals, such as Danton, before he was himself arrested, declared an outlaw, and guillotined.
ROUSSEAU, Jean-Jacques (1712-1778). French philosopher. His treatise *The Social Contract* argues that government is based on the consent, direct or implied, of the governed through their exercise of "free will." The argument is really eloquent but only apparently cogent, and logically full of gaping holes that are insufficiently patched over by sometimes ingenious rhetoric.
SAINT-JUST, Antoine-Louis-Léon de (1767-1794). French revolutionary elected to the Convention in 1792, where he supported Robespierre and was named to the Committee of Public Safety. Inspired by the ideals of Sparta and the Roman Republic, his intransigent politics were uncompromisingly egalitarian. A supporter of Robespierre in numerous political battles, he was executed after the fall of the Jacobins.
SAINT-SIMON, Count de (1760-1825). Title of Claude-Henry de Rouvroy. French social philosopher, one of the most important precursors of socialism. He foresaw the advent of technocracy but believed in meritocracy.
SCHWITZGUÉBEL, Adhémar (1844-1895). Charter member of the Sonvillier section of the International in the Swiss Jura, delegate to the Geneva Congress (1866) of the International. He also collaborated on *L'Égalité.*
SERRANO y Domínguez, Francisco (1810-1885). Duke de la Torre and Count de San Antonio. Spanish general and politician. He participated in the 1868 insurrection that led to

the fall of Queen Isabella, after which he constituted a provisional government that elected him regent, 1869-71.

SIMON, Jules-François (1814-1896). French politician and Professor of Philosophy who published many studies on the condition of the working class during the 1860s. After the fall of the Second Empire, he became Minister of Public Education in the Government of National Defense; under the Third Republic he was head of government.

TERTULLIAN (c. 155-222?). Anglicized name of Septimius Florens Tertullianus, the "father of Christian Latin literature" and first author of the Church in Africa. His writings display a zeal and combativeness which led him to expound an illuminist doctrine that condemned flight in time of persecution and included a "strict penitentialist" argument on the unpardonability of sin.

THIERS, Louis-Adolphe (1797-1877). French politician and historian who held a succession of cabinet posts under Louis-Philippe until 1836, when he resigned in a conflict over foreign policy. Under Napoleon III he opposed the imperial wars, but he negotiated with Bismarck to facilitate the crushing of the Paris Commune. Under the Third Republic he evolved toward conservative republicanism, aligning himself with Gambetta.

VICTOR-EMMANUEL II (1820-1878). Constitutional monarch of Piedmont-Sardinia who expanded his realm to include Lombardy (in exchange for Nice and Savoy), central Italy, and eventually Naples, thanks to the campaign of Garibaldi. Proclaimed King of Italy in 1861, he added Venice in 1866 but had to wait until 1870 to enter Rome and make it his capital. His foreign policy was close to that of Germany and Austria.

VOGT, Gustav (1829-1901). Berne lawyer, active participant at the Berne Congress (1868) of the League of Peace and Freedom. He was professor and administrator at the University of Berne and later at that of Zürich.

VOLTAIRE (1694-1778). Name adopted by François-Marie Arouet. French novelist and playwright.

Bibliography

I. Principal Editions of Bakunin's Works and Guides to the Literature

The ongoing project to publish all of Bakunin's extant writings, headquartered in the International Institute for Social History, Amsterdam, is:

Archives Bakounine. Edited by A. Lehning. 8 volumes in 9 by 1984. Leiden: E.J. Brill, 1961- .

These volumes are also available in an identical but less expensive edition:

Œuvres complètes. Edited by A. Lehning. 8 volumes by 1984. Paris: Champ libre, 1973- .

All texts are presented in the original language and, where that is not French, they are also translated into French. Copious notes and an extended Introduction accompany each volume. Works are arranged chronologically within each volume and are accompanied by supporting Appendices. Each volume is devoted to a single topic, around which theme Bakunin's works in that volume are gathered. Subjects treated so far include, for example, Bakunin's relations with Nechaev, his relations with Slavs more generally, his relations with Italy, and the split in the International. All works published so far are from the period 1870-1876, and each volume contains in its title the dates covered by the works it contains. (Bakunin's relations with Italy, for instance, are covered only for 1871-1872.) The numeration of the two editions differs slightly: Volume I, parts 1 and 2, of the *Archives Bakounine* are, respectively, Volumes I and II of the *Œuvres complètes*; Volume II of the former is then Volume III of the latter; and so on.

There are various editions of Bakunin's works in different languages, none of which is complete. The following list gives reference to the most useful of these:

Œuvres. 6 volumes. Volume I edited by Max Nettlau, volumes II-VI edited by James Guillaume. Paris: P.V. Stock, 1895-1913. The standard set before the *Archives Bakounine* began, this still contains texts which are otherwise difficult to find. Volume I was reprinted by the publisher in 1972.

Gesammelte Werke. 3 volumes. Edited by Max Nettlau. Berlin: Verlag "Der Syndikalist," 1921-1924.

Scritti editi e inediti. 3 volumes. Edited by P.C. Masini. Bergamo: Novecento grafico, 1960-1963. Concentrates on Bakunin's Italian period in the 1860s.

Izbrannye sochineniia [Selected Works]. 5 volumes. Petrograd-Moscow: "Golos truda," 1919-1921.

Sobranie sochinenii i pisem [Collection of Works and Letters]. 4 volumes. Edited by Iu. M. Steklov. Moscow: Izdatel'stvo vsesoiuznogo obshchestva politkatorzhan i ssyl'no-poselentsev, 1934-1936. Bakunin's writings up to his escape from Siberia in 1861, including letters to family and friends. Valuable for his formative period and contains extensive commentaries. All texts are in Russian.

Various editions also exist in Japanese, Polish, and Spanish. This brief list does not exhaust Bakunin's works available in print. The best guide to the literature, secondary, as well as primary, in any language is:

Lehning, Arthur. "Michel Bakounine et les historiens: un aperçu historiographique." In *Bakounine: Combats et débats.* [Edited by Jacques Catteau]. Paris: Institut

d'études slaves, 1979. Pages 18-43.
This essay also appears in German as the Introduction to the reprint edition of:
Michail Bakunins sozialpolitischer Briefwechsel mit Alexander Iw. Herzen und Ogarjow. Edited by Michail Dragomanov. Translated by Boris Minzès. Stuttgart: Cotta, 1895; reprint ed., Berlin: Karin Kramer, 1975. Pages 7-48.
The best survey of the extremely disparate state of the corpus of Bakunin's published writings in all languages is:
Péchoux, Pierre. "Bilan des publications." In *Bakounine: Combats et débats.* Pages 45-59. The "Bibliographie" in this volume, also established by Péchoux, is compact but comprehensive, and the best of its kind: pages 241-47.
The following interesting item should also be noted:
Dzhangirian, V.G. *Kritika anglo-amerikanskoi burzhuaznoi istoriografii M.A. Bakunina i bakunizma* [Critique of Anglo-American Bourgeois Historiography of M.A. Bakunin and Bakuninism]. Moscow: "Mysl'," 1978. Although the concluding evaluations in this book are ideologically constrained, the commentaries on individual works are sometimes more objective than much Soviet literature on Bakunin.
Also deserving mention is a collection of reminiscences about Bakunin, by his contemporaries:
Lehning, Arthur (ed.). *Michel Bakounine et les autres.* Collection 10/18, no. 1051. "Noir et Rouge" series. Paris: Union générale d'éditions, 1976.

II. Bakunin's Works Published Separately in English

This list does not include serialized items, such as may have appeared in newspapers or journals. Four categories are evident: editions of *God and the State,* which has been the most widely available of Bakunin's works; other individual works published separately; collections of Bakunin's writings; and anthologies in which he appears.

A. God and the State

With a preface by Carlo Cafiero and Élisée Reclus. Translated from the French by Benj. R. Tucker. Boston, Mass.: B.R. Tucker, 1883; 5th ed., 1885; 6th ed., 1888; 7th ed., 1890; 8th ed., New York: Benj. R. Tucker, 1895; London: London Anarchist Groups, 1893; with an Appendix dated 1894, signed "N[ettlau]," London: London Anarchist Groups, 1893 [1894 on cover]; London: "The Commonweal," 1894; reprint ed.?, with a preface by the editors and translators, Liberty Library, no. 2, Columbus Junction, Iowa: E. H. Fulton, February, 1896; reprint of 1893 ed., San Francisco, Calif.: A. Isaak, 1900; reprint of 1896 ed., Boston, Mass.?: G.K. Hall?, 1959?.
With a preface by Carlo Cafiero and Élisée Reclus. A New edition, revised [by Nettlau from Tucker's translation] from the original manuscript. [With an Introductory Remark by Nettlau]. London: Freedom Press, 1910; 1st American ed. [of this New ed.], New York: Mother Earth Publishing Association, [1916 or 1917]; reprint ed., with a new introduction and index of persons by Paul Avrich, New York: Dover Publications, 1970; reprint ed., Freeport, N.Y.: Books for Libraries Press, 1971; reprint ed., New York: Arno, 1978.
Edited and slightly abridged, with an introduction by Guy A. Aldred, "Spur" Glasgow Library, no. 2, Glasgow: Bakunin Press, 1920.
Indore, Bombay: Modern Publishers, [c. 1920].

B. Other Individual Works and Fragments Published Separately

The "Confession" of Mikhail Bakunin: With the Marginal Comments of Tsar Nicholas I.

Translated by Robert C. Howes. Introduction and notes by Lawrence D. Orton. Ithaca, N.Y.: Cornell University Press, 1977.

A Criticism of State Socialism. With an Afterword on Modern State Socialism. London: Coptic Press on behalf of Cuddon's Cosmopolitan Review, 1968.

The Organization of the International. Translated [from a German translation] by Freda Cohen. Spur Series, no. 5. London: Bakunin Press, 1919.

The Paris Commune and the Idea of the State. London: Centre International de Recherches sur l'Anarchisme, 1971.

The Policy of the International. To which is added an essay on "The Two Camps" by the same author. [Translated by K(arl). L(aber). from a German translation; "The Two Camps" is translated by "Crastinus" (pseud. of Silvio Corio).] Spur Series, no. 6. London: Bakunin Press, 1919. [Contains only the first installment.]

Statism and Anarchy. Edited by J. Frank Harrison. Brooklyn, N.Y.: Revisionist Press, 1974.

Dubium: *The Catechism of the Revolutionary.* [With an Introduction by Eldridge Cleaver]. [Berkeley, Calif.: "Black Panther," c. 1969]. This translation is reproduced from Max Nomad, *Apostles of Revolution* (Boston, Mass.: Little, Brown & Co., 1939), pp. 228-33, which is also printed with a preface by Nicolas Walter, London: Kropotkin Lighthouse Publications, [c. 1970]. The edition, Red Pamphlet No. 01 (Berkeley, Calif.?: "Black Panther"?, [c. 1971]), is a new translation.

C. Collections of Bakunin's Writings

Aldred, Guy A. (ed.). *Bakunin's Writings.* Indore, Bombay: Modern Publishers, 1947; reprint ed., New York: Kraus, 1972; reprint ed., New York: Gordon Press, 1973.

Important texts, but too freely translated and all too often abbreviated. Severely edited fragments.

Dolgoff, Sam (ed.). *Bakunin on Anarchy: Selected Works by the Activist-Founder of World Anarchism.* Edited, translated [by various hands] and with an Introduction by Sam Dolgoff. Preface by Paul Avrich. New York: Alfred A. Knopf, 1971; paperback ed., New York: Random House, Vintage Books, 1972.

This substantial collection is marred by over-editing, serious mistranslations, and an uneven and unsystematic selection of texts. It nevertheless contains important works, demonstrating partially the scope of Bakunin's activity, and a commendable bibliography and notes.

Kenafick, K.J. (ed.). *Marxism, Freedom and the State.* Translated with a biographical sketch by K.J. Kenafick. London: Freedom Press, 1950.

The title of this relatively short compilation adequately conveys the issues addressed in the unattributed texts which it contains.

Lehning, Arthur (ed.). *Michael Bakunin: Selected Writings.* Edited and introduced by Arthur Lehning. Translations from the French by Steven Cox. Translations from the Russian by Olive Stevens. London: Jonathan Cape, 1973; 1st Evergreen ed., New York: Grove Press, 1974.

The best one-volume survey of the varied activities and interests of the pre-anarchist as well as the anarchist Bakunin.

Maximoff, G.P. (comp. and ed.). *The Political Philosophy of Bakunin: Scientific Anarchism.* Preface by Bert F. Hoselitz. Introduction by Rudolf Rocker. Biographical Sketch of Bakunin by Max Nettlau. Glencoe, Ill.: Free Press of Glencoe, 1953; paperback ed., New York: Macmillan Co., Free Press of Glencoe, 1964.

An admirably conceived but, due to the compiler's death in mid-project, poorly executed and hard-to-use collection. Brief excerpts from this collection have been separately published as *Rebellion: Mikhail Bakunin* [Mountain View, Calif.: Sraf print, c. 1969].

D. Anthologies Containing Selections from Bakunin's Works

Abramowitz, Isidore (ed.). *The Great Prisoners.* New York: E.P. Dutton & Co., 1946. Pages 625-47.
Excerpts from Bakunin's *Confession* and his 1857 letter to the Tsar from prison.

Berman, Paul (ed.). *Quotations from the Anarchists.* New York: Praeger, 1972. Passim.
Topically organized with copious examples of Bakunin at his aphoristic best.

Confino, Michael (comp.). *Daughter of a Revolutionary: Natalie Herzen and the Bakunin-Nechaev Circle.* Edited with an Introduction by Michael Confino. Translated [from the Russian] by Hilary Sternberg and Lydia Bott. London: Alcove Press, 1974. Passim.
Contains a number of letters from Bakunin and much information about his relations with Nechaev, Herzen, and Ogaryov.

Fried, Albert, and Sanders, Ronald (eds.). *Socialist Thought.* Garden City, N.Y.: Anchor Books, Doubleday & Co., 1964. Pages 332-44.
The majority of the "Open Letters to Swiss Comrades of the International."

Horowitz, Irving L. (ed.). *The Anarchists.* New York: Dell Publishing Co., 1964. Pages 120-44.
Selections reproduced from Maximoff's compilation.

Krimerman, Leonard I., and Perry, Louis (eds.). *Patterns of Anarchy.* Garden City, N.Y.: Anchor Books, Doubleday & Co., 1966. Pages 80-97.
Excerpts from Kenafick's collection.

Shatz, Marshall S. (ed.). *The Essential Works of Anarchism.* New York: Bantam Books, 1971. Pages 126-86.
Extensive selections from *God and the State* and *Statism and Anarchy.*

Woodcock, George (ed.). *The Anarchist Reader.* Atlantic Highlands, N.J.: Humanities Press, 1977. Pages 81-88, 108-10, 140-43, 309-14.
Fragments of Bakunin's most famous essays.

III. Articles and Monographs on Bakunin in English

Aldred, Guy A. *Bakunin.* "The Word" Library, ser. 2, no. 1. Glasgow: Strickland Press, Bakunin Press, 1940. Reprint ed., Studies in Philosophy, no. 40. Brooklyn, N.Y.: Haskell, 1971.
Sheds light on Bakunin's thought by viewing Bakunin and Marx as complementary. Includes an assessment of Bakunin's influence and of Marx's conflict with him.

———. *Michael Bakunin, Communist.* "Spur" Glasgow Library, no. 3. Publication of the Glasgow Communist Group. Glasgow-London: Bakunin Press, 1920.
A very good appreciation of Bakunin, concentrating almost exclusively on his pre-anarchist years.

Avrich, Paul. "Bakunin and His Writings." *Canadian-American Slavic Studies,* 10 (Winter 1976): 591-96.
A useful bibliographic commentary on the editions of Bakunin's works in various languages and on major studies of him.

———. *Bakunin and Nechaev.* London: Freedom Press, 1974.
A pamphlet reappraising their relationship in light of historical sources which have only recently been made generally available.

———. "Bakunin and the United States." *International Review of Social History,* 24 (pt. 3, 1979): 320-40.
Recounts Bakunin's sojourn in the United States in late 1861, en route from Siberia to London; explores his attitude towards the country; and traces his influence on its anarchist movement. A first-rate piece of historical investigation.

———. "The Legacy of Bakunin." *Russian Review,* 29 (April 1970): 129-42.
A meditation on the influence of Bakunin on Fanon, Debray, Marcuse, and Cohn-

Bendit, including reflections on Marx's dispute with Bakunin and the relevance of the latter's ideas for understanding the revolutions of the twentieth century in the Third World.

———. *The Russian Anarchists.* Studies of the Russian Institute, Columbia University. Princeton, N.J.: Princeton University Press, 1967. Paperback ed., New York: W.W. Norton & Co., 1978. Chapter 1, esp. pages 20-28; chapter 3, esp. pages 91-96.

Brief treatments of how Bakunin's ideas affected those in Russia who may have been disposed to put them into action.

"Bakunin, Ôsugi and the Yokohama-Paris Connection." *Libero International* (Kobe, Japan), no. 5 (September 1978).

A special issue of an apparently defunct quarterly ("quarterly when we've got our stuff together"), published in English by Japanese sympathizers of anarchism. Includes discussion of Bakunin's sojourn in Yokohama during his flight from Siberia to London and of the Japanese historiography of Bakunin. Also treats the praxis of the Japanese anarchist Ôsugi Sakae as well as his interpretation of Bakunin.

Beneš, Václav L. "Bakunin and Palacký's Concept of Austroslavism." *Indiana Slavic Studies,* 2 (1958): 79-111.

Discusses Bakunin's revolutionary Panslavism of the late 1840s, in comparison with Palacký's concept of Austroslavism, using the two principals' presence at the 1848 Prague Congress as a convenient point of departure. It relies a bit too heavily on Bakunin's *Confession* for some evidence, without considering how its testimony may have been affected by the circumstances of its composition.

Berlin, Isaiah. "Herzen and Bakunin on Individual Liberty." In Joint Committee on Slavic Studies [of the ACLS and SSRC], *Continuity and Change in Russian and Soviet Thought.* Edited with an introduction by Ernest J. Simmons. Cambridge: Harvard University Press, 1955. Pages 473-99. Reprinted in: Berlin, Isaiah. *Russian Thinkers.* Edited by Henry Hardy and Aileen Kelly. With an introduction by Aileen Kelly. New York: Viking Press, 1978. Pages 82-113.

An influential essay which, despite its title, does not treat equally its two principals, reading sometimes like a eulogy for the first, who gets most of the attention; the author uses Bakunin only as a foil to Herzen. The erudition of the argument exceeds the judiciousness of the conclusion.

Bose, Atindranath. *A History of Anarchism.* Calcutta: World Press, 1967. Pages 179-220.

A workmanlike analysis of Bakunin's ideas, more than of his life, covering well his philosophical background in German idealism but failing to connect it with his later anarchist writings, to which it skips with hardly a word on the intervening quarter-century. Of those writings, it nevertheless presents a good exegesis of selected fragments, selected unfortunately without any clear design. Because of inattention to the historical environment in which Bakunin lived, the author's concluding critique becomes a somewhat insubstantial discussion of the anarchist's personality.

Bowlt, John E. "A Monument to Bakunin: Korolev's Cubo-Futurist Statue of 1919." *Canadian-American Slavic Studies,* 10 (Winter 1976): 577-90.

Includes five illustrations.

Braunthal, Julius. *History of the International.* Translated [from the German] by Henry Collins and Kenneth Mitchell. 2 volumes. New York: Praeger, 1967. I, *1864-1914,* 136-41, 175-87.

A somewhat cursory discussion of Marx's differences with Bakunin and Proudhon.

Brenan, Gerald. *The Spanish Labyrinth: An Account of the Social and Political Background of the Civil War.* New York: Macmillan, 1943. Second ed., 1950. Paperback ed., 1964. Pages 131-45.

A summary of the reception given Bakunin's ideas in Spain, and his influence on the origins of workers' federations there.

Brown, Edward J. "The Circle of Stankevich." *American Slavic and East European Review,*

16 (September 1957): 349-68.

Concerns mainly Belinsky, with hardly a mention of Bakunin, but includes significant notes on the circle's study of Schelling.

______. *Stankevich and His Moscow Circle, 1830-1840.* Stanford, Calif.: Stanford University Press, 1966. Chapter 5.

Deals mainly with Stankevich's emotional relations with Bakunin's sisters Liuba and Varvara, but includes interesting passages on relations among Stankevich, Belinsky, and Bakunin. In particular, the author observes that the younger generation's campaign to liberate Bakunin's sister from her betrothal to a man she did not love "was not peculiarly [Bakunin's] project." The conclusion that "it is a mistake to suppose that he was the sole instigator" of the project contravenes the widely accepted interpretation that this was, in Bakunin's eyes, an episode in the struggle for human freedom and the first of his conspiracies.

Bucci, John Anthony. "Philosophical Anarchism and Education." Ph.D. dissertation, Boston University School of Education, 1974. Pages 67-71, 113-17, 164-78.

Explicates Bakunin's ideas on the relationship between education and freedom, both theoretically and in practice.

Camus, Albert. *The Rebel.* Translated by Anthony Bower. With an introduction by Sir Herbert Read. New York: Knopf, 1956. Paperback ed., New York: Vintage Books, n.d. Pages 150-64 passim.

The author's penetrating philosophical insights carry him beyond attention to historical continuity.

Carr, E.H. "Bakunin's Escape from Siberia." *Slavonic and East European Review,* 15 (January 1937): 377-88.

A good story, retold from Russian-language materials.

______. *Michael Bakunin.* London: Macmillan, 1937. Paperback ed., New York: Vintage Books, 1961. Reprint of first ed., New York: Octagon Books, 1975.

The standard English biography, by now quite dated.

______. *The Romantic Exiles: A Nineteenth-Century Portrait Gallery.* New York: Frederick A. Stokes Co., 1933. Paperback ed., Boston, Mass.: Beacon Press, 1961. Reprint of first ed., New York: Octagon Books, 1975. Chapter 10; chapters 11, 14 passim.

A necessarily superficial treatment of Bakunin, in a volume concerned primarily with the Herzen household.

Chastain, James G. "Bakunin as a French Secret Agent in 1848." *History Today,* 31 (August 1981): 5-9.

Argues, on the basis of new documents, that Bakunin acted as agent and instigator on behalf of the revolutionary French government when he travelled about Europe in 1848; and adduces this interpretation to explain, in part, the origin of rumors (which plagued Bakunin for the rest of his life) that he was an agent of the Russian Empire.

Christoff, Peter K. "The Radical Slavophilism of Alexander Herzen and Michael Bakunin (1847-1857)." Ph.D. dissertation, Brown University, 1948. Chapters 6-7.

Follows Bakunin's philosophical development and involvement in Polish and Austroslav affairs in the late 1840s.

Clark, John. "Marx, Bakunin and the Problem of Social Transformation." *Telos,* 42 (Winter 1979-80): 80-97.

An interesting and useful comparison which appreciates Bakunin's call "for extending the critique of ideology to the emergence of techno-bureaucracy."

Cochrane, Stephen T. *The Collaboration of Nečaev, Ogarev, and Bakunin in 1869: Nečaev's Early Years.* Osteuropastudien der Hochschulen des Landes Hessen: Ser. 2, Marburger Abhandlungen zur Geschichte und Kultur Osteuropas; vol. 18. Giessen: W. Schmitz, 1977. Chapter 3.

This chapter, which takes up two-thirds of the entire monograph, is an analysis, based on both internal and external criticism, of the collaboration indicated in the title.

In particular, it analyzes the contents and authorship of nearly two dozen pieces of literature which the three produced, including the famous "Catechism of the Revolutionary." Difficult-to-obtain and little-used primary sources enable the author to reach judiciously reasoned conclusions concerning the roles and contributions of the three principals (and the non-role of Herzen) to their triumvirate.

Cole, G.D.H. *A History of Socialist Thought.* 5 volumes in 7. New York: St. Martin's Press, 1953-60. II, *Socialist Thought: Marxism and Anarchism, 1850-1890,* chapters 6, 8-9.

Chapters 6 and 8 tell the story of Bakunin's participation in the International (including his "secret societies") against the background of that organization's evolution and the varying social conditions in which it developed across Europe. Marx's attitudes toward this evolution are also noted. Chapter 9 is an excellent summary of Bakunin's major ideas; the author explains not only what they are but also what they are not. He also makes some unique and valid observations on the connections between Bakunin and figures such as Saint-Simon and Comte. This is superlative intellectual history.

Cranston, Maurice. "A Dialogue on Anarchy: An Imaginary Conversation between Karl Marx and Michael Bakunin." *Anarchy,* no. 22 (December 1962): 353-71. Reprinted in: Cranston, Maurice. *Political Dialogues.* London: British Broadcasting Corporation, 1968. Pages 116-38.

An artful invention, originally broadcast over radio.

Cutler, Robert M. "The Thought of Michael Bakunin: Its Origins, Anarchist Shape, and Points of Contrast with That of Marx." S.B. thesis, Massachusetts Institute of Technology, 1974.

An attempt to demonstrate the continuity of the evolution of Bakunin's ideas from his pre-anarchist through his anarchist periods.

D'Agostino, Anthony. *Marxism and the Russian Anarchists.* San Francisco, Calif.: Germinal Press, 1977. Chapter 2.

The author presents a reasoned and dispassionate conspectus of Bakunin's main ideas. Two interpretations which may be disputed, however, are that Bakunin's criticism of the State as a ruling class is an "extension" of Marx's economic analysis, and that the coincidence of Bakunin's view of the State with that of Machiavelli's led him to advocate a "Machiavellism from below."

Del Giudice, Martine. "Bakunin's 'Preface to Hegel's "Gymnasium Lectures"': The Problem of Alienation and the Reconciliation with Reality." *Canadian-American Slavic Studies,* 16, no. 2 (Summer 1982): 161-89.

A brilliant piece which argues that Bakunin's 1838 essay is not the politically conservative and philosophically idealist statement that it is usually taken to be, but rather a critique of abstraction and subjectivism heralding the development of critical consciousness on the part of the Russian intelligentsia of the 1840s. Following Hegel, Bakunin establishes education as the crucial link between theory and practice; the "reconciliation with reality" is not a naive and uncritical endorsement of the status quo but a direct response to the modern crisis of alienation.

______. "The Young Bakunin and Left Hegelianism: Origins of Russian Radicalism and Theory of Praxis, 1814-1842." Ph.D. diss., McGill University, 1982.

Demonstrates that the Left Hegelianism of Bakunin's Berlin period is in fact a logical continuation of his earlier philosophical development.

Dirscherl, Denis. "Great Russia's Nationalist Ideology." *American Benedictine Review,* 20 (no. 1, 1969): 130-56.

Discusses selected aspects of the thought of Bakunin, Herzen, Gogol, and Belinsky, in order to illustrate a predetermined thesis. The author equates Bakunin's early Panslavism with Great Russian nationalism, ignoring his internationalist anarchism.

Dunn, Patrick P. "Belinski and Bakunin: A Psychoanalytic Study of Adolescence in Nineteenth-Century Russia." *Psychohistory Review,* 7 (no. 4, 1979): 17-23.

A sometimes flawed essay, contrasting Belinski's "productive adulthood" and Bakunin's "prolonged adolescence." Really too brief to be illuminating.

Dziewanowski, M.K. "Herzen, Bakunin, and the Polish Insurrection of 1863." *Journal of Central European Affairs,* 8 (April 1948): 58-78.

A workmanlike narrative of the two men's relations in respect of mostly Polish, but also other Slav, affairs, from Bakunin's arrival in London in January 1862 through the insurrection's reverberations in early 1864. The conclusions drawn are addressed more to the personalities of the two principals than to any other issue.

Eaton, Henry L. "Marx and the Russians." *Journal of the History of Ideas,* 41 (January-March 1980): 89-112.

Bakunin figures prominently in the first half of this essay, which enumerates Marx's contacts with Russians.

Edwards, H. Sutherland. *Personal Recollections.* London: Cassell, 1900. Chapter 17-18.

Reminiscences of an English journalist and music critic who had a special interest in the Slavic affairs of his time.

______. *The Russians at Home and the Russians Abroad.* 2 volumes. London: Wm. H. Allen & Co., 1879. II, chapters 1 and 6.

More of the same.

Eltzbacher, Paul. *Anarchism: Exponents of the Anarchist Philosophy.* Translated [from the German] by Stephen T. Byington. Edited by James J. Martin. With an appended essay on "Anarcho-Syndicalism" by Rudolf Rocker. New York: Benj[amin] R. Tucker, 1908. Reprint ed., New York: Libertarian Book Club, 1960. Chapter 6.

A concise and admirable almanac of Bakunin's ideas, in his own words wherever possible, under the rubrics: General, Basis, Law, The State, Property, and Realization.

Fadner, Frank. *Seventy Years of Pan-Slavism in Russia: Karamzin to Danielevskii, 1800-1870.* Washington, D.C.: Georgetown University Press, 1962. Pages 147-70.

A good treatment of a delimited subject, forsaking an interpretation of what Panslavism meant to Bakunin (though not unaware of this), emphasizing his speeches and writings from 1847-48 and 1862-63, but addressing more generally the years 1845-69.

Fattal, D. "Three Russian Revolutionaries on War." *New Review,* 11, nos. 2-4 (December 1971): 132-43.

A summary comparison of Bakunin, Tkachev, and Kropotkin, which argues that their views on war derive from their attitudes towards the State; a series of interesting but only topically related observations.

Fischer, Gerhard. "'The State Begins to Wither Away . . .': Notes on the Interpretation of the Paris Commune by Bakunin, Marx, Engels, and Lenin." *Australian Journal of Politics and History,* 25 (no. 1, 1979): 29-38.

An interesting comparison which suggests that what happened in the Commune corresponded closely with Bakunin's view of the necessity of destroying the state and creating working-men's federations. Concludes that these views are closer to Marx's and Engels's than to Lenin's.

Fleming, Marie. *The Anarchist Way to Socialism: Élisée Reclus and Nineteenth Century European Anarchism.* Totawa, N.J.: Rowman & Littlefield, 1979. Chapter 4 passim.

Discusses what the few extant historical sources tell us about Reclus's relations with Bakunin, but unnecessarily downplays Bakunin's possible influence on him.

Freymond, Jacques, and Molnár, Miklós. "The Rise and Fall of the First International." In *The Revolutionary Internationals, 1864-1943.* Edited by Milorad M. Drachkovitch. Stanford, Calif.: Stanford University Press, 1966. Pages 3-35.

While not directly concerned with Bakunin, parts of this chapter (especially the section on "The Collapse of the First International") display rare and acute perceptiveness concerning Marx's motives and actions between 1869 and 1872.

Gray, Alexander. *The Socialist Tradition: Moses to Lenin.* London: Longmans, Green & Co.,

1946. Pages 352-62.

An exegetic grab-bag of quotations which stresses Bakunin's opposition to State and Church but omits mention of his federalism, and puts none of this into historical context.

Halbrook, Stephen P. "Lenin's Bakuninism." *International Review of History and Political Science,* 8 (February 1971): 89-111.

Relies heavily on secondary sources for crucial judgments without evaluating them critically, leading to several factual errors and tendentious assessments of Marx and Lenin, as well as of Bakunin.

———. "The Marx-Bakunin Controversy: Intellectual Origins, 1844-1870." Ph.D. dissertation, Florida State University, 1972.

Despite an interpretation of Marx and Engels which sees them only in the perspective of their social-democratic continuators, this dissertation contains occasionally illuminating contrasts between them and Bakunin. The best is in the second part of chapter 2, where their analyses of the 1848-49 revolutions in East Central Europe are compared. Neither the formation of Bakunin's ideas nor their clash with Marx's within the International is covered. For this reason, the treatment of Bakunin's activities in the 1860s is not fully satisfactory; the texts discussed in chapter 4 are nevertheless analyzed well.

Hall, Burton. "Another View of Marx: A Closer Look at Bakuninism." *New Politics,* 7 (no.1, 1968): 78-83.

A brief discussion of Bakunin's criticism of Marx, including some remarks on Machajski in Bakuninist perspective. Concludes that "radical and permanent opposition toward authoritarian State power" is perhaps more important than a vision of post-revolutionary society.

Hardy, Deborah. "Consciousness and Spontaneity, 1875: The Peasant Revolution Seen by Tkachev, Lavrov, and Bakunin." *Canadian Slavic Studies,* 4 (Winter 1970): 699-720.

An illuminating but in some ways inconclusive essay in comparative intellectual history, wherein *Statism and Anarchy* is the almost exclusive source for Bakunin's ideas.

Hare, Richard. *Portraits of Russian Personalities between Reform and Revolution.* London: Oxford University Press, 1959. Chapter 2.

A not unsympathetic biographical sketch of Bakunin which gives his ideas some serious consideration.

Harrison, J. Frank. "Bakunin's Concept of Revolution." *Our Generation,* 11, no. 4 (Winter 1977): 27-35.

This summary is as good as its brevity permits. It is prevented from addressing very deeply the issue of the secret revolutionary organization.

Haynal, André; Molnar, Miklos; and De Puymège, Gérard. *Fanaticism: A Historical and Psychoanalytical Study.* Translated [from the French] by Linda Butler Koseoglu. New York: Schocken, 1983. Pages 169-85 passim.

Discusses Bakunin's relations with Nechaev and Dostoevsky's use of the sensational murder committed by the latter.

Hecht, David. *Russian Radicals Look to America, 1825-1894.* Cambridge: Harvard University Press, 1947. Chapter 4.

A summary of Bakunin's sojourn in the United States, limited by paucity of sources mostly to his stay in Boston, plus a survey and evaluation of the opinions he expressed on the country, both at the time and during his later activities in Europe.

Herzen, Alexander. *My Past and Thoughts.* 4 volumes. Translated [from the Russian] by Constance Garnett. Revised by Humphrey Higgins. With an Introduction by Isaiah Berlin. London: Chatto & Windus, 1968. III, 1351-78.

Bakunin in London in 1862 and 1863.

Heuman, Susan Eva. "Bakunin's Influence on the Russian Studentchestvo Movement in the

Eighteenth Seventies." Certificate essay, The Russian Institute, Columbia University, 1968.

An instructive account based on secondary and some primary sources.

Hodges, Donald Clark, "Bakunin's Controversy with Marx: An Analysis of Tensions within Modern Socialism." *American Journal of Economics and Sociology,* 19 (April 1960): 259-74.

A survey and delineation of conflicts among various trends in twentieth-century revolutionary theory and practice (Kautsky, Lenin, Mao, the syndicalists, etc.), in the perspective of the conflict between Bakunin and Marx.

Hostetter, Richard. *The Italian Socialist Movement.* 1 volume. Princeton, N.J.: D. Van Nostrand Co., 1958. I, *Origins (1860-1882),* chapters 4-5, 8-12.

Provides a summary of Bakunin's contacts with Italian revolutionaries in the context of his Florentine and Neapolitan circles, and a digest of the ideas current among them at that time. Recapitulates in detail the Bakunin-Mazzini polemic and minutely traces its effects on the various branches of the Italian socialist movement. Subsequent chapters also trace the activities, and their effects, of Bakunin's Italian adherents, though not of Bakunin personally.

Hyams, Edward. *The Millenium Postponed.* London: Secker & Warburg, 1973. Pages 88-93.

An atrociously dilettantish biographical sketch, valuable as an example of how Bakunin's ideas and activities have too often been treated.

Jakobsh, F.K. "Günter Eich: Homage to Bakunin." *Germano-Slavica,* no. 3 (Spring 1974): 37-46.

Bakunin as a thematic figure in Eich's poetry.

Joll, James. *The Anarchists.* Second ed., London: Methuen, 1979. Chapter 4.

A portrayal of Bakunin's conflict with Marx, painted with a broad brush yet with good attention to detail.

Jourdain, M. "Mikhail Bakunin." *Open Court,* 34 (October 1920): 591-99.

A biographical sketch of Bakunin, accompanied by an impressionistic evaluation of his ideas.

Kelly, Aileen. *Mikhail Bakunin: A Study in the Psychology and Politics of Utopianism.* London: Clarendon Press, Oxford University Press, 1983.

A thorough and unsympathetic work which treats Bakunin as a case study in the social psychology of millenarianism. Treats the entire range of Bakunin's writings, but tends less to reconstruct the meaning of the evolution of Bakunin's thought over time than to place his ideas in the mold of a seemingly precast interpretive design. The attempt to establish connections between the "early Bakunin" and the "late Bakunin" is nevertheless instructive.

Kenafick, K.J. *Michael Bakunin and Karl Marx.* London: Freedom Press, 1949.

An uneven but useful monograph which attends to Bakunin much more than to Marx. It contains some interesting observations concerning various intellectual influences on Bakunin.

Kennard, M.P. "A Russian Anarchist Visits Boston in 1861: Text of an Account Written Some Twenty Years After, Edited by O. Handlin." *New England Quarterly,* 15 (March 1942): 104-9.

A contemporary memoir of Bakunin's sojourn in Boston, containing remarkable anecdotes and a fair-minded appraisal of the principal.

Kline, George F. *Religious and Anti-Religious Thought in Russia.* Chicago, Ill.: University of Chicago Press, 1968. Chapter 1.

This essay is focused more on atheism than on Bakunin.

Kofman, M. "The Reaction of Two Anarchists to Nationalism: Proudhon and Bakunin on the Polish Question." *Labour History,* no. 14 (May 1968): 34-45.

An interesting comparison of what Poland meant to the two anarchists, their analysis of social conditions in Eastern Europe, and their divergent positions within the revolutionary myth.

Kohn, Hans. *Panslavism: Its History and Ideology.* Notre Dame, Ind.: Notre Dame University Press, 1953. Pages 74-81. Second revised ed., New York: Vintage Books, 1960. Pages 90-98.

A fairly accurate summary of Bakunin's views, as he presented them at the 1848 Prague Congress.

Kostka, Edmond. "Schiller's Impact on Bakunin." *Monatshefte,* 54 (January 1962): 109-16.

A discussion of Bakunin's encounter with Schiller's prose, contrasting his reaction to it with Belinsky's, in the context of the German studies of the Stankevich circle, with special attention to the years 1838-40.

Kun, Miklós. "Bakunin and Hungary (1848-1865)." *Canadian-American Slavic Studies,* 10 (Winter 1976): 503-34.

An episodic but extremely valuable study, drawing on unpublished archives, of a subject which has never really been directly addressed in English in a sustained and focused manner.

Lampert, E. *Studies in Rebellion.* London: Routledge & Kegan Paul, 1957. Chapter 3.

A flavorful and artfully written personality study, spiced with plentiful quotations from Bakunin's contemporaries, which gives serious attention to his ideas but not to the historical circumstances in which he lived.

Lavrin, Janko. "Bakunin the Slav and the Rebel." *Russian Review,* 25 (April 1966): 135-49.

A rather insubstantial sketch of the Slavic theme in Bakunin's revolutionary ideas, concentrating on the 1848-49 period, largely ignoring his anarchism.

Lehning, Arthur. "Bakunin's Conceptions of Revolutionary Organizations and Their Role: A Study of His 'Secret Societies'." In *Essays in Honour of E.H. Carr.* Edited by C. Abramsky, assisted by Beryl J. Williams. Hamden, Conn.: Archon Books, 1974. Pages 57-81.

A sympathetic account of Bakunin's revolutionary praxis, with supporting material from his published and unpublished manuscripts. It does not attempt to answer the question why Bakunin chose to operate through "secret societies" but clearly establishes that he had great impact through them.

Masaryk, Thomas Garrigue. *The Spirit of Russia.* Translated by Eden and Cedar Paul. 3 volumes. Second ed., London: Allen & Unwin, 1955. I, 430-71.

A discursive essay which does not pretend to comprehensive coverage of Bakunin's career and emphasizes the early 1840s and early 1870s. It contains a first-rate exegesis of "The Reaction in Germany" and does a respectable job of evaluating Bakunin's ideas, but errs in calling him a positivist and an individualist.

McClellan, Woodford D. *Revolutionary Exiles: The Russians in the First International and the Paris Commune.* Totawa, N.J.: Frank Cass & Co., 1979. Chapters 2, 3, 10 passim.

Treats Bakunin in relation to the Russian emigration in Switzerland, with respect to the First International.

Masters, Anthony. *Bakunin: The Father of Anarchism.* New York: E.P. Dutton & Co., 1974.

Not a serious work of scholarship.

Mehring, Franz. *Karl Marx: The Story of His Life.* Translated [from the German] by Edward Fitzgerald. London: Allen & Unwin, 1936. Reprint ed., with a new introduction by Max Schachtman. Ann Arbor, Mich.: University of Michigan Press, 1962. Chapters 13-14.

A dispassionate narrative of events related to the struggle in the International between Marx and Bakunin.

Meijer, J.M. *Knowledge and Revolution: The Russian Colony in Zuerich (1870-1873). A Contribution to the Study of Russian Populism.* Assen: Van Gorcum, 1955. Passim, esp. chapter 3.

Concerns the Russian students and the influences on them of Bakunin and Lavrov.

Mendel, Arthur. "Bakunin: A View from Within." *Canadian-American Slavic Studies,* 10

(Winter 1976): 466-88.

Interprets Bakunin's behavior as the result of an unresolved Œdipal conflict but does not successfully connect this interpretation with his activities as a revolutionary.

______. *Michael Bakunin: Roots of Apocalypse.* New York: Praeger, 1981.

A psychobiography occasionally useful for tracing Bakunin's early philosophical development. But the author's oversubjectivity is acknowledged in his admission that he relies "only sparingly on secondary sources"; and internal evidence suggests that, as a nonprofessional psychologist, he fell victim to the phenomenon of counter-transference.

Molnár, Miklós. "Bakunin and Marx." *The Review: A Quarterly of Pluralist Socialism,* 5, no. 3 (1963): 70-84.

An excerpt from the author's doctoral thesis, which was published in French, this article is a good integration of the history of the International during 1871-72 with a comparative study in intellectual history. The author's conclusion is that the root cause of the International's dissolution was its inability to reconcile within a single program the desires for freedom from exploitation and oppression, diversely expressed in different geographical regions within the European workers' movement, according to their local conditions.

Nettlau, Max. *Anarchy through the Times.* Translated [from the Spanish] by Scott Johnson. New York: Gordon Press, 1979. Pages 143-208.

A rambling assemblage of facts and events relative to the intellectual and social history of Bakunin's influence and activities in the First International.

______. "Bakunin, Michael." In *Encyclopaedia of the Social Sciences.* 15 volumes. New York: Macmillan, 1935. II, 393-94.

A good, brief, balanced assessment.

______. "Bakunin's 'Confession' to Tsar Nicholas I (1851)." *Freedom: A Journal of Anarchist Communism,* 36 (May 1922): 28-29.

A discussion of the historical background against which, and circumstances in which, Bakunin wrote the document.

______. "Bakunin's So-Called 'Confession' of 1851." *Freedom: A Journal of Anarchist Communism,* 35 (December 1921): 75-76.

An interpretation of Bakunin's motives in writing the document, in rebuttal to contemporary attacks on him.

______. "Élisée Reclus and Michael Bakunin." In *Élisée and Élie Reclus: In Memoriam.* Compiled and edited by Joseph Ishill. Berkeley Heights, N.J.: Oriole Press, 1927. Pages 197-208.

A valuable account of their acquaintance and friendship.

______. "An English Life of Bakunin." *Spain and the World,* 2, no. 27 (5 January 1938): 3-4; no. 28 (21 January 1938): 3-4; no. 29 (2 February 1938): 4; no. 30 (18 February 1938): 4.

A severely critical review of E.H. Carr's biography.

______. "A Last Word on Bakunin's 'Confession'." *Freedom: A Journal of Anarchist Communism,* 29 (September 1925): 42-43.

A review of a Russian study of the middle period of Bakunin's life (A.A. Kornilov, *Gody stranstsvii Mikhaila Bakunina).*

______. "New Bakunin Documents." *Freedom: A Journal of Anarchist Communism,* 28 (March-April 1924): 18-19.

A review of a volume of a collection of Russian documents on Bakunin, including his "Confession" (V.P. Polonskii [ed.], *Materialy dlia biografii M. Bakunina*).

Nomad, Max. "The Anarchist Tradition." In *The Revolutionary Internationals, 1864-1943.* Edited by Milorad M. Drachkovitch. Stanford, Calif.: Stanford University Press, 1966. Pages 57-92.

An interesting survey which includes some topical observations.

______. *Apostles of Revolution.* Boston, Mass.: Little, Brown & Co., 1939. Pages 146-210;

211-55 passim.

An uncritically hostile and episodic account of Bakunin's life as a revolutionary.

———. "Marx and Bakunin." *Hound and Horn,* 6 (April-June 1933): 381-418.

A judicious examination mainly of their struggle inside the International, written from the interesting perspective of an era antedating Stalin's purges and Hitler's Reich.

Odlozilik, Otakar. "The Slavic Congress of 1848." *Polish Review,* 4, no. 4 (Autumn 1959): 3-15.

A valuable essay-review of the definitive edition of sources relating to the 1848 Prague Congress, including an evaluation of previous work on the subject and a discussion of Bakunin's participation in the Congress as revealed by the documents.

Orton, Lawrence. "Bakunin's Plan for Slav Federation, 1848." *Canadian-American Slavic Studies,* 8 (Spring 1974): 107-15.

Introduces and translates the three brief papers which Bakunin presented at the Prague Congress.

———. "The Echo of Bakunin's 'Appeal to the Slavs' (1848)." *Canadian-American Slavic Studies,* 10 (Winter 1976): 489-502.

A very competent study of the influence, and of the events surrounding the publication, of the pamphlet in its various translations during 1848-49.

———. *The Prague Slav Congress of 1848.* Boulder, Colo.: East European Quarterly, 1978. Chapter 7.

Discusses Bakunin's participation at the Congress and the views he expressed.

Palmieri, F. Aurelio. "A Theorist of the Russian Revolution." *Catholic World,* 110 (December 1919): 331-43.

Views Bakunin's "religious anarchism" as a final development of the ideas of Hegel and especially of Feuerbach, and concentrates on this atheism in order to rebut the argument that the Bolsheviks' anti-religiosity was the product of a Jewish intelligentsia.

Payne, Robert. *The Fortress.* New York: Simon & Schuster, 1967. Pages 101-32.

A slightly romanticized and somewhat anecdotal sketch of Bakunin's life which devotes much of its unevenly spread attention to his imprisonment by the Tsar in the Peter-and-Paul Fortress.

Pech, Stanley J. *The Czech Revolution of 1848.* Chapel Hill, N.C.: University of North Carolina Press, 1969. Pages 240-50.

Discusses Bakunin's links with the originators of the "May Conspiracy" but does not provide a rigorous evaluation of his role or his activities.

Petersen, Arnold, and Johnson, Olive M. *The Virus of Anarchy: Bakuninism vs. Marxism.* New York: New York Labor News Co.. 1932.

A pamphlet published by the U.S. Socialist Labor Party during the Great Depression. Describes itself illuminatingly as a collection of "three articles demonstrating the danger to the proletariat, as well as folly and imbecility[,] of Anarchism in general and Anarcho-Communism in particular, which latter is the twentieth century form of Bakuninism so bitterly fought in the early seventies of the last century by Marx, Engels and other revolutionary Socialist leaders."

Pieters, K. "The 'Pervoe Znakomstvo' of Herzen and Bakunin (1839-1840): A Contribution to the Study of Their Mutual Relations." *Slavica Gandensia,* 1 (1974): 85-123.

A useful study.

Pirumova, Natalia. "Bakunin and Herzen: An Analysis of Their Ideological Disagreements at the End of the 1860s." *Canadian-American Slavic Studies,* 10 (Winter 1976): 552-67.

A curious and somewhat muddled assessment. The author, a Soviet historian, had been officially criticized for having published, in Moscow some years earlier, a biography of Bakunin that reached conclusions displeasing to ideological purists there.

Plechanoff, George [Plekhanov, Georgii]. *Anarchism and Socialism.* Translated [from the

German] by Eleanor Marx-Aveling. Chicago, Ill.: Charles H. Kerr & Co., 1909. Chapters 5-6.

A Marxist polemic, interesting for historical reasons, which attacks Bakunin as "a Proudhonian adulterated by Marxism."

Pomper, Philip. "Bakunin, Nechaev, and the 'Catechism of the Revolutionary': The Case for Joint Authorship." *Canadian-American Slavic Studies,* 10 (Winter 1976): 535-51.

A cogent analysis which utilizes techniques of internal and external criticism, and is sensitive to textual subtleties.

Postgate, Raymond W. *The Workers' International.* New York: Harcourt, Brace & Howe, 1920. Pages 42-83.

A popular history, in which Bakunin's activities are depicted according to Marxist canon, no other historical sources being widely available at the time the author wrote.

Pyziur, Eugene. *The Doctrine of Anarchism of Michael A. Bakunin.* Marquette Slavic Studies, no. 1. Milwaukee, Wisc.: Marquette University Press, 1955. Paperback ed., Chicago, Ill.: Henry Regnery Co., 1968.

A useful but rather antipathetic digest.

Ravindranathan, T.R. "Bakunin and the Italians." Ph.D. dissertation, Oxford University, 1980.

A serious work of reconstruction.

———. "Bakunin in Naples: An Assessment." *Journal of Modern History,* 53, no. 2 (June 1981): 189-212.

Rigorously reevaluates Bakunin's influence on the emergence of Italian socialism. Uses archival documents and printed primary sources (including Bakunin's difficult-to-find articles in the Neapolitan press) to conclude that his presence and activity in Italy during a critical period for Italian socialism were determining influences on the first fifteen years of its evolution.

Reichert, William O. "Art, Nature, and Revolution." *Arts in Society,* 9, no. 3 (1972): 399-410.

Elaborates an anarchist theory of aesthetics through a survey of Proudhon's, Kropotkin's, and Bakunin's attitudes towards art and nature, and toward man's relation to them. Quite good in view of its brevity.

Reszler, André. "Bakunin, Marx, and the Aesthetic Heritage of Socialism." *Yearbook of Comparative and General Literature,* 22 (1973): 42-50.

A discussion of the relation of revolution to creation and art. Bakunin's aesthetic is treated as "liberating," Marx's as "critical."

Ridley, F.F. *Revolutionary Syndicalism in France.* Cambridge: Cambridge University Press, 1970. Pages 38-44.

Usefully discusses the link between syndicalism and Bakunin's anarchism.

Rühle, Otto. *Karl Marx: His Life and Work.* Translated [from the German] by Eden and Cedar Paul. New York: Viking Press, 1929. Pages 269-307 passim.

A dispassionate, interpretive narrative of Marx's relations with Bakunin.

Saltman, Richard P. *The Social and Political Thought of Michael Bakunin.* Westport, Conn.: Greenwood Press, 1983.

A good attempt to explicate certain important elements of Bakunin's mature anarchism, and to demonstrate their interrelationship, treating mainly the 1866-1874 period. Asserts but does not establish a Lamarckian influence on Bakunin, while ignoring the significant influence of Comte. The inattention to Bakunin's philosophical development must be balanced against the attempt to work out the metaphysical groundings of Bakunin's "theory of freedom."

Scherer, John Lowell. "The Myth of the 'Alienated' Russian Intellectual: Mikhail Bakunin, Aleksei Khomyakov, Vissarion Belinsky, Nikolai Stankevich, Alexander Herzen." Ph.D. dissertation, Indiana University, 1968. Chapters 1, 3.

Somewhat useful for the years 1837-42 in Bakunin's development.

Senese, Donald L. "Bakunin's Last Disciple: Sergei Kravchinskii." *Canadian-American*

Slavic Studies, 10 (Winter 1976): 570-76.

A summary of Kravchinskii's career and views and of Bakunin's influence on them.

Seymour, Henry. *Michael Bakounine: A Biographical Sketch*. London: By the Author, 1888.

Extremely brief, with some chronological errors.

Silberner, Edmund. "Two Studies on Modern Anti-Semitism." *Historia Judaica*, 14 (October 1952): 93-118.

The first half of this article establishes the character of Bakunin's anti-Semitism, compares it with Marx's, and attempts to trace the origin and development of this trait.

Stekloff, G.M. [Steklov, Iu. M.]. *History of the First International*. Translated from the third Russian edition, with notes from the fourth, by Eden and Cedar Paul. New York: International Publishers, 1928. Reprint ed., New York: Russell & Russell, 1968. Pages 147-83.

An account relatively sympathetic to Bakunin but often polemicizing against him. The author, a Marxist historian, died in a West Siberian labor camp after having edited, still more sympathetically and less polemically, Bakunin's correspondence up to 1861.

Thomas, Paul. *Karl Marx and the Anarchists*. London: Routledge & Kegan Paul, 1980. Chapter 5.

This lengthy chapter evenhandedly and usefully emphasizes Bakunin's and Marx's perceptions and misperceptions of one another, excluding, however, the social history which was the ground for them. The author is concerned primarily with Marx, and so is able to choose to avoid some difficult historiographic issues concerned with interpreting Bakunin.

Thorp, Annie Longfellow. "Laughing Allegra Meets an Ogre: A Brief Sketch by Longfellow's Youngest Daughter, Edited by D. Hecht." *New England Quarterly*, 19 (June 1946): 243.

The amusing reminiscence of a young girl, brought up on fairy tales, who comes downstairs one evening to see Bakunin seated in her place at the dinner table.

Varlamov, V[olodymyr]. *Bakunin and the Russian Jacobins and Blanquists as Evaluated by Soviet Historiography*. New York: Research Program on the USSR, 1955. Reprinted, minus the valuable annotated bibliography, in: *Rewriting Russian History: Soviet Interpretations of Russia's Past*. Edited by Cyril E. Black. Second ed., revised, New York: Vintage Books, 1962. Chapter 11.

A valuable narrative of the pre-Stalin historiographic debate on Bakunin in the USSR, and an assessment of its political undercurrents.

Venturi, Franco. *Roots of Revolution: A History of the Populist and Socialist Movements in Nineteenth Century Russia*. Translated from the Italian by Francis Haskell. With an introduction by Isaiah Berlin. New York: Knopf, 1960. Paperback ed., New York: Grosset & Dunlap, 1966. Chapters 2, 17.

The first of these chapters deals comprehensively with Bakunin's development up to 1848; the second, sporadically, with his relations among Russian students in Switzerland in the early 1870s.

Vizetelly, Ernest Alfred. *The Anarchists: Their Faith and Their Records, including Sidelights on the Royal and Other Personages Who Have Been Assassinated*. New York: John Lane Co., 1911. Reprint ed., New York: Kraus, 1971. Pages 21-38.

A popular biographical sketch.

Voegelin, Eric. "Bakunin's Confession." *Journal of Politics*, 8 (February 1946): 24-43.

Perceptively analyzes Bakunin's motives in writing the document and accurately summarizes its contents, but concludes unsatisfactorily.

______. "Revolutionary Existence: Bakunin" and "Bakunin: The Anarchist." In *From Enlightenment to Revolution*. Edited by John H. Hallowell. Durham, N C.: Duke University Press, 1975. Chapters 8 and 9.

Two extremely perceptive and lucid essays. The first is concerned to make comprehensible the motivation for Bakunin's choice of lifestyle, called "revolutionary existence." To this end, Bakunin's metaphysics are closely scrutinized. The examination includes a brilliant exegesis of his 1842 article, "Reaction in Germany," as well as reflections on the formation of his ideas and their relation to Marx's.

The second essay begins with an excursus on the meaning of "anarchism" as exemplified by its most noted exponents since Bakunin, then returns to an interpretation of Bakunin's post-1861 activities, and of some of his writings, in light of the considerations concluded upon in the previous essay. Despite the author's view of Bakunin as a "Satanist," these essays are distinguished by the serious attention they give to Bakunin's ideas and their metaphysical bases.

Von Eckardt, J.W.A. *Russia before and after the War.* Translated [from the German] by Edward Fairfax Taylor. London: Longmans, Green & Co., 1880. Chapter 6.

An offhandedly tendentious account of Bakunin's career, containing several factual errors.

Wagner, Richard. *My Life.* Authorized translation [anonymous from the German]. New York: Dodd, Mead & Co., 1911. New ed., New York: Tudor Publishing Co., 1936. Pages 466-99 passim.

Bakunin and the 1849 revolt in Dresden, where Wagner knew him.

Walicki, Andrzej. "Hegel, Feuerbach and the Russian 'Philosophical Left,' 1836-1848." *Annali dell'Istituto Giangiacomo Feltrinelli,* 6 (1963): 105-36.

Contains a brief discussion of Bakunin's encounter with the writings of Fichte and Hegel; discusses the influence of Feuerbach on Belinsky and on Herzen, but not on Bakunin.

______. *A History of Russian Thought: From the Enlightenment to Marx.* Translated [from the Polish] by Hilda Andrews-Rusiecka. Stanford, Calif.: Stanford University Press, 1979. Pages 118-21, 268-80.

A not injudicious summary of Bakunin's life, philosophical views, and social theories, which attempts to overcome the one-sidedness of Marxist historiography on these subjects but does not entirely succeed.

Weintraub, Wiktor. "Mickiewicz and Bakunin." *Slavonic and East European Review,* 28 (November 1949): 72-83.

Their acquaintance and its significance in light of the Polish question. Mainly treats Mickiewicz.

Wilson, Edmund. *To the Finland Station: A Study in the Writing and Acting of History.* New York: Harcourt, Brace & Co., 1940. With a new Introduction, New York: Farrar, Strauss & Giroux, 1972. Chapter 14.

An idiosyncratic essay, almost as much about Marx as about Bakunin. Its title, "Historical Actors: Bakunin," reveals its major flaw. Bakunin is treated as an actor, an artful invention. This is easy to do, as his life was certainly colorful; but his ideas get ignored in the process. For the author, this chapter is in fact only an interlude in the midst of several chapters on Marx and Engels.

Woodcock, George. *Anarchism: A History of Libertarian Ideas and Movements.* New York: World Publishing Co., 1962. Chapter 6.

A detailed, colorfully written biographical essay.

______. "Bakunin: The Destructive Urge." *History Today,* 11 (July 1961): 469-78.

A short and artful biographical sketch.

Wright, C. Hagberg. "Bakounine." *Fortnightly Review,* 115 (May 1921): 759-71.

A biographical sketch containing an impressionistic evaluation of some of Bakunin's ideas.

Zenker, E.V. *Anarchism: A Criticism and History of the Anarchist Theory.* [Translated anonymously from the German]. New York: G.P. Putnam's Sons, 1897. Chapter 4, esp. pages 149-63.

An unappreciative assessment.

Zenkovsky, V.V. *A History of Russian Philosophy.* Translated by George L. Kline. 2 volumes. New York: Columbia University Press, 1953. I, 245–57.

A summary of Bakunin's philosophical development from Fichte through Hegel, with some unsystematic reflections on how this evolution (and what he retained from its earlier phases) may have created predispostions which influenced his subsequent political activity.

ADDENDUM TO THE BIBLIOGRAPHY (1992)

Constraints on space prevent any exhaustive listing or discussion of works that have appeared since the first edition of this book. The purpose of this brief essay, therefore, is to highlight and evaluate recent trends in Bakunin studies that have become more evident with the passage of time.

The published corpus of Bakunin's writings by the middle of the twentieth century had two major components: the Russian edition of his papers, covering his life up to the time of his escape from Siberia in 1861; and the French edition of his writings focusing, less comprehensively, on the period of his activity in the First International in the late 1860s and early 1870s. The *Arhcives Bakounine* wisely began their publishing with the end of Bakunin's life in 1876 and have worked backwards, covering by now much of the period upon which the earlier French edition of Bakunin's works touched. T. R. Ravindranathan worked through Bakunin's Italian period in the mid-1860s, consulting many rare texts, including journalistic works that are quite different from Bakunin's programmatic statements of the period; the latter have long been available. (The revision of Ravindranathan's doctoral thesis, listed above, is now published as *Bakunin and the Italians* [Kingston and Montreal: McGill-Queen's University Press, 1988]. It is worth adding that a good English translation of Bakunin's last major work, *Statism and Anarchy,* has finally appeared, edited by Marshall S. Shatz [Cambridge: Cambridge University Press, 1991].)

Before settling for a time in Italy, Bakunin spent 1863–1864 in Scandinavia; he landed in Stockholm after the failure of an expedition from London in aid of the Polish rebels in 1863. Despite the publication and study of texts from this "Scandinavian interlude," no work covers this period comprehensively. That is most likely because such a work would logically have to take into account the London period following Bakunin's escape as well; but sources for this period are scattered, and some that are known to exist remain unpublished. (But see Silvio Furlani, "Bakunins svenska förbindelser," *Historisk tidskrift,* No. 1 [1985]: 3–25; Michel Mervaud, "Bakunin, le *Kolokol* et la question finlandaise," *Cahiers du monde russe et soviétique* 7, no. 1 [January–March 1966]: 5–36; Mervaud's introduction to his edited volume *Lettres inédites: Herzen, Ogarev, Bakounine* [Paris: Librairie des cinq continents, 1975]; and the texts by Bakunin that Mervaud presents in *Bakounine: Combats et débats.*)

The fourth volume of Bakunin's collected works in Russian includes his activity in Siberia from 1857 to his escape in 1861. Comparisons of the material it contains with texts from Bakunin's later career show a continuity between his social and political concerns in Siberian exile and those of his London, Scandinavian, and Italian phases. This relatively uncharted period in Bakunin's life and activity—from 1857 through the mid-1860s—has to be explored more fully before his "conversion" to anarchism can properly be reassessed in relation to his earlier period before 1849. Let it be said, nevertheless, that Bakunin's beliefs about political organization were basically federalist. They appeared as anarchist only because his opponents were the strongest unitary multinational empires in Europe.

The historical record of this interim period from 1857 to the mid-1860s needs fuller exploration and elaboration. Such work remains handicapped by the absence of a critical edition, or even a compilation, of Bakunin's writings extant from the period. Just as the analysis of the so-called *Grundrisse,* Marx's notebooks from the 1850s, has in recent years established beyond dispute the continuity of the "young Marx" of 1844 with the "mature Marx" of *Das Kapital,* so will a proper examination of what has appeared as Bakunin's "lost decade" demonstrate the organic evolution of his social and political thought. (Miklós Kún has found important archival sources, but they do not prove his argument that Bakunin turned to conspiracy as a principal means of revolution after encountering Freemasonry in Florence in 1864–1865. For an example of his work, see "Un tournant décisif dans la vie de Bakounine: Données inédites sur son évolution idéologique et sur son activité conspiratrice," *Acta Historica* 26, nos. 1–2 [1980]: 27–75. Important unpublished primary sources dating from Bakunin's Siberian and London periods have also recently been uncovered in Russian archives.)

R. M. C.

Index

ORDER FORM

GREAT BOOKS IN PHILOSOPHY PAPERBACK SERIES

ETHICS

Aristotle—*The Nicomachean Ethics*	$8.95
Marcus Aurelius—*Meditations*	5.95
Jeremy Bentham—*The Principles of Morals and Legislation*	8.95
Epictetus—*Enchiridion*	3.95
Immanuel Kant—*Fundamental Principles of the Metaphysic of Morals*	4.95
John Stuart Mill—*Utilitarianism*	4.95
George Edward Moore—*Principia Ethica*	8.95
Friedrich Nietzsche—*Beyond Good and Evil*	8.95
Bertrand Russell On Ethics, Sex, and Marriage (edited by Al Seckel)	17.95
Benedict de Spinoza—*Ethics* and *The Improvement of the Understanding*	9.95

SOCIAL AND POLITICAL PHILOSOPHY

Aristotle—*The Politics*	7.95
The Basic Bakunin: Writings, 1869–1871 (translated and edited by Robert M. Cutler)	10.95
Edmund Burke—*Reflections on the Revolution in France*	7.95
John Dewey—*Freedom and Culture*	10.95
G. W. F. Hegel—*The Philosophy of History*	9.95
Thomas Hobbes—*The Leviathan*	7.95
Sidney Hook—*Paradoxes of Freedom*	9.95
Sidney Hook—*Reason, Social Myths, and Democracy*	11.95
John Locke—*Second Treatise on Civil Government*	4.95
Niccolo Machiavelli—*The Prince*	4.95
Karl Marx/Frederick Engels—*The Economic and Philosophic Manuscripts of 1844* and *The Communist Manifesto*	6.95
John Stuart Mill—*Considerations on Representative Government*	6.95
John Stuart Mill—*On Liberty*	4.95
John Stuart Mill—*On Socialism*	7.95